AN UNCOMMON CASEBOOK

The Complete Clinical Work of
Milton H. Erickson

AN
UNCOMMON
CASEBOOK

The Complete Clinical Work of
Milton H. Erickson

Summarized and Compiled by

William Hudson O'Hanlon
and Angela L. Hexum

W·W·NORTON & COMPANY · *NEW YORK* · *LONDON*

Library of Congress Cataloging-in-Publication Data

An Uncommon casebook : the complete clinical work of Milton H.
   Erickson / summarized and compiled by William Hudson O'Hanlon and
   Angela L. Hexum.
      p.   cm.
   "A Norton professional book" — P. facing t.p.
   Includes bibliographical references.
   Includes index.
   ISBN 0-393-70101-8
   1. Psychotherapy — Case studies.   2. Erickson, Milton H.
   I. O'Hanlon, William Hudson.   II. Hexum, Angela L.
   [DNLM: 1. Erickson, Milton H.   2. Psychotherapy — methods — case
   studies.   WM 420 U54]
RC465.U53   1990   616.89'14 — dc20   90-7739

W. W. Norton & Company, Inc., 500 Fifth Avenue, New York, N.Y. 10110
W. W. Norton & Company, Inc., 10 Coptic Street, London WC1A 1PU

1 2 3 4 5 6 7 8 9 0

To my grandparents, Lofton and Jessie Hudson, who have given me a wealth of love, laughter, and learning.—A.L.H.

To my uncommon family, Pat, Patrick, Zack, Nick and Angie.—W.H.O.

Contents

Preface

This book chronicles and summarizes the clinical work of one of the most unusual and innovative psychotherapists who ever lived. If that seems an unbelievable claim, I suggest you read this book. I am certain you will be convinced.

I first met Dr. Milton Erickson in 1973. I was a psychology student at Arizona State University near Phoenix, where Erickson resided in his later years. I was working at my part-time job in the campus gallery when Erickson, his wife, and a daughter came to buy some of the Seri Indian Ironwood carvings for which he had such a passion (he had one of the largest collections in the world, all crammed into his rather modestly sized home). After I helped them down to the car with their purchase, a co-worker told me that that was the famous Dr. Erickson. I had never heard of him, but became intrigued by an article in *Time* magazine that appeared that very week ("A Svengali in Arizona," October 22, 1973). The case example I read in the article was so intriguing, so distinctive, and so very different from my previous studies in psychology that I set out to find out more about Erickson's work.

I eventually read everything I could find written by and about Erickson's work (a habit that continues to this day) and spent some time with Erickson learning from him personally.

After his death, I became associated with the Milton Erickson Foundation, which was set up to carry on his work. As the Foundation's newsletter editor from 1981 to 1987, I was at the hub of the ever-expanding network of people and information about Erickson and "Ericksonian" approaches (a perfect position for an avowed "information junkie"). Then as now I frequently lectured around the U.S. and in other countries on Erickson's work.

I compiled this book first and foremost for myself. I continue to learn so much from Erickson's work that I wanted to have it available in a summarized, coherent form. This is useful in several respects: First, I can now quickly locate particular cases without having to search through many books; second, I can easily cull out the cases that exemplify Erickson's approach to a particular type of problem (e.g., bedwetting or marital difficulties) or his use of particular techniques (e.g., hypnosis or symptom scheduling); third, I or someone else might be able to discern previously undiscovered patterns running through Erickson's work, which might help in our understanding of his rich and complex methods.

I thought the time was ripe for such a compilation, as there are only a finite number of Erickson's cases and it appears as if most of them have been reported in one place or another by now. The cases have been derived from books, articles, tapes and personal reports available both publicly and privately. The title was derived from Jay Haley's classic book about Erickson's work, *Uncommon Therapy*.

My co-author (or co-compiler, one might say) is my stepdaughter, Angela Hexum. As a psychology student at Swarthmore College, she was interested in participating in the project as a good introduction to clinical work. I was glad for her help, both for assistance in summarizing the cases and for her help with making the writing and analyses clear and jargon-free.

We have limited ourselves to complete clinical cases, that is, cases in which there was a clear presenting problem and/or request for treatment and a conclusion, whether success, failure, or dismissal. We have left out case fragments. We have also deliberately excluded personal and family anecdotes. As amusing, interesting, and instructive as these anecdotes may be, they are not, in and of themselves, psychotherapy.

There may be more case examples in Erickson's work than are reported here. We would be happy to hear from individuals, couples, or families treated by Erickson, either to elaborate on cases described here or to describe further examples. It is interesting to hear, from Erickson's patients, their side of the story, as we do in several of the cases included in the book.

We have organized the cases in a rather arbitrary way. Since the material itself suggested no clear divisions, we have grouped the cases in a way that made sense to us and made the material easier to handle. There are clearly many cases that would have fit just as well in a different section than the one we chose. The index should make up for this. Cases are cross-referenced as to techniques and modalities used, as well as by the nature of the presenting complaint and age group of the patient.

A NOTE ON THE FORM OF THE CASES

The cases are presented in a standard form:

Case Summary: A case description which, while not always being as dramatic or detailed as Erickson's telling of it, attempts to summarize in descriptive (nonspeculative, atheoretical) language and in the shortest possible manner the main points of the treatment.

Presenting Problem: A summary of the problem the patient presented with or sought treatment for. We have tried, again, to be as descriptive as possible and avoid theoretical formulations (such as "reaction formation" or "inferiority complex"). If the presenting problem is uncertain but can be inferred from the description, we have placed it in parentheses to indicate that it is speculative.

Age Group: The age group of the primary patient or patients. We have specified three: child, adolescent, and adult.

Modality: Whether treatment was done with an individual, a couple or a family. Sometimes several modalities were used. We have also indicated whether treatment was done on an outpatient or an inpatient basis.

Problem Duration: Information on the duration of the presenting problem.

Treatment Length: The length in clock and calendar time, as well as number of sessions, of Erickson's treatment.

Result: Whether or not the presenting problem was reported resolved and a brief statement summarizing those results.

Follow-up: Post-therapy information, if any is available, including the length of time of the follow-up.

Techniques: A summary of the techniques used. Where possible, we have used categories of techniques that are most universally recognized and agreed upon in therapy literature or in the "Ericksonian" literature. As this is the category that will be most unfamiliar to the newcomer to Erickson's work, a Glossary of Techniques is included in the back of the book.

Sources: Every source for the case description. Where the source is a written one, page numbers are provided. The reader may refer to the original for more details and nuances. One might also be interested in comparing different versions of the case. The names for the books and articles are shortened in some cases, but a look at the list at the back of the book called Source Materials will make it obvious if there is any uncertainty. Behind each source is the abbreviation we have used in the summary.

Case #:   To assist in identifying cases, we have given each a number.

In any of the categories, when the information is uncertain, we have placed it in parentheses. When the information is unavailable, we have indicated this by the abbreviation NA (for "not available").

William Hudson O'Hanlon

AN
UNCOMMON
CASEBOOK

The Complete Clinical Work of
Milton H. Erickson

1

Habits and Compulsions

THUMBSUCKING

Case Summary: A 16-year-old girl (15 in another version) sucked her thumb. Her parents, her church congregation, her teachers and her school-mates were all exasperated with her. Her school psychologist had told her that her thumbsucking was an aggressive behavior. The parents requested that the therapy be religious in orientation. MHE declined to take this approach. He told the parents that they had to promise to offer the girl no admonition whatsoever for her thumbsucking for one month. When the girl arrived at the office MHE dismissed her parents. MHE told her that he did not like the way her parents had ordered him to cure her thumbsucking. "It's your thumb and your mouth, and why in hell can't you suck it if you want to?" MHE wondered, if her thumbsucking was supposed to be aggressive, why didn't she really get aggressive? (In another version he told her she was "stupid" about her thumbsucking.) MHE told her to suck her thumb noisily for a half an hour (20 minutes in another version) while her father read the paper each night and to do the same during her mother's nightly sewing. When she went to school she was to pick out the teacher and the student

1

whom she disliked the most and to suck her thumb whenever either looked at her. After the session the girl only sucked her thumb when following MHE's instructions. After a while she got bored with following his instructions and quit sucking her thumb altogether. A year later MHE encountered the girl in a social context. She said, "I don't know whether I like you or not, but I am grateful to you."

Presenting Problem: Thumbsucking

Age Group: Adolescent

Modality: Individual; outpatient

Problem Duration: NA

Treatment Length: (One session)

Result: Success. The girl stopped sucking her thumb.

Follow-up: One year later she had not returned to thumbsucking and was better adjusted in all regards.

Techniques: Symptom prescription; symptom scheduling; matching (MHE not liking the parent's demands to cure the thumbsucking)

Sources: *Collected Papers I*, pp. 174–175; *Uncommon Therapy*, pp. 195–197; *My Voice Will Go With You*, pp. 158–160

Case #1

Case Summary: A six-year-old boy sucked his thumb and chewed his nails. His parents, a doctor and a nurse, had tried a variety of punishments and warned him that he was ruining his teeth, all to no avail. Finally they told him they were getting a nut doctor to treat him. The little boy met MHE with clenched fists. His parents were told that they were to stay out of the matter, since the boy was now MHE's patient. MHE reminded the parents and the boy that doctors and nurses knew not to interfere with another doctor's treatment. In the presence of the boy's parents, MHE told the boy that his parents just didn't know that little six-year-old boys needed to suck their thumb and bite their nails. He had a perfect right to suck his thumb and bite his nails. To test MHE, the boy stuck his left thumb in his mouth and started sucking. MHE congratulated him and reminded him that he had learned at school that everyone needed to have a turn on the playground when using the playground equipment. Similarly, he told the boy, each of his fingers and his right thumb also needed sucking if he were going to be fair. So MHE encouraged the boy to suck his thumbs and his other fingers all he wanted. MHE then pointed out that he did not know any big boys who sucked their thumbs, so he recommended that the boy get all his thumbsucking done in the next few weeks, since he would then be a big boy of seven and would want to join the other big boys. The boy quit sucking his thumb and biting his nails just before his seventh birthday.

Presenting Problem: Thumbsucking; nailbiting

Age Group: Child

Modality: Individual/family; outpatient

Problem Duration: NA

Treatment Length: One session

Result: Success. Jackie quit sucking his thumb and biting his nails.

Follow-up: NA

Techniques: Splitting (six-year-old little boys from seven-year-old big boys); pattern intervention; symptom prescription

Sources: *Healing in Hypnosis*, pp. 117–118 and pp. 262–264; *Phoenix*, pp. 82–83; *Teaching Seminar*, pp. 112–113

Case #2

NAILBITING

Case Summary: A couple had two sons and a daughter. The father wanted the eldest son to become a doctor and the mother wanted him to become a concert pianist. The mother made the boy practice four hours per day. At age four, he started biting his fingernails until his fingers bled as a way of getting out of practicing, but his mother made him practice anyway. In college, he still had to continue his four hours of daily practice to receive his allowance and pay for his education. He deliberately flunked out of two medical schools, then cheated on a test, which got him blacklisted from all medical schools. He earned an M.A. in psychology and reluctantly sought hypnotherapy from MHE for his nailbiting, only at his father's insistence. (His father had attended one of MHE's hypnosis courses.)

MHE told the young man that he felt sorry for him because he had never had the pleasure of chewing on a long juicy nail. MHE recommended that, instead of always frustrating himself, the man let one nail grow so that he could experience the pleasure of biting a long juicy nail, as well as continuing to frustrate himself by nibbling the others. The man grew the one nail and MHE encouraged him to bite it, but the man refused. He gradually let two, then three, then all his nails grow (it took either six months or 16 months, depending on the version). Then he decided to play the organ for enjoyment, married a Catholic woman despite his parents' objections (MHE attended the wedding), and decided to attend law school. His father was furious at MHE for allowing this.

The parents had decided that the other son should become an Episcopalian minister. Instead he became a used car salesman, got engaged to a Jewish woman, and abused alcohol. After seeing his brother defy his parents and go to law school, he decided to break off the engagement, give up alcohol, and get a new job selling new cars. The daughter ran away at the age of 16 and married a boy her age. The two brothers insisted that the girl and her husband get college educations.

Presenting Problem: Nailbiting

Age Group: Adult

Modality: Individual; outpatient

Problem Duration: 22 years

Treatment Length: NA

Result: Success. The man stopped biting his nails and chose his own career.

Follow-up: Eight years later, he was well adjusted, had normal fingernails, was successful in his career and a personal friend of MHE.

Techniques: Pattern intervention (getting the man to stop biting only one fingernail); redirecting attention (towards enjoying biting his nails)

Sources: *Collected Papers I*, pp. 414–416; *Healing in Hypnosis*, pp. 259–262; *My Voice Will Go With You*, pp. 137–140

Case #3

ALCOHOL AND DRUG MISUSE

Case Summary: A 52-year-old businessman suffered from severe panic attacks whenever he left his home to go to work or left work to go home. He had been in psychoanalysis for three years but his problem had only gotten worse. During that time he had been on tranquilizers, which interfered with his ability to do his job. He had tried other drugs, with no results, and finally began drinking alcohol to help control the panic. He started with one drink in the morning and one drink at the end of his workday, but soon he was up to three drinks in the morning and at day's end with one in the middle. He sought MHE's help, despite the objections of his analyst, because he decided hypnosis couldn't be any worse than the alcohol, which was turning him into an alcoholic. He was openly skeptical towards hypnosis and MHE, but desperate.

MHE wrote down the man's words verbatim; noticing that, the man slowed down his rate of speaking. After hearing the man's story, MHE read him an article containing an induction that was used with resistant patients. The man was rather disgusted with MHE's having taken so long to make a verbatim record of his history and taking this time to read an article, but he sat through it. He responded to the induction, however, and was soon in trance. MHE aroused him by reorienting him to the time right before the reading of the article. The man was surprised by the amount of time that had passed and realized that he was late for a business appointment. As he rushed out, MHE made another appointment with him and told him to be sure to bring a full bottle of alcohol to the next session.

The man returned to the next session three days later reporting that he had been resentful about MHE's telling him to bring a full bottle and about taking all that time in the session to take laborious detailed notes and to read him the article. But he had noticed that he hadn't been drinking nearly as much to help him get places. Sometimes he realized that he just got places without drinking a thing and that he hadn't even thought about it. He told MHE that he thought he could be helped, if MHE would just stop writing things down and start doing hypnosis. The man reported that he felt strangely excited and expectantly hopeful, but didn't know why.

Again, MHE induced a trance and reoriented the man to the time right before the trance induction, so the man again forgot that he was in trance. Five days later he returned for his next session and told MHE that, despite the fact that he hadn't yet done anything therapeutically for him, something was changing. The man had only experienced one panic, but had gotten angry twice when people had delayed him when he was trying to go somewhere. He had only had two drinks, cocktails with his wife one evening after work. At his next appointment a week later, the man reported that he had had a lot of little panics all week, but at unusual times. They would last only a few seconds. He decided that he was tearing up his problem and spreading it around like confetti. He had also come to suspect that the underlying meaning of the panic attacks was that he was irritated with his wife for dominating him and this was his way of getting back at her. He wondered why he was telling MHE this insight, after not discussing it with his analyst for three years.

He was again hypnotized and given amnesia for the experience. A week later he was back for another session, reporting that he had successfully asserted himself with his wife and had deliberately induced panic attacks until he became convinced that he could now control them. Although the man said his problem was over, he decided that he would continue seeing MHE, because he found it so pleasant and useful.

Presenting Problem: Panic attacks; alcohol abuse

Age Group: Adult

Modality: Individual; outpatient

Problem Duration: Eight years

Treatment Length: More than four sessions

Result: Success. The man stopped drinking excessively and stopped having panic attacks.

Follow-up: MHE continued to see him and wrote that he was still free of the problem.

Techniques: Hypnosis; amnesia; linking (the man's rate of speech to MHE's note-taking); implication (the instruction to bring a full bottle indirectly suggested that the man not drink)

Source: *Collected Papers I*, pp. 311–318

Case #4

૭ₑ૭

Case Summary: A 42-year-old man came to MHE after a three-month drinking binge. He was filthy and unshaven. He believed MHE could help him because they were both "Norskys" and "squareheads" (of Norwegian ancestry) and Norskys can "talk straight from the shoulder" to one another. The man was a pilot who had set several early aviation records. He went through cycles of being a penniless drunk and then a successful, accomplished man. He brought MHE his scrapbook to prove it. MHE told him he had no right to carry the scrapbook because he was just a lush and a sponge and the person in that scrapbook was a man. MHE threw the scrapbook in the wastebasket. He berated the man for several hours about sponging off his parents and his wife.

MHE found out that the man's binges always began with ordering two schooners of beer, chasing them down with a whiskey. MHE instructed the man to go to a nearby beer garden, order two schooners and a whiskey. When he got ready to drink them, he was to curse MHE, saying with the first, "Here's to that bastard Erickson. May he drown in his own spit!" and with the second, "Here's to that bastard Erickson. May he rot in Hell!"

The man ordered the drinks but realized he was doing exactly what Erickson had told him to do and so didn't drink them. He went and joined a health club and got himself back in shape. He was taken back into the air force. A couple of months later the man returned, still without having had a drink. MHE asked him if he though he deserved a halo and then proceeded to berate him some more.

Several months later the man called MHE and told him he was having a battle with himself and wanted a drink. MHE invited him come to MHE's apartment with the bottle and they'd get drunk together. He told the man that he would match him drink for drink. The man arrived, but after MHE poured the drinks he said, "You bastard, you really would get drunk with me. You'll have to drink alone." Another time, he called MHE up and told him he was going to take him up on his offer to get drunk with him. As they were riding to the bar, however, the man decided not to. After that he would call MHE every once in a while and talk.

The man became a colonel and pilot in the air force and did not drink for at least 21 years. Several times over the years, others would spike his drink or food with alcohol, but he would always recognize it and spit it out after feeling nauseated.

Presenting Problem: Alcohol misuse

Age Group: Adult

Modality: Individual; outpatient

Problem Duration: 30 years. He had been drinking since he was 12.

Treatment Length: Three sessions

Result: Success. The man stopped drinking.

Follow-up: Success continued for at least 20 years. The man stopped drinking in 1942 and visited MHE in 1963.

Techniques: Task assignment (behavioral); symptom prescription; interpersonal evocation (of anger and rebellion at MHE's suggestions that he drink)

Sources: *Conversations I*, pp. 110–113; *Experiencing Erickson*, pp. 162–166; "Caring and Clarity," p. 33

Case #5

Case Summary: A man came to MHE because he could not pass a beer garden without going in and drinking. Because he passed beer gardens on his way to work, this interfered with his job. MHE assigned a path for the man to take to work which would not lead him past any beer gardens. They experimented with how close the man could get to a beer garden without going in. The distance gradually diminished from one block to the opposite side of the street to walking right past the door. The man found that he was free to do as he pleased and had no more drinks.

Presenting Problem: Alcohol misuse

Age Group: Adult

Modality: Individual; outpatient

Problem Duration: NA

Treatment Length: NA

Result: Success. The man was able to resist going into beer gardens and drinking.

Follow-up: Continued success.

Techniques: Task assignment (behavioral/perceptual); implication (that the man could go near a beer garden without going in)

Source: *Conversations I*, pp. 113–114

Case #6

Case Summary: A woman abused alcohol for 12 years. She drank in secret while her husband was at work and then hid her whiskey bottles. They fought bitterly when he came home and found her drunk. MHE told the husband that if he could find the bottles then he could keep them, but what he did not find was hers.

The husband's idea of an enjoyable weekend was reading a business periodical cover to cover. The wife preferred to garden and to sneak drinks of whiskey. They both hated fishing. MHE instructed them to go fishing, justifying it with health reasons. They went and did not enjoy it; however, it did lead to their taking frequent camping trips together. The quality of their time spent together improved and the wife cut back on her drinking.

Presenting Problem: Alcohol abuse; marital difficulties

Age Group: Adult

Modality: Marital; outpatient

Problem Duration: 12 years

Treatment Length: NA

Result: Success/partial success. The couple spent more enjoyable time together and the wife cut back on her drinking.

Follow-up: NA

Techniques: Task assignment (behavioral); ordeal

Sources: *Conversations II*, pp. 170–172; *Uncommon Therapy*, pp. 239–240

Case #7

Case Summary: A man from New York called MHE to ask him to treat his 16-year-old son, who had been on drugs and alcohol since he was 12. The parents had fought for years and finally divorced. The mother had disowned the son. The father had taken the boy to a number of psychiatrists of different schools, trying to find help for him. MHE told the father over the phone that the boy would require a great deal of effort and since he (MHE) was in a wheelchair and did not have much physical strength, he would not treat the boy. MHE remarked after hanging up the phone that there was no hope for the boy.

Presenting Problem: Drug and alcohol misuse

Age Group: Adolescent

Modality: Family (phone call); (outpatient)

Problem Duration: NA

Treatment Length: (10 minutes)

Result: Refusal. MHE did not take the case.

Follow-up: NA

Techniques: NA

Source: *Experiencing Erickson*, p. 151

Case #8

❧

Case Summary: A man came to see MHE for his alcohol abuse. He told him that every member of his immediate family had a problem with drinking. He had very little time for treatment since he was about to transfer to a job in a different state. MHE told the man to go to the Botanical Gardens and marvel at the cacti that can go three years without water.

Many years later a young woman came to see MHE. MHE asked her why she wanted to see him. She told him that she wanted to meet the kind of man who would send an alcoholic out to the Botanical Gardens to look around, to learn how to get around without alcohol, and have it work. She told him that her mother and father had been sober ever since MHE sent her father out to the Botanical Gardens years before.

Presenting Problem: Alcohol misuse

Age Group: Adult

Modality: Individual; outpatient

Problem Duration: NA

Treatment Length: (One session)

Result: Success. The man quit drinking.

Follow-up: The man switched from working occasionally in the newspaper business to working regularly for a magazine.

Techniques: Task assignment (behavioral and symbolic)

Source: *My Voice Will Go With You*, pp. 80–81

Case #9

꙯

Case Summary: A wealthy man asked MHE to help him quit drinking. MHE asked if he was married. He said, "Yes, very much married." When MHE asked him what he meant, he said he and his wife had a secluded cottage by a stream which was well stocked with booze and food where they would spend two or three weeks per summer in the nude. MHE told him to get his wife to remove all the booze from the cottage and to leave him there without any clothes. Then the wife could have a friend drop her off at the cottage and take her clothes away. The man decided he was mistaken about wanting to quit drinking.

Presenting Problem: Alcohol misuse

Age Group: Adult

Modality: Individual; outpatient

Problem Duration: NA

Treatment Length: (One session)

Result: Failure. The man continued to drink.

Follow-up: NA

Techniques: Task assignment (behavioral); utilization (of enjoyable activities and isolation)

Source: *My Voice Will Go With You*, pp. 128–129

Case #10

Case Summary: After getting out of prison, a 30-year-old man named Pete was sent to MHE by the staff of a halfway house. Pete had been in prison on and off for 20 years. MHE saw him for a few sessions and offered some treatment. At the end of each session Pete politely told him, "You know where you can stuff that." MHE also saw Pete's girlfriend. She told MHE that she was eager for her daughters to grow up so they could start earning a living as prostitutes. MHE told her he didn't approve. Pete was an alcoholic. He worked as a bouncer at taverns and took his pay in drinks. Tavern after tavern fired him because he got into too many fights. Finally his girlfriend got fed up with him and kicked him out. He couldn't get a job.

Pete walked eight miles in 109° heat to MHE's office. "What was that you tried to tell me?" he asked. "I'm sorry, Pete, but I've stuffed it," MHE answered. However, he did offer Pete the use of a mattress in his backyard and some basic food. MHE knew that convicts have a code of honor and asked Pete if he needed him to take his boots so he would not run away. Pete told him he didn't need to.

Pete stayed in the Erickson's backyard for several days and sobered up. MHE's youngest daughter and his granddaughter spent a lot of time getting to know Pete out in that backyard. He seemed to appreciate their company. After several days of sitting in the backyard, Pete got his girlfriend and took her to an Alcoholics Anonymous meeting and he got a job in a factory. Pete's girlfriend eventually decided she wanted her daughters to get an education and have a better life that she had had. Pete had been sober for five years when the case was recorded.

Presenting Problem: Alcohol misuse; fighting; problems keeping a job

Age Group: Adult

Modality: Individual/couple; outpatient

Problem Duration: NA

Treatment Length: NA

Result: Success. Pete and his girlfriend both got help for their alcohol problems by attending Alcoholics Anonymous.

Follow-up: Five years.

Techniques: Direct suggestion; utilization (of the man's phrase); interpersonal evocation (of commitment to not run away)

Sources: *Phoenix*, pp. 54–57; *Teaching Seminar*, pp. 216–220

Case #11

Case Summary: A physician discovered that a woman had liver damage from tranquilizers and asked MHE to take her as a patient. The woman took a tranquilizer over the slightest thing. From her appearance MHE surmised that she wanted to be thought of as normal and would be resistant if he labeled her as neurotic. The woman was very knowledgeable about classical music. MHE told her that he had a classical solution to her tranquilizer problem—one that would last her for many years. Each time she felt the need to swallow a tranquilizer she was to sit down and emphatically say every profanity and obscenity she knew. MHE pointed out that classical profanity had been going on since the days of the cave man and had been found effective. The woman was pleased with this solution. The woman and her husband returned for one more session, where they decided they had no other problems that necessitated solving.

Presenting Problem: Overuse of tranquilizers

Age Group: Adult

Modality: Individual/couple; outpatient

Problem Duration: NA

Treatment Length: Two sessions

Result: Success. The woman was able to cut back on her use of tranquilizers.

Follow-up: NA

Techniques: Task assignment (behavioral); utilization (of the woman's interest in classical music)

Source: *Uncommon Therapy*, pp. 242–243

Case #12

SMOKING

Case Summary: A 50-year-old man with numerous behaviorally-related ailments (Buerger's disease, diabetes, cardiac disease and high blood pressure) sought a consultation with MHE. He reported that he had been in psychoanalysis for eight months and during that time had required an insulin increase, gained 40 lbs., had his blood pressure go up 35 points and had gone from smoking one and a half packs of cigarettes per day to four and a half. His analyst had assured him that he was making progress in uncovering the causes of his self-destructive behavior, but he himself thought that he was digging his own grave with power tools. He wondered if it would be unethical of MHE to do some hypnotherapy with him.

MHE replied that every competent physician would put the patient's welfare above his desire to keep the patient, so the matter of ethics did not enter into the situation. MHE had the man go into trance by repeating his problem slowly and clearly and then had him tell MHE what he thought would be the proper therapy for his condition. The man came up with a clear treatment plan and MHE told him to repeat the plan four times and then to feel a compulsion to follow it, since it had come from inside him. A year later the man, now physically fit and healthy, returned with a friend in poor physical shape and asked MHE to help the friend in the same way MHE had helped him.

Presenting Problem: Obesity, cigarette smoking, hypertension, Buerger's disease

Age Group: Adult

Modality: Individual; outpatient

Problem Duration: NA

Treatment Length: One session

Result: Success. The man changed his habits and got fit.

Follow-up: One and a half years

Techniques: Hypnosis; linking (repeating his problem induces trance); posthypnotic suggestion; utilization (of compulsive behavior)

Source: *Collected Papers IV*, pp. 207–209

Case #13

꒦

Case Summary: A man who had emphysema and a bad heart and was a chain smoker was brought to MHE for hypnotherapy by a former patient for whom MHE had done some similar work. He repeated the procedure he had used with the referring patient. He had the man repeat his problem as a means of inducing trance, then to outline the treatment that was indicated for his condition. Once the man had repeated the treatment plan several times, MHE told him he would now have a compulsion to follow the plan, since it derived from him.

Presenting Problem: Cigarette smoking

Age Group: Adult

Modality: Individual; outpatient

Problem Duration: NA

Treatment Length: One session

Result: Success. The man stopped smoking. He left his cigarettes behind in MHE's office and never smoked another.

Follow-up: Six months later, the man died of coronary disease.

Techniques: Hypnosis; utilization (of compulsive behavior); linking (of repetition of problem to induce a trance); posthypnotic suggestion

Source: *Collected Papers IV*, p. 209

Case #14

꒦

Case Summary: A 32-year-old man asked MHE for hypnosis to make him stop smoking. He had been in therapy twice a week for the past two years. When he started therapy he only had to have two packs with him at all times so he wouldn't run out, but now he was up to having to have six packs with him. MHE assured him that he couldn't make him stop smoking; however he had him repeat his story and, by listening to it, enter a trance. Then, while in trance, the man was asked to outline what he needed to do to stop smoking. He wasn't seen again for two years, when he returned for an emergency appointment. He had stopped smoking right after the hypnosis session, which his analyst took credit for. He had stayed in psychoanalysis for the two years, but now he had a job offer and wanted to get over a recurrent problem of never being able to keep a job more than a few months. He asked MHE to put him in a trance and do what he should have had him do two years before, to resolve the job problem. MHE repeated the same procedure with him and the man was able to stay at the job and get promoted.

Presenting Problem: Cigarette smoking; job instability

Age Group: Adult

Modality: Individual; outpatient

Problem Duration: NA

Treatment Length: Two sessions

Result: Success. The man stopped smoking and was able to keep a job.

Follow-up: Four years for the smoking; two years for the job problem. The man was then married and had a child. His wife gave up smoking voluntarily.

Techniques: Hypnosis; linking (the repetition of his problem with trance induction); posthypnotic suggestion; utilization (of compulsive behavior)

Source: *Collected Papers IV*, pp. 209–210

Case #15

Case Summary: A 40-year-old man with a chronic respiratory disease sought hypnosis from MHE to stop smoking. The way he talked, it seemed clear to MHE that the man was convinced that he could not be hypnotized. After 30 minutes of direct, formal trance induction had failed due to the man's hypervigilance, MHE had the man fix his gaze on the clock in the office. This, he was told, would hold his eyes still. Next he was to fix his hearing on the ticking of the clock. This was to hold his ears still. He was to be hypervigilant and attend to any outside noises as well as monitoring and disrupting any obvious trance suggestions MHE would offer. After 10 minutes of this, the man was in trance, although he didn't recognize it as such.

MHE tested this by removing the clock; the man didn't even notice it was gone.

In trance, MHE talked to him about having his unconscious mind reorganize his thinking and about his health goals. The man stopped smoking all but four cigarettes per day after 11 hours of treatment over the course of one month (down from his previous three or four packs per day). He still hadn't realized that he had been going into trance. He returned a month later and asked that the cigarette smoking be totally eliminated, as it might return to its previous level if he continued to smoke even one per day. MHE then saw him for 16 hours over a period of eight days and primarily focused on the man's financial and family problems. During these discussions, the man stopped smoking altogether.

Presenting Problem: Excessive smoking

Age Group: Adult

Modality: Individual; outpatient

Problem Duration: Over 30 years. The man had been smoking since he was a teen.

Treatment Length: 27 hours over the course of six weeks (14 sessions)

Result: Success. The man stopped smoking.

Follow-up: NA

Techniques: Hypnosis; linking; utilization (of hypervigilance and resistance)

Source: *Collected Papers IV*, pp. 439–440

Case #16

Case Summary: MHE saw a man who wanted to stop smoking and to have less anxiety in social situations. MHE told him he would not stop smoking and, in fact, the man did not stop until many years later. MHE told the man to repeat to himself as he walked into a room full of people, "Don't give a damn, don't give a damn, don't give a damn." The man followed MHE's advice and it worked to relieve his social anxiety.

Presenting Problem: Smoking; anxiety in social situations

Age Group: Adult

Modality: Individual; outpatient

Problem Duration: NA

Treatment Length: NA

Result: Success and failure. The man stopped being so anxious in social situations but kept smoking.

Follow-up: Jeffrey Zeig, one of MHE's students, treated the man many years later and helped him stop smoking. The man reported that he was still using the social anxiety intervention with good results.

Techniques: Task assignment (cognitive)

Source: *Experiencing Erickson*, p. 78

Case #17

❧

Case Summary: A man who was homosexual but did not want others to know about it sought MHE's help to stop smoking. MHE told him that the way he smoked gave his homosexuality away. MHE also gave him a number of tasks to do with his hands to help him stop. The man did not stop smoking.

Presenting Problem: Smoking

Age Group: Adult

Modality: Individual; outpatient

Problem Duration: NA

Treatment Length: NA

Result: Failure. The man did not stop smoking.

Follow-up: Jeffrey Zeig, one of MHE's students, saw the man some time later. The man told him that MHE had made it so easy to stop that he hadn't bothered to.

Techniques: Reframing; task assignment (behavioral)

Source: *Experiencing Erickson*, p. 80

Case #18

Case Summary: A doctor in Chicago was a compulsive cigarette smoker. He had to have four to six packs of cigarettes with him at all times and he chain-smoked one after another. MHE hypnotized him and suggested that he would have a compulsion to quit before the middle of August, but that he would be so eager to know when he'd quit that he might stop earlier. The man stopped smoking in July and had a compulsion to carry a full pack of cigarettes with him at all times.

Presenting Problem: Cigarette smoking

Age Group: Adult

Modality: Individual; outpatient

Problem Duration: NA

Treatment Length: NA

Result: Success. The man stopped smoking cigarettes.

Follow-up: Three months

Techniques: Hypnosis; symptom transformation (compulsion to smoke cigarettes—compulsion to quit and obsession about knowing when it would happen)

Source: *Life Reframing*, pp. 127–128

Case #19

Case Summary: A policeman was forced to retire for medical reasons. He had emphysema and high blood pressure and was obese. He came to MHE to get help with cutting down on his eating, drinking, and smoking. MHE told the man that when he wanted a meal he should walk to a grocery store a mile and a half away to buy food for one meal. When he wanted a drink he should walk to a bar a mile away and if he wanted another drink he should walk another mile. When he wanted a pack of cigarettes he should walk across town to get them. The man left MHE's office angry and swearing at him. A month later a new patient came in saying that the policeman had referred him to MHE as "the one psychiatrist who knows what he is doing."

Presenting Problem: Excessive smoking, drinking and eating; health problems

Age Group: Adult

Modality: Individual; outpatient

Problem Duration: NA

Treatment Length: One session

Result: (Success. A friend's statement implies that the man changed his habits.)

Follow-up: One month

Techniques: Task assignment (behavioral); ordeal; linking (the man's bad habits to healthful activities); utilization (of the man's motivation)

Sources: *My Voice Will Go With You*, pp. 149–150; *Phoenix*, pp. 111–112

Case #20

ౣ

Case Summary: A woman wanted to quit smoking and lose weight. She didn't like to exercise. MHE gave her two suggestions. First she was to keep her cigarettes in the attic and her matches in the basement. When she wanted a cigarette she was to go down to the basement, take a match and set it on top of the box. Then she was to up to the attic, get a cigarette and bring it down to the basement. Second, MHE suggested that when she wanted some cake she should cut a thin slice and then run around the outside of the house as fast as she could before eating it. Each time she wanted another slice she had to run around the house twice as many times. She soon found that she wanted fewer and fewer cigarettes and snacks.

Presenting Problem: Cigarette smoking; obesity

Age Group: Adult

Modality: Individual; outpatient

Problem Duration: NA

Treatment Length: NA

Result: Success. The woman cut back on her smoking and her eating.

Follow-up: NA

Techniques: Task assignment (behavioral); ordeal; linking (eating with exercise)

Sources: *Phoenix*, pp. 21–22; *Teaching Seminar*, p. 195, #27

Case #21

OVEREATING/OBESITY

Case Summary: Ann came to MHE for obesity. She said that her mother, father and sister were dead and that if he couldn't or wouldn't help her she might as well join them. MHE immediately decided that the girl needed to be treated with unkindness and brutality so that she would be convinced of his honesty. He asked her how tall she was and how much she weighed. 4'10" and 250–260 lbs., she told him. MHE cataloged all the reasons why she was the most astoundingly hideous person he'd ever seen. He was particularly appalled by the multitude of polka dots on her dress. He told her he didn't think she could take the whole truth about herself.

Ann said she wanted hypnosis to help her lose weight. MHE said that hypnosis would be good for her because then she could listen to the horrible truth about herself. He put her in trance and asked her what was important about each of her family members. Her parents were alcoholics and were horribly cruel to her. Her sister was even more pathetic than she was but the sisters had loved each other and Ann was devastated by her sister's death. After the death of all her family members Ann had gotten a job scrubbing floors. The men at work tried to bribe each other to have sex with her but none of them would do it. She lived alone in an old shack.

In a very unsympathetic tone MHE asked her if she knew what a library was. He instructed her to go there and read anthropology books to find out about the hideous kinds of women men will marry. Then she was to read about the way people disfigure themselves with tattoos and the like. She was to return in two weeks.

At the next session he put her into trance again. He asked about what she'd read and then told her to spend the next week sitting in the busiest section of the city looking at the "peculiar shapes and faces of the things men will marry" as well as those women marry. Her next two assignments were to study books on cosmetology to learn what is considered desirable in humans and to study human dress and appearance. Then MHE told her that for two weeks she was to go into one women's clothing store after another, wearing her polka dot dress, to ask the clerks for advice about what she ought to wear. Finally, he told her to obsess for the next two weeks about why she had added such enormous poundage and if there was a reason for it. MHE told her to become curious about what she might look like if she weighed 150 lbs.

After all of her assignments she finally asked MHE if she could be permitted to try to change herself. Within one year she weighed 150 lbs. In time she enrolled in and graduated from the university, got engaged, got a job as a fashion artist, and got her teeth fixed. She brought her fiancé in to meet MHE. "The darn fool is so stupid," she said, "He thinks I'm pretty. But I'm never going to disillusion him."

Presenting Problem: Obesity

Age Group: Adult

Modality: Individual; outpatient

Problem Duration: Since childhood

Treatment Length: NA

Result: Success. The young woman lost weight and made a good social adjustment.

Follow-up: Fifteen years later she was still married with three children.

Techniques: Task assignment (behavioral and cognitive); hypnosis; utilization (of her poor self-image); reframing (of what attractiveness includes)

Sources: *Collected Papers IV*, pp. 66–70; *Uncommon Therapy*, pp. 115–119

Case #22

Case Summary: A physician's wife in her late forties wanted one session of hypnosis to help her lose weight. She currently weighed 240 lbs. and had weighed over 200 lbs. for many years, despite many futile attempts to lose weight. She feared for her future because she had such a love of eating that she felt she could spend all her time just eating. MHE induced trance and taught her to experience time distortion. He then instructed her to go home and follow the diet prescribed for her by her husband and to eat all her meals in a state of time distortion that would make eating seem to last for hours. She and her husband were seen nine months later and she weighed 120 lbs. She had lost the weight easily and without medical complications and reported that the time distortion suggestion had worked well.

Presenting Problem: Obesity

Age Group: Adult

Modality: Individual; outpatient

Problem Duration: NA

Treatment Length: One session

Result: Success. The woman lost 120 lbs.

Follow-up: Nine months. Not only did the woman's weight improve, but her social and recreation activities were also more satisfying.

Techniques: Hypnosis; time distortion; direct suggestion; posthypnotic suggestion.

Source: *Collected Papers IV*, pp. 181–182

Case #23

Case Summary: A woman came to MHE for help with weight loss. Her normal weight was 125 lbs. She would diet faithfully and as she approached 125 lbs. she would begin to weigh herself compulsively and frequently. When she hit exactly 125, she would rush to the kitchen and begin to gorge on food. This would always lead to regaining the lost weight. Now she weighed 180 lbs.; this was the heaviest she had ever been and she was desperate for MHE's help, even though she expected to fail again. She did not want psychiatric help, only help with weight loss through hypnosis.

MHE spent the first session getting the history and inducing a trance. He noted that she had a tendency to develop amnesia for the trance. MHE elicited a promise of full cooperation. She readily gave it, saying she was very good at following doctors' orders, as she had already lost weight successfully under several doctors' programs. He told her she wouldn't like his program, but she said she was desperate and would agree to anything. MHE told her he was going to give her medical orders. He told her that the diet he was prescribing, and which she had agreed to unconditionally, involved her gaining between 15 and 25 pounds. After that she would be allowed to lose not more than three pounds per week.

The woman protested, both in trance and out of trance, but finally agreed. When she had gained 10 pounds, she asked to be allowed to begin dieting, but MHE reminded her that it was between 15 and 25 lbs. As she approached the 15-lb. gain, she began weighing herself compulsively and frequently, and as she hit 15 lbs. she demanded that she be allowed to lose. MHE reminded her that he had said she must gain between 15 and 25 lbs. She returned when she had gained exactly 20 lbs. and began a weight loss that was slow and steady. She finally got to 123 lbs. because she had begun to forget to weigh herself near the end of the diet.

Presenting Problem: Obesity

Age Group: Adult

Modality: Individual; outpatient

Problem Duration: NA

Treatment Length: NA

Result: Success. The woman lost weight and kept it off.

Follow-up: Nine months. The woman had become active in her community, playing golf and joining a book review club, contacts she had avoided in the past due to her weight.

Techniques: Hypnosis; behavioral contract; pattern intervention (symptom amplification/increase/reversal)

Sources: *Collected Papers IV*, pp. 182–185; *My Voice Will Go With You*, pp. 123–125

Case #24

Case Summary: A physician's wife in her mid-thirties sought hypnosis from MHE to lose weight, but declared that she knew she would fail. She had started gaining weight in her late teens and had steadily gained until she was now 280 lbs. She was so convinced that she would overeat as she always had that she kept interrupting MHE's trance induction to ask him why he was wasting his time with her. MHE assured her that he knew she was going to overeat and that all her behavior would be utilized in her psychotherapy. In trance he told her that between then and the next session she should overeat enough to maintain a weight of 260 lbs. She returned for the next session reporting that she had enjoyed eating for the first times in years and that she now weighed 260. She was again put in trance and instructed to overeat enough to maintain a weight of 255 lbs. by the next session. She complied. Then she was to maintain 250. Again it worked. She was worried about a visit to her parental home, but she and MHE jointly decided that she should overeat enough to maintain 238 lbs. and MHE added that she should probably add three, four, or five lbs. to that. When she returned she weighed exactly 242 lbs. She told MHE that it seemed to be a silly game that they were playing, but since it seemed to be working she didn't care. MHE instructed her to maintain the same weight for two weeks in a row, but she grew impatient to lose again. When the case was written, she weighed 190 lbs. and was shopping for clothes that would look good on a chubby 130 or 140 lb. woman.

Presenting Problem: Obesity

Age Group: Adult

Modality: Individual; outpatient

Problem Duration: 20 years

Treatment Length: NA

Result: Success. The woman lost 90 lbs. and was still losing when the case was written up.

Follow-up: NA

Techniques: Hypnosis; utilization (of her need to overeat)

Sources: *Collected Papers IV*, pp. 185–187

Case #25

Case Summary: An extremely overweight 26-year-old woman lived with her mother. When she came to MHE for therapy she summarized her life in a very confrontive, aggressive manner. MHE asked her why she was so defensive, emphasizing the *why*. She said she didn't know why and said to

MHE, "I think that I need help." MHE spent the rest of the session chatting with her about unimportant details of her life. As she was leaving, MHE instructed her to think about why she hated her mother. She insisted that she didn't hate her mother. MHE insisted that, though she didn't yet recognize it, that was the problem she was going to work on between now and the next appointment. At the next appointment she burst out laughing and told MHE that she had hated him all week and had debated not returning. She also said that she hated her mother quite a bit and in the process of thinking about the hate she lost 15 lbs.

Presenting Problem: (Obesity)

Age Group: Adult

Modality: Individual; outpatient

Problem Duration: NA

Treatment Length: NA

Result: (Partial success. The woman lost some weight.)

Follow-up: NA

Techniques: Implication; task assignment (cognitive)

Source: *Conversations I*, pp. 169–172

Case #26

Case Summary: A young woman was brought by her father to MHE for therapy. She had difficulty coordinating her tactile sensations with the visual ones. She could feel things but she couldn't locate them visually. She was also very overweight and had been mistreated (verbally and physically) since childhood by her mother. Her mother had always told her she was hideous and that her father was no good. MHE put her in a light trance and told her he was very curious about the pretty girl underneath that layer of blubber. MHE called the mother a flat slob. He said that the father had every right to sleep with other women, so that the girl would become an advocate of her father's rights. (The father never actually was unfaithful, but the mother had constantly told the daughter that he was.) When MHE criticized the mother, the girl would tense up. When she was tense, MHE would distract her by asking questions like whether or not her elbow was comfortable on the arm rest. MHE saw the father in therapy and told him to separate from his wife. He also saw the mother in therapy. The daughter lost weight and got engaged. MHE had her tell her mother exactly how she was expected to behave at the wedding. The mother complied. The marriage was happy although nine months into it the woman found she was not sexually satisfied. MHE taught her to recognize her sexual rights and to assert herself when she had sexual needs. The mother came to rely on MHE as a sort of father-figure. When she did something wrong she would call MHE and he would scold her over the phone.

Presenting Problem: Obesity; difficulty coordinating tactile sensations with visual ones; (acute schizophrenia)

Age Group: Adult

Modality: Individual; outpatient

Problem Duration: (Lifelong)

Treatment Length: NA

Result: Success/partial success. The woman lost weight. It is unclear whether or not she learned to coordinate her sensations.

Follow-up: The young woman had a happy marriage and was expecting a child.

Techniques: Implication (that the woman would be pretty once she lost weight); refocusing attention; hypnosis; interpersonal evocation (of identification with father rather than mother)

Sources: *Conversations I*, pp. 235–240; *Uncommon Therapy*, pp. 269–272

Case #27

Case Summary: Judy was extremely overweight. She came to MHE about wanting to lose weight. The girl though that she "would still be about the ugliest girl in creation" even after she lost weight. While she was talking about her unattractiveness, MHE spent most of his time looking at a paperweight, glancing up at her occasionally. At the end of the session MHE apologized for not looking at her. He said that he found her rather difficult to look at because he could not help but imagine that she would be "even more sexually attractive" after reducing. He said that her sexual attractiveness was not a matter that they should discuss, but that it was the reason he couldn't look at her. At a later session Judy told MHE that she had fallen in love with a man old enough to be her father. MHE said it was very complimentary to the man for her to be in love with him. Then he suggested that her affections would gradually turn towards someone her own age. Later she lost interest in MHE and got engaged to a man her own age.

Presenting Problem: Obesity; poor body-image

Age Group: Adolescent

Modality: Individual; outpatient

Problem Duration: NA

Treatment Length: NA

Result: NA

Follow-up: NA

Techniques: Implication (that she was sexually attractive); indirect suggestion (that she would turn her affections towards someone her own age)

Sources: *Conversations III*, pp. 18–21; *Uncommon Therapy*, pp. 89–90

Case #28

Case Summary: An obese woman came to MHE for help with weight loss. She had dieted and dieted but always broke down and gorged. Then, in despair, she would gorge some more. MHE told her he was going to give her medical orders. She was to diet for three weeks and then gorge on Sunday. After Sunday she should return to dieting for another three weeks. The diet was effective and the woman wanted to change her eating habits so that she could enjoy being hungry and then satiated each day.

Presenting Problem: Obesity

Age Group: Adult

Modality: Individual; outpatient

Problem Duration: NA

Treatment Length: NA

Result: (Success. The woman lost weight and decided to change her eating habits.)

Follow-up: NA

Techniques: Symptom prescription; symptom scheduling; utilization (of dieting/gorging pattern)

Sources: *My Voice Will Go With You*, pp. 125–126

Case #29

Case Summary: An obese woman came to MHE for help losing weight. MHE told her to climb Squaw Peak at sunrise. She said she wanted company so MHE suggested she take her obese son. When the woman returned she said she didn't think she or her son wanted to lose weight. She asked, "Do you mind if I stop trying to fool myself?" "Not at all," replied MHE.

Presenting Problem: Obesity

Age Group: Adult

Modality: Individual; outpatient

Problem Duration: NA

Treatment Length: (Two sessions)

Result: Failure. The woman did not lose weight.

Follow-up: NA

Techniques: Task assignment (behavioral)

Sources: *My Voice Will Go With You*, pp. 126–127

Case #30

Case Summary: A woman neglected her husband, her four children, and her home. All she ever did was cook and eat. Because of her obesity, she was too ashamed to come to see MHE in person so she called him on the phone. He told her that he was sorry that her children would have to grow up ignorant. They would never know many of the wonderful experiences the Southwest had to offer, like the Botanical Gardens, the Grand Canyon, the Petrified Forest, Casa Grande, etc. He suggested she post a note on her mirror that said, "Let the damn kids grow up ignorant." He suggested that she take her kids out of school and travel with them around Arizona, New Mexico, Utah and California for the next year (through Arizona only in another version). A year (two years in another version) later she called MHE and told him her weight had returned to normal and her interest in her family had been renewed.

Presenting Problem: Obesity; overinvolvement with food

Age Group: Adult

Modality: NA

Problem Duration: Two years

Treatment Length: One phone call

Result: Success. The woman lost weight and her interest in her children returned.

Follow-up: NA

Techniques: Task assignment (behavioral); utilization (of guilt); redirecting attention

Sources: *My Voice Will Go With You*, pp. 127–128; *Phoenix*, p. 85

Case #31

ANOREXIA/WEIGHT LOSS/FOOD REFUSAL

Case Summary: A woman named Mary got up one night around 2 a.m. She didn't want to wake up her children so she took a big swig out of a cough syrup bottle in the bathroom. She had forgotten that she had carelessly filled that bottle with lye. The result of this trauma was that she went into a severe psychotic state with a profound withdrawal. She was checked into Arizona State Hospital. Mary's normal weight was about 110 lbs. After six months of hospitalization her weight was 80 lbs., despite the fact that she was on a stomach tube receiving 4000 calories per day. The doctors wanted her to gain weight so that she would be able to endure an operation to reconstruct her esophagus. When MHE joined the staff at the hospital he decided to take over her feeding. He reduced the calories to 2500. Before feeding her, he gave her some fresh horseradish to chew. At subsequent feedings he used chewing gum, catsup, tabasco sauce, cinnamon bark and cloves. Mary built up to 110 lbs. very rapidly. After her recovery she looked up MHE to discuss her marital, social, and family adjustments. She also told him that she had started cooking with her kids to teach them to enjoy food.

Presenting Problem: Inability to gain weight

Age Group: Adult

Modality: Individual; inpatient

Problem Duration: (Six-seven months)

Treatment Length: (One month)

Result: Success. The woman returned to a normal weight.

Follow-up: She developed a great appreciation of food.

Techniques: Utilization (of connection between taste and digestion)

Source: *Conversations I*, pp. 220–222

Case #32

❧

Case Summary: Barbie, a 14-year-old anorexic, was in the hospital. She weighed 61 lbs. and had lost five lbs. while hospitalized in the previous month. She ate only an oyster cracker and a glass of ginger ale per day. She thought she didn't deserve food. She was close to dying. Her parents were both physicians. They had read *Uncommon Therapy* and decided that if anyone could help their daughter, MHE could. MHE did not immediately agree to take the case and had them call back in a few days. They lived out of state and had to travel to see MHE. Barbie's mother brought her to see MHE. MHE talked to the mother privately first and told her that in the hospital they treated anorexic patients with dignity, very properly, and they all died. MHE had her sign papers saying that MHE had explained all the risks to her and that she agreed to cooperate with whatever treatment he would provide.

When MHE asked Barbie questions her mother answered them. The first sessions were passed in this manner. On the third day the mother complained that Barbie had kept her awake all night by whimpering. MHE got Barbie to agree that she should be punished for keeping her mother awake. MHE told the mother to scramble an egg and feed it to Barbie as punishment. On the same day MHE told the mother that she was to "keep her trap shut" when he asked Barbie a question. MHE also told the girl that he was not going to try to make her eat, as her parents wanted him to. Eating was her problem and she would have to deal with it.

During the following sessions, MHE told Barbie stories about his mother's life in a mining camp, about how she invented a cinnamon pie to get the miners something interesting after all the dried pies they had to eat. He told Barbie how they had to plan ahead for six months' provisions. He told her many other stories, which all involved food and social situations. The stories were very suspenseful and fascinating to Barbie. MHE said that as a physician it was his obligation to look after her health so he advised that she should brush her teeth twice a day. After brushing she should rinse out her mouth with raw cod liver oil. She was to make certain she did not swallow any of the toothpaste or mouthwash.

After two weeks of treatment, Barbie's mother asked if she might take Barbie to the Grand Canyon. Barbie promised to brush and rinse but she left the cod liver oil behind. After Barbie gained three pounds, MHE asked Barbie's mother her height and her weight. She said she was 5′6″ (although MHE suspected she was taller) and she said she weighed 118 lbs., just as she had when she was married. MHE told her she was severely underweight and that she ought to be ashamed of herself. MHE accused the girl of being a liar and a coward. She denied it.

To prove his claim, MHE told her to hit him hard on the arm. When she tapped him lightly, he told her he had proved his point. He encouraged her to try again. She got angry and hit him a little harder, but then ran out of the room crying. When she returned with no tear marks on her face, he again accused her of being a liar and a coward for running out of the room and trying to hide the evidence of her emotions.

MHE continued to evoke many emotions in the girl. He told Barbie to make sure that her mother cleaned her plate at every meal. Two sessions later Barbie reported that she had forgotten to mention that her mother didn't finish her hamburger two evenings previous to the session. MHE punished both of them by having them come to his house and eat large grilled cheese sandwiches. The mother started gaining weight. MHE gave them both several weight goals (75 or 85 for the girl, 125 or 130 for the mother) to reach before he would let them leave Phoenix and return home. They reached the weight goals. MHE told the mother if the girl did not gain five pounds in the first month at home, she was to return to Arizona to be under his supervision.

Later, the father brought the rest of the family to see MHE. MHE told the father he was underweight and demanded he gain five pounds before leaving Arizona, as his underweight condition was jeopardizing his daughter's health. Then he saw each of the siblings alone and told them that they should not have allowed their sister to refuse their gifts of fruit or candy when she started to get sick. They deprived her of her constitutional right to receive presents. MHE also reprimanded Barbie for depriving her siblings of the right to give. Barbie returned home with her family but kept in touch with MHE, on several occasions sending him gifts made of foodstuff. He gave her a recipe that he had gotten from his mother. He also wrote her a letter reminding her that her weight was between her and her conscience and requesting a picture of her the next year. He received a picture of her on vacation in a bathing suit, looking well-nourished and healthy.

Presenting Problem: Anorexia

Age Group: Adolescent

Modality: Individual / family; outpatient

Problem Duration: One year

Treatment Length: 20 hours over the course of one month, with some follow-up interviews with family members some time later

Result: Success. The girl gained weight and kept it on.

Follow-up: At least 11 years. Barbie continued to correspond with MHE until his death in 1980, and with Mrs. Erickson at least until 1985. She continued to do well, physically and socially.

Techniques: Utilization (of family member's guilt and Barbie's belief that food was punishment); symptom displacement (having the daughter make sure the mother cleaned her plate and gained weight); task assignment (behavioral); reframing; metaphor; ordeal

Sources: *Experiencing Erickson*, pp. 43–47; *Hypnotherapy*, pp. 268–276; *Phoenix*, pp. 153–163; *Teaching Seminar*, pp. 132–143

Case #33

Case Summary: A woman in the state mental hospital vomited up all the food she was given. She was starving to death in spite of being tube fed. MHE asked the superintendent of the hospital if he could do anything he had to do to save her and got permission. MHE had her strapped to a chair and told her he was going to continue the tube feedings until she kept them in her stomach. He fed her the first one and she vomited it up into a tray a nurse was holding. MHE poured the vomit back down the tube. She vomited again, but less than the last time. He continued to pour the vomit back down the tube until she kept it all in her stomach. She stopped vomiting her food. The nurses were very angry at MHE and wanted him fired.

Presenting Problem: Vomiting; starving

Age Group: Adult

Modality: Individual; inpatient

Problem Duration: NA

Treatment Length: NA

Result: Success. The woman stopped vomiting her food.

Follow-up: NA

Techniques: Ordeal

Sources: *Experiencing Erickson*, p. 166

Case #34

MISCELLANEOUS COMPULSIONS AND OBSESSIONS

Case Summary: A college student who suffered from obsessional fears about leaving doors, refrigerators and lockers open was hypnotized by MHE for experimental purposes. She was called Miss Damon, but she was told that she would have another name, Miss Brown, while in trance. Hand levitation, catalepsy of the arm and amnesia were induced in trance. The next day, Miss Damon was observed to be talking to herself and self-inducing trance and hand levitation, oblivious to her surroundings and others' attempts to talk with her. She appeared intensely interested and curious at times and at other times terrified.

When asked about her interest in these phenomena, she replied that her salary was so low that she deserved to at least get whatever experience she could on the job. MHE offered to help her explore more automatic trance movements by helping her experience automatic handwriting. She thought she wouldn't be able to accomplish this but was eager to try. MHE induced a trance and she began to write automatically while her conscious attention was absorbed in a magazine article she was reading. She became distressed while she was writing and couldn't understand it as she wasn't really aware that she had written anything and couldn't identify anything in the article she was reading that had disturbed her. Very quickly, however, she seemed to forget about her distress and became curious about what she had written. Much of it was indecipherable.

When the procedure was repeated, much the same result was obtained—unconscious writing, disturbed feelings, indecipherable writing and amnesia. MHE decided she was unconsciously seeking his help so he arranged to have an assistant and a stenographer sit in to aid in the investigation. During questioning, an alternate personality emerged, who claimed that Miss Damon did not and could not know the information written as she was too afraid to know it. After a long written exchange with Jane Brown, the alternate personality, Miss Damon became upset and confused because all she was aware of was MHE's fragmented questions. She was then introduced to Jane Brown. Thereafter many hours were spent in "conversation" with Jane Brown through automatic handwriting and a system of abbreviations developed to hasten the communication. The participants all became convinced of the distinctness of Jane Brown and accepted her as a separate entity.

Jane Brown gradually revealed that there was something that MHE had to help Miss Damon know and that Jane could only answer direct questions. If MHE asked the wrong question, he would get the wrong answer; if he asked the right question, he would get the right answer. After several false inquiries during which Miss Damon and Jane Brown at times got upset, they appeared closer to the information, but still it remained elusive. MHE declared that he had an evening appointment and demanded a commitment for a time that the answer would be provided. Jane Brown agreed to provide it at 7:30 p.m. As the hour approached, Miss Damon got very scared. At 7:30, Jane Brown provided the translation for the earlier automatic handwriting.

It was revealed that Miss Damon had gotten lost when she was three years old while staying with her grandfather. He had scolded her and accused her of leaving the door open. She hadn't left the door open and afterwards had left the doors open to spite him. Later she developed her obsessions about doors. The obsessions were relieved after the realization.

Presenting Problem: Obsessions (about closing doors)

Age Group: Adult

Modality: Individual; outpatient

Problem Duration: 17 years

Treatment Length: One session, several hours

Result: Success. The door-closing obsessions stopped.

Follow-up: NA

Techniques: Hypnosis; automatic handwriting; splitting (waking identity/ trance identity)

Sources: *Collected Papers III*, pp. 231–260; [probably repeated in part with some details changed in *Collected Papers III*, pp. 267–270]

Case #35

Case Summary: A woman had a "silly grin" that was plastered on her face at irregular intervals. MHE talked to her while she was in trance about how smiles come on gradually and leave gradually, how long smiles endure and how pleasing smiles can be to others and to oneself. Since it was such a natural thing, the smile shouldn't be called a grin, or silly, but it should be appreciated as a normal and meaningful expression of a person, whether male or female. At the next session and while in trance, the woman asked MHE to explain menstruation to her. MHE asked her if she wanted it explained in or out of trance and she informed him that he should explain it to her in both states. After this explanation, she lost her "silly grin" as well as her severe and painful menstrual cramps.

Presenting Problem: Compulsive grinning

Age Group: Adult

Modality: Individual; outpatient

Problem Duration: NA

Treatment Length: NA

Result: Success. The woman stopped having her compulsive grins as well as the severe menstrual cramps that usually made her take to her bed for three days during her period.

Follow-up: NA

Techniques: Hypnosis; reframing; normalizing

Source: *Collected Papers IV*, p. 117

Case #36

Case Summary: A 17-year-old retarded boy was sent to a training school for delinquents and while there developed a compulsive arm movement and anesthesia of his right arm. As a result, he had to be transferred to the hospital. Psychotherapy proved unworkable due to his low intelligence level (65 I.Q.). Hypnosis was difficult to use because the boy kept falling asleep during the induction. Finally the boy, seen daily for three weeks, was able to develop a good trance. Direct suggestions for symptom reduction didn't work and no good explanation for the symptoms emerged.

Then MHE had an intern count the number of arm movements and they were found to be 135 times per minute. MHE suggested that the frequency would increase to 145 times per minute until the next session. The boy complied. At the next session the frequency was reduced and again the boy followed the suggestion. This increasing-decreasing process was used again several times. Gradually, MHE used this technique to increase and decrease the movements by five and 10 times per minute until there were only 10 per minute. Then they were increased to 50 per minute and again reduced to 10. When they were at five per minute, MHE suggested that they could become as frequent as 20 or 30 or more per day. After a few days they were only occurring occasionally throughout the day.

The boy started keeping count of his movements and was given the suggestion that the count would reduce until it was five per day and then would increase to as high as 25 times per week. Finally, MHE suggested that the boy guess which day of the week the movements would stop for a day and then entirely. The boy guessed correctly. The anesthesia followed the movements in waxing and waning and disappeared entirely along with the movements. MHE arranged to have him assigned to the bakery at the school to knead bread.

Presenting Problem: Compulsive arm movements; anesthesia of the hand and arm

Age Group: Adolescent

Modality: Individual; inpatient (residential)

Problem Duration: Six weeks

Treatment Length: More than a month of daily sessions

Result: Success. Both the anesthesia and the compulsive movements ceased.

Follow-up: One year. The boy returned to the training school and the symptoms remained absent for at least a year.

Techniques: Hypnosis; direct suggestion; pattern intervention; increasing the symptom; implication

Sources: *Collected Papers IV*, pp. 158–160; *Conversations II*, p. 207; *Mind-Body Communication*, p. 85

Case #37

Case Summary: A man had developed a compulsion to visit his mother's grave. His mother had died when he was 12 and his father had insisted that he visit the grave every Sunday. His father had become an alcoholic after his wife's death. When he found out that his son had skipped visiting the grave one week, he beat him severely. His father had soon abandoned him and he had gone to live with a distant relative. The man found that if he didn't visit his mother's grave every day, he would develop somatic symptoms such as diarrhea and gastric symptoms, as well as anxiety and panic. He had been offered a new and better job in a distant city, but was afraid that he couldn't leave due to the compulsion.

   MHE did hypnosis and had the man think that it was two weeks in the future. Then MHE engaged in some playful banter with the man and asked him whether he was strong enough to take a shock. The man assured MHE that he could take anything MHE could dish out. MHE then informed him that he had not visited his mother's grave for two weeks. The man was shocked and wondered how he had accomplished it. MHE quickly distract-ed him with a detailed discussion of all that the man would have to do to get ready to move to get to his new job. He then induced an amnesia and reoriented the man to the present time. The man returned in two weeks for his next appointment and proceeded to discuss how busy he had been get-ting ready to move. MHE had secretly called his wife and found out that he hadn't visited the grave, so he pointed out to the man that he hadn't visited the grave in the past two weeks. The man was a bit surprised, but attributed it to having been so busy and having decided to take the new job.

Presenting Problem: Compulsion to visit mother's grave; anxiety; insom-nia; panic; gastric symptoms; diarrhea

Age Group: Adult

Modality: Individual; outpatient

Problem Duration: 15 years

Treatment Length: Two sessions; two weeks.

Result: Success. The man stopped having the compulsion to visit his moth-er's grave and was able to take a new job far away from his mother's grave.

Follow-up: 10 years later he was only visiting his mother's grave when he revisited his old home town and only if it were convenient during those visits. He seemed well adjusted otherwise.

Techniques: Hypnosis; age progression; amnesia

Source: *Collected Papers IV*, pp. 404–407

Case #38

Case Summary: A woman in her thirties sucked her thumb and scratched her nipple and her navel until both were constantly scabbed. She had had these habits since childhood and requested therapy for them from MHE. He told her that he wouldn't give therapy for it, but that he would simply cure it in less than 30 seconds' time. All she had to do was to say "yes" and mean "yes." She was skeptical. He told her that the next time she wanted to scratch her nipple, she should come to his office, expose her breasts and do it. He then asked her if she would do it. As she had previously agreed, she an-swered "Yes," and then said, "You know I'll never do it. I never will."

Presenting Problem: Scratching nipple and navel; thumbsucking

Age Group: Adult

Modality: Individual; outpatient

Problem Duration: (Approximately 20 years)

Treatment Length: (One session)

Result: Success. The woman quit sucking her thumb and scratching her nipple and her navel.

Follow-up: NA

Techniques: Task assignment (behavioral); ordeal; pattern intervention; symptom prescription

Sources: *Conversations I*, p. 15; *Uncommon Therapy*, p. 101

Case #39

Case Summary: A boy compulsively picked a pimple on his forehead so that it turned into an ulcer that would not heal. Father had punished the boy by selling his bicycle and breaking his bow and arrow set in an attempt to get him to stop, but to no avail. The boy was angry at his whole family. The boy refused to see MHE, so he made a house call. MHE asked what the proper treatment for an ulcerated forehead was. Father and son both informed him that it involved bandages and salves. MHE asked how breaking a bow and arrow could be a treatment for the sore. Father acknowledged that it was inappropriate and MHE got the boy to agree that he could give his father credit for good intentions at least, even if his behavior was stupid. MHE found out that the boy dropped letters out when he wrote things, so he got the boy to agree to practice his handwriting by writing the sentence, "I do not think it is a good idea to pick at that sore on my forehead" (in another version, "I fully agree with Dr. Erickson and I understand that it is neither wise nor good, nor desirable, to keep picking at that sore on my forehead"), in order to eliminate the sore. The boy was to write that on weekends, during which time his father was to take over the boy's weekend chores. The boy was to count the number of lines he had written and was to bring them in to show MHE. His forehead was healed within a month and his grades had improved.

Presenting Problem: Ulcerated forehead; compulsion (to pick a scab)

Age Group: Child

Modality: Family; outpatient

Problem Duration: Two years

Treatment Length: (Four or five sessions)

Result: Success. The ulcer healed.

Follow-up: One year: no recurrence.

Techniques: Ordeal; task assignment (behavioral and cognitive)

Sources: *Conversations III*, pp. 100–106; *Uncommon Therapy*, pp. 209–212; *Teaching Seminar*, pp. 109–110

Case #40

Case Summary: A 10-year-old girl was brought to a demonstration of hypnosis that MHE was doing. She forbid her parents to give MHE any information. She also did not want to tell him anything about her problem, since it was too embarrassing. She was wearing gloves over her gloves, so MHE surmised that she had a fear of getting dirty. She confirmed this and asked him to keep the information confidential and not talk to her like a psychiatrist, but just like an ordinary person having a conversation during the demonstration. She also requested that he not touch her dress and that he let her sit on a chair that had not been used that day. He agreed to her conditions.

She sat in an armchair while MHE lectured about the use of hypnosis for children. Then MHE had her extend her arm out in front of her and stare at the thumb until it enlarged in her view to fill her visual field. When this happened, he said, it would lead to her arm bending at the elbow and her hand would touch her face. When that happened, she was to go deeply asleep with her eyes open, seeing, feeling and hearing nothing but MHE.

After having her experience various trance phenomena, MHE asked her when her birthday was. She replied that it was December 29th. He told her that since it was September, she probably did not yet know what birthday present she would receive. Whatever it was, it could be something special, he told her, and something that she could make herself, like sewing a dress. That birthday was very important, because she would be leaving the little girls and becoming a big girl when she turned 11. Then MHE, in the guise of continuing the lecture, offered a series of posthypnotic suggestions for amnesia and a growing sense of certainty that things were changing inside. The audience members, including her father, who was trained in hypnosis, were not aware of the suggestions given.

MHE told her parents to just watch the girl for any signs of change. The father wrote MHE one month after the girl's birthday and told him that she had been less and less moody and picky about clothing in the months before her birthday. She had also been in a state of anticipation, running to the door when the doorbell rang, answering the phone and rushing for the mail, and when asked had merely said she thought there might be something there. On her birthday she had awakened everyone in the household by running around the house screaming, "It's gone, it's gone!" From then on she was free of the fears and the behavior that had accompanied them. She still refused to let her father tell MHE what her problem had been. Her behavior at school improved as well (she had been having tantrums when some of the other children had accidentally violated her taboos).

Presenting Problem: Fear of getting dirty

Age Group: Child

Modality: Individual; outpatient (demonstration)

Problem Duration: Six months

Treatment Length: One session

Result: Success. The girl stopped having her fears and the corresponding bizarre behavior.

Follow-up: Three years later the young woman came up to him at a hypnosis meeting and told him that she only wore one pair of gloves now, and only when it was appropriate. She still refused to tell him what her fear had been, but told him that the results had lasted.

Techniques: Hypnosis; amnesia; negative hallucination; indirect suggestion; posthypnotic suggestion; linking (getting over her fears with her birthday); splitting (10-year-old little girl from 11-year-old big girl)

Source: *Hypnotherapy*, pp. 278–281

Case #41

Case Summary: A woman came to MHE because she had become obsessed with thoughts of killing herself and her son with a knife. She had seen a number of psychiatrists who had not helped her. She did not want electric or insulin shock therapy and she did not want hypnosis, she told MHE, she only wanted therapy to rid herself of this disturbing idea. MHE challenged her and asked her if she really knew what her son was, how old he was, and what a knife was and what a knife could do. She answered that of course she knew what her son was and how old he was. She was not sure what he meant about whether she knew what a knife was.

MHE used this as an opening to give a long rambling lecture about the varieties of knives and the different kinds of stab techniques one could use. After a while, the woman asked, "Do I need to stab him?" MHE replied that he did not know, but sometimes her son was downstairs, sometimes he was upstairs, and again went off on a long lecture about the various places her son could be and the various places on his body she might stab him. After a number of hours of this, the woman had calmed down enough to go home and feel calm that night. She returned the next day and began to examine her feelings towards her son and her husband. In a short time, she had gained insight into her problem.

Presenting Problem: Obsession (about stabbing self and son)

Age Group: Adult

Modality: Individual; outpatient

Problem Duration: NA

Treatment Length: NA

Result: Partial success reported. The woman stopped having such urgent and intrusive thoughts and was able to get some insight into her problem. MHE does not say whether or not she finally got rid of the obsession totally.

Follow-up: NA

Techniques: Reframing; utilization (of obsessive thinking)

Sources: *Life Reframing*, pp. 206–207; *Mind-Body Communication* pp. 175–177

Case #42

Case Summary: MHE told a woman who compulsively pulled her hair out that she should pull one hair out per day and wrap it very tightly around a matchstick for one month. She got so tired of having to do this that she asked MHE if she could stop. He told her she could pull out two or three hairs and wrap them around a matchstick. She pleaded with him to let her stop. He let her substitute hairs that had naturally come out of her scalp while she was combing her hair and wrap them around a matchstick. She quickly stopped pulling her hair out.

Presenting Problem: Compulsive hair pulling (trichotillomania)

Age Group: Adult

Modality: Individual; outpatient

Problem Duration: NA

Treatment Length: NA

Result: Success. The woman stopped pulling her hair out.

Follow-up: NA

Techniques: Symptom prescription; ordeal

Source: *Phoenix*, pp. 144–145

Case #43

Case Summary: A woman who drank 40 colas per day sought MHE's help to curb her cola habit. MHE told her he could not help her and refused to treat her. When MHE was asked later by a supervisee why he did not just utilize the pattern and have her drink 30 colas, then 20, and gradually reduce the pattern, he replied, "She did not drink 30 colas or 20 colas, she drank 40 colas per day!"

Presenting Problem: Excessive cola drinking

Age Group: Adult

Modality: Individual; outpatient

Problem Duration: NA

Treatment Length: (One session)

Result: Refusal. MHE refused to treat the woman.

Follow-up: NA

Techniques: NA

Sources: Stephen Gilligan, personal communication, 1989

Case #44

2

Physical Problems
and Pain

PHYSICAL GROWTH/DEVELOPMENT

Case Summary: A doctor referred his 17- or 18-year-old-daughter to MHE because she had developed no breasts and had become very withdrawn, hiding behind the furniture and in the corner at home and avoiding all social contacts. Her father was afraid she would become schizophrenic. The girl had been treated with hormones for several years starting at age 12, but although she developed normally physically in other areas, she had no breasts. The girl's mother was quite unpleasant and the girl disliked her.

MHE put the girl in deep trance and explained that, as a man, he was very ignorant about how to develop breasts. But she, as a woman, knew a lot about the subject. He told her that when she was alone at night, she would develop a tremendous surging feeling in her breasts, in her rudimentary nipples. She was to develop amnesia for this and other suggestions. MHE reminded her of the old song, about how the toe-bone's connected to the foot-bone and so on. In a similar manner, her "adrenal-bone" was connected to her "thyroid-bone," and they could support and help each other. She was also led to develop various temperature and sensation changes in trance. She was also given the suggestion that she would develop an unbearable itch in

46

her feet that would soon transfer to the "barren nothingness" of her breast area. She was also instructed to constantly imagine herself in embarrassing social situations that would somehow involve her breasts. She would then feel the weight of that embarrassment sink to her breasts. She was also to act as if she had breasts by lifting her arm up to her face in the way that she would have to if she had breasts.

In the next few weeks, she would develop a growing conviction that she was actually growing breasts. She had a good sense of humor, so MHE instructed her to have a good time during her first year in college and to enjoy mystifying and entertaining her fellow students by wearing different size padding in her bra at different times. She did indeed develop breasts and as a side effect she became less withdrawn and started dating. Her social and academic adjustment in college was good.

Presenting Problem: Lack of breast development; avoiding people

Age Group: Adolescent

Modality: Individual; outpatient

Problem Duration: Five-six years

Treatment Length: Once a week for two months; eight sessions

Result: Success. The young woman grew breasts and became less socially withdrawn.

Follow-up: Nine months. She came in to see MHE at the end of her first year in college and told him that she was not wearing padding. She had grown medium-sized breasts and asked him to stop the growing process at that size.

Techniques: Hypnosis; posthypnotic suggestion (behavioral and perceptual); amnesia; analogy; utilization (of embarrassment and humor)

Sources: *Collected Papers II*, pp. 183–185, pp. 204–206; *Mind-Body Communication*, pp. 9–11; *Uncommon Therapy*, pp. 112–115

Case #45

Case Summary: A 20-year-old woman was brought by her sister to MHE for therapy because she had failed to develop breasts. She had failed some of her college courses, was afraid to seek a job, was maladjusted emotionally, and was engaged to a 47-year-old alcoholic welfare recipient. She had been raised in a very severe religious manner, with concomitant harsh views of the physical body. MHE put her in trance and suggested that she read the Song of Solomon from the Bible and realize that, while it glorifies the church, it also glorifies the female body. He told her that she should develop a similar attitude towards her body and patient expectancy towards her breasts. She was further instructed to develop an intense feeling of goodness and promise about her breasts. Two years after the one session of hypnosis she had broken up with the alcoholic and was engaged to a young man her own age, returned to college and passed the courses she previously failed, was reading the Song of Solomon weekly, and had grown breasts.

Presenting Problem: Lack of breast development

Age Group: Adult

Modality: Individual; outpatient

Problem Duration: NA

Treatment Length: One session

Result: Success. The woman had developed breasts and was making a better personal and social adjustment.

Follow-up: Two years

Techniques: Direct suggestion; reframing; task assignment (behavioral and cognitive)

Source: *Collected Papers II*, pp. 203–204

Case #46

UNRECOGNIZED ORGANIC PROBLEMS

Case Summary: MHE saw a 20-year-old man with stunted growth. MHE found that the man saw everything as if he were much smaller than he really was, as if he were looking at the world from his waist height. MHE got him to hallucinate his world as if he were standing partway up a staircase. After a time of this, the man grew 12 inches in one year. MHE never wrote the case up because he was certain no one would believe it.

Presenting Problem: Stunted growth

Age Group: Adult

Modality: Individual; outpatient

Problem Duration: NA

Treatment Length: NA

Result: Success. The man grew 12 inches in one year.

Follow-up: NA

Techniques: Positive hallucination; utilization (of the man's ability to alter his visual perspective); symptom transformation (seeing the world from a short to a taller perspective)

Source: *Ericksonian Approaches*, p. 282

Case #47

Case Summary: A student who was attending college on the G.I. Bill reported to the Veterans Administration Hospital with fatigue and concern about his heart. Despite being very intelligent, he was failing all his classes. MHE examined him and suspected that he had broken some bones in his feet several weeks earlier after jumping down some stairs. The student had spontaneously developed an anesthesia in his feet, however, so that he was not aware of the injury. MHE determined from his history that the man was in danger of becoming an invalid if he discovered the extent of his injuries, as he reacted with complete collapse at the slightest injury. [In one version of the case, however, the young man is shown the X-rays and exclaims, "But I thought broken bones hurt!"] Therefore, he set up an elaborate ruse, telling the man that he had a skin condition that would have to be treated by X-ray (this was really done to verify and assess the fracture) and kept in some medicated gauze protected by a cast with iron supports. The student accepted the explanation and with some hypnotic suggestions from MHE he continued to have the "stocking anesthesia" that had protected him from experiencing the pain of his injury until it was cured. The student subsequently made all A's in his college classes.

Presenting Problem: Fatigue; worry about heart; academic failure; (fractured bones in feet)

Age Group: Adult

Modality: Individual; outpatient

Problem Duration: Two weeks

Treatment Length: (One session)

Result: Success. The student was successfully treated without undue upset.

Follow-up: NA

Techniques: Hypnosis; reframing; utilization (of denial and anesthesia)

Sources: *Collected Papers II*, p. 182, pp. 313–314 and p. 346; *Mind-Body Communication*, pp. 6–8

Case #48

Case Summary: A middle-aged nurse was referred to MHE by another physician. She was suffering from vague intestinal pain, fatigue, insomnia, a lump in her throat and weakness. She had diagnosed the lump in her throat as "hystericus globus." MHE said that it sounded to him as if she had a peptic ulcer and he recommended she get an X-ray. She refused and demanded hypnosis. In hypnosis, she agreed to seek an X-ray, which showed that she did have a peptic ulcer. She informed MHE that she intended to ignore the medical advice she was given regarding the ulcer. In trance, MHE told her that she should take charge and to dominate her therapy. She could do this by freely following the medical advice she had been given and by taking a happier attitude toward her situation. She complied and returned two more times for more help in treating herself. The nurse was Armenian and liked spicy food. He told her to go on eating the food. He told her that she was always saying that she couldn't stomach the daily calls she received from her sister and her niece. He suggested that she stop the frequent visits and phone calls she was getting from her sister and her niece. Her ulcer cleared up after the second session.

Presenting Problem: Vague gastric pains, fatigue, weakness, lump in throat

Age Group: Adult

Modality: Individual; outpatient

Problem Duration: NA

Treatment Length: Four sessions

Result: What the woman thought was a hysterical condition was shown to be an ulcer, which cleared up with help from hypnotic suggestions.

Follow-up: NA

Techniques: Hypnosis; utilization (of the woman's resistance and domineering nature)

Sources: *Collected Papers IV*, p. 50; *Mind-Body Communication*, pp. 148–149; *My Voice Will Go With You*, pp. 233–234

Case #49

Case Summary: A woman from Baja, California was referred to MHE because she was thought to have hysterical paralysis. She had been examined by many physicians and, since no organic cause had been found, they had come to the conclusion that it was a psychiatric problem that might yield to hypnotic treatment. The woman told MHE her body felt strange and that her paralysis would shift from her arm to her leg at different times. MHE did not think it was psychological, so he sent her back to her doctor and told him he thought it was organic. Her doctor hypnotized her out of her symptoms, but after a time they returned. Again he hypnotized her and the symptoms left. The next day she died. The autopsy report showed that she had a diffuse brain tumor.

Presenting Problem: Intermittent paralysis of arms and legs

Age Group: Adult

Modality: Individual; outpatient

Problem Duration: NA

Treatment Length: One session

Result: Dismissal. MHE thought the woman's problem was organic, not psychiatric. MHE was correct.

Follow-up: The woman's doctor sent MHE the autopsy report.

Techniques: NA

Source: *Mind-Body Communication*, pp. 102–103

Case #50

Case Summary: A secretary who was a good hypnotic subject called MHE on the phone. She wanted hypnotic anesthesia for menstrual cramps. Over the phone he put her into a trance and told her that her menstrual cramps would cause her no further pain. He awakened her and she said, "Thank you, the pain is all gone." Twenty minutes later she called back and said the anesthesia had worn off. He hypnotized her for menstrual cramps again. A half-hour later she called back with the same complaint. MHE told her to call her doctor and tell him she had acute appendicitis. The next morning her appendix was removed.

Presenting Problem: Pain (from menstrual cramps)

Age Group: Adult

Modality: Individual; outpatient

Problem Duration: NA

Treatment Length: Three short phone calls

Result: Success. MHE discovered that her pain was not due to menstrual cramps but to appendicitis. Her appendix was removed.

Follow-up: NA

Techniques: Hypnosis; anesthesia; direct suggestion

Source: *Teaching Seminar*, pp. 62–63

Case #51

NON-ORGANIC PARALYSIS/DEAFNESS

Case Summary: A 59-year-old laborer one year from retiring on a company pension injured his right arm slightly at work and reacted by developing a hysterical paralysis of the right arm. The company physician was threatening to terminate the man without his pension if he did not recover, "stop this nonsense," and return to work within a week. MHE arranged to have two other physicians examine the man with him. They discussed his case in front of him using complicated medical terms and giving the man the impression that they had discovered his true condition, which was physical, not mental, in origin. This was all an elaborate ruse used to deliver hypnotic suggestions to the man. They decided that he was suffering from an "inertia syndrome" which would, if it were really physical, have a predictable course. First the muscles in his right shoulder would relax and then he would recover the feeling in his arm and would be left with a stiff wrist that would never go away. It would get fatigued after use, but not so much as to interfere with his job performance. MHE convinced the man that he would have to use hypnosis to verify the diagnosis. The man responded to the suggestions and was able to work until his retirement, at which time his stiff wrist symptom left.

Presenting Problem: Paralysis of the right arm

Age Group: Adult

Modality: Individual; outpatient

Problem Duration: One week

Treatment Length: One session

Result: Success. The man was able to regain use of his arm and return to work.

Follow-up: At least one year. When he retired, the man lost the stiff wrist that was substituted for the paralysis of the arm.

Techniques: Anchoring the symptom; hypnosis; indirect suggestion; reframing; symptom substitution.

Source: *Collected Papers IV*, pp. 150–151

Case #52

Case Summary: A 33-year-old woman who was married to a doctor was carried into MHE's office by the doctor and his partner. The doctor and his wife had been arguing in his office when she had suddenly started to scream hysterically. When her husband could not bring her out of her screaming fit, the partner came into the office. The two men had agreed that if they slapped her she might respond. When she was slapped, she froze and went catatonic. Shining a bright light in her eyes had no effect. She wouldn't respond to requests for answers or movement. The husband recommended MHE give her a shot of something to knock her out and let her sleep it off or, if he had to, give her electroshock.

MHE dismissed both men from his office and decided to use a psychological approach. MHE turned on a blinking toy light in his office and timed suggestions to the blinking of the light. He suggested that at first she could see a light in the distance, then it would disappear. He repeated this for about 20 minutes; then, when he saw a light quivering of her eyelids, he added the suggestion that she should try harder to see timed to coincide with the light being on. After five more minutes her eyelids began to quiver and her pupils began to contract. MHE started to link suggestions for eye closure with the blinking light. When she responded to those suggestions, he suggested that she rest and sleep deeply. Then he suggested that she feel so comfortable that she could tell him whatever he asked.

Within 45 minutes, she had related to him an incident from her childhood in which a neighbor woman had started to scream and then gone catatonic, which had resulted in the woman's being committed to the mental hospital. When the woman had begun to argue with her doctor husband about where they would go on vacation (she wanted to visit her hometown and he wanted to go elsewhere), she realized he would get his way and started to scream in frustration. Suddenly she wondered whether she would be able to stop. She had become scared at that thought. Then when her husband slapped her, she had become paralyzed and mute, unable to see or hear anything. The next thing she became aware of was a distant light and MHE's voice.

She was most shaken by the experience, but MHE reassured her that it would not happen again. She asked that her husband and his partner be brought in and informed of the situation and her recovery. They listened to the story and all went home. The problem never recurred and the woman adjusted well.

Presenting Problem: Catatonia

Age Group: Adult

Modality: Individual; outpatient

Problem Duration: Several hours

Treatment Length: Two hours

Result: Success. The woman came out of her catatonic stupor.

Follow-up: Six years. There had been no recurrence of the problem.

Techniques: Linking (blinking of the light with suggestions)

Source: *Hypnotherapy*, pp. 353–356

Case #53

꩜

Case Summary: A woman was brought to MHE's office by her husband after she had developed paralysis and mutism during an argument. She had gotten into a minor car accident the night before and had waited to tell her husband until morning, fearing that he would be upset and unpleasant. When she told him the next morning, he exploded in anger and yelled at her. An argument ensued and she had gotten so angry with him that she had thrown her purse at him. The purse fell on the floor and her pocket mirror fell out. As the sun hit the mirror and reflected into her eyes, she became fixated just the way she was at her moment of anger. She was unresponsive to her husband. After trying for some time to get a response from her, he had desperately brought her to MHE.

MHE dismissed the man from his office and gently touched her on the shoulder. She immediately became rigid and looked as if she would scream, but no sound emerged. MHE placed a blinking toy light within her field of vision and started to time his suggestions with the blinking light. He then added suggestions that she was frightened but beginning to feel better. When he saw her relax, he added that it was just a light fright and she could relax more and more and go deeper and deeper asleep.

In this way he induced a trance and told her to relate the recent incident as if she were talking about someone else. She related a long-forgotten incident from childhood in which she had run out in front of a car and had been paralyzed with fright when she had seen the glare of the oncoming headlight. During the argument, when the light hit her eyes, it had triggered that memory. She was brought out of trance and had no recurrence of the problem. She and her husband were seen three more times for their current needs.

Presenting Problem: Paralysis; mutism; catatonia

Age Group: Adult

Modality: Individual/couple; outpatient

Problem Duration: Several hours

Treatment Length: Four sessions

Result: Success. The woman came out of her paralyzed state and it never recurred.

Follow-up: NA

Techniques: Hypnosis; matching; linking (the blinking light to the suggestions); utilization (of light, which had brought on the symptom); dissociation

Source: *Hypnotherapy*, pp. 356–358

Case #54

ASTHMA

Case Summary: A 35-year-old woman who had been seeing MHE wondered if he could help her figure out why she had asthma and why she had it at only during the winter months. She was certain that it was organic, although many allergists and doctors had told her that it was psychological. He told her that he thought they could discover if it was psychological in that very session. She was skeptical, but he predicted that she would have an asthma attack at a certain time during the session.

MHE had noted while he was gathering some background information that her father only wrote to her during the winter months, when he had time off from his farm work. She had had a disagreement with her father right after her mother's death and had come down with a cold at the same time. She attributed the asthma to the cold, but MHE suspected it had a psychological trigger.

He put her in trance and told her that he was going to tap his pencil at a certain time after she aroused from the trance and that would trigger a very important memory. He also arranged for her to have amnesia for what had transpired in trance. After she came out of trance, he reminded her that it was a very hot July in Phoenix and wondered whether she thought she could have an asthma attack at that time. She maintained that she could not because the attacks were brought about by the cold weather. She agreed that, if she were to have one then, they would certainly be psychological.

From 2:17 until 2:34, they sat in silence in the session; then MHE mentioned that it was three minutes until she would either have or not have an asthma attack. At the specified time, MHE tapped his pencil and told her she could remember the content of any of the nasty letters that her father was in the habit of sending her. The woman began to have an asthma attack. MHE reinduced trance with a previously established cue and told her that the attack could stop. It did. The woman was then awakened and instructed to fully recall the events of the session and the trance. It turned out that her father had been rather cruel to her mother and that her mother had left some of the mother's property to her daughter instead of her husband. Every year, during certain predictable times of the year, her father would send her letters bitterly criticizing her. Once the woman made the connection in MHE's office, she stopped having asthma. MHE continued to see her and helped her write some letters in reply to her father's nasty letters to her and to secure her legal rights in the matter of the property.

Presenting Problem: Asthma

Age Group: Adult

Modality: Individual; outpatient

Problem Duration: 10 years

Treatment Length: NA

Result: Success. Her asthma cleared up.

Follow-up: Five-year follow-up. The treatment took place in July of 1949 and she was last seen by MHE in a casual visit in June 1954.

Techniques: Hypnosis; amnesia; posthypnotic suggestion; guiding associations

Sources: *Collected Papers IV*, p. 91; *Hypnotherapy*, pp. 235–237

Case #55

Case Summary: A 12-year-old boy had severe asthma and was constantly using his inhaler to help him breathe. MHE asked the boy to describe his fears regarding his breathing problem in great detail. As the boy became absorbed in telling MHE about his fears of dying, he started relaxing and breathing more easily. MHE pointed this freer breathing out to the boy and told him that a certain percentage of his asthma might be due to his fears, while other parts of it were organic. They decided together that only 20 percent of the asthma was organic. After the boy had made this shift in his asthma, he made other positive changes in his life as well.

Presenting Problem: Asthma

Age Group: Child

Modality: Individual; outpatient

Problem Duration: NA

Treatment Length: NA

Result: Partial success. The boy was able to reduce the amount of his asthma.

Follow-up: NA

Techniques: Reframing; splitting (asthma into emotional and organic aspects)

Source: *Healing in Hypnosis*, pp. 198–199

Case #56

Case Summary: A woman and her husband had been living in San Diego in a converted garage with no electricity trying to save money to buy a house. After a while the woman noticed that their savings account was not building up as rapidly as they had planned. Her investigation led to the discovery that her husband was having an affair. When she confronted the mistress, the mistress laughed at her. The woman developed a severe asthma attack and had to be hospitalized. When she was released, she found that she could not stay in San Diego without having severe asthma attacks. The couple moved to Phoenix and her husband gave up the affair and promised not to have affairs in the future. She found that she could still not return to San Diego, where both she and her husband very much wanted to live. MHE used hypnosis with her and told her that what had happened to her was enough to make any woman catch her breath. He used many other puns and common idioms involving breathing while she was in trance. After four hours, he suggested that she drive to San Diego and drive around. She did so and had no trouble breathing, even when she visited and reconfronted the former mistress. She wired her husband and had him return. She was very happy to be back in San Diego.

Presenting Problem: Asthma; affair

Age Group: Adult

Modality: Individual; outpatient

Problem Duration: NA

Treatment Length: Four hours

Result: Success. The woman was able to return to San Diego and breathe comfortably.

Follow-up: NA

Techniques: Hypnosis; metaphor

Source: *Mind-Body Communication*, pp. 88–89

Case #57

INFERTILITY

Case Summary: A woman had been married twice, both times to husbands who had had children in previous marriages. Although she desperately wanted to have children, she had not been able to get pregnant. She saw MHE reluctantly after being referred by her physician and informed him that she had no need for more psychotherapy as she had already had some. She wanted only to get pregnant. MHE induced a profound trance with her and began to direct her to experience various physiological changes. She learned that one arm could get very warm and the other very cold; that one of her legs could get very relaxed and at the same time an arm could get very cold; that she could blush as she sat quietly in the chair; that her chest could get cold and then her breasts could start to get warm; that her pelvis could get warm and relaxed and then lose that relaxed feeling and then get it back. He then explained to her that he thought she might be having tubal spasms that were preventing her pregnancy and that she should relax her pelvis completely during sex. She soon reported that she had a surprisingly cramp-free menstrual period. Later she became pregnant and attributed that result to MHE's teaching her to relax.

Presenting Problem: Infertility

Age Group: Adult

Modality: Individual; outpatient

Problem Duration: 12 years

Treatment Length: Less than three months

Result: Success. The woman got pregnant.

Follow-up: NA

Techniques: Hypnosis; apposition of opposites; direct suggestion; reframing

Source: *Collected Papers II*, pp. 200–202

Case #58

꙳

Case Summary: Two single college professors got married. They both were 30 years old, and both wanted children desperately. They described their difficulty to MHE in very stilted professional language. Due to their ages, they had decided that they would begin procreative intercourse immediately after their wedding. They told MHE that they believed that for procreative purposes their physical union must be accompanied by complete emotional and intellectual union. They had physical union twice daily, continuing until both had orgasms. On Sundays and holidays they did it up to four times. At the end of three years they were still childless. They had both been examined and no medical reason could be found for their infertility. They came to MHE with their story and complained that they had become emotionally intolerant of each other and that intercourse had become a burden and a duty.

Noting their stiff posture and the polysyllabic vocabulary they used to describe everyday events, MHE told them that they needed shock therapy. He told them it would not be electric shock therapy, but emotional or psychological shock therapy and he was not sure that they were ready for it.

He left them alone in the office for 30 minutes to contemplate and discuss whether or not they were ready for shock treatment. When MHE reentered the office and they assured him were ready, he gave them their shock and ordered them to ride the 40 miles back home in complete and utter silence after he had given them the shock. He had them both hold onto the seats of their chairs and asked them, "Why in hell don't you fuck for fun and pray to the devil she doesn't get pregnant and spoil your fun for three months?" A month later MHE dropped in on the couple unexpectedly. The couple looked very embarrassed, but the subject of sex didn't come up. Three months later they came in to tell MHE the wife was pregnant.

Presenting Problem: Sexual dissatisfaction; infertility

Age Group: Adult

Modality: Marital; outpatient

Problem Duration: Three years

Treatment Length: One session

Result: Success. The couple developed fertility.

Follow-up: Three months. During the follow-up visit they told MHE a number of dirty stories.

Techniques: Reframing; task assignment (behavioral and cognitive); shock

Sources: *Collected Papers IV*, pp. 447–450; *Conversations II*, pp. 123–125; *Healing in Hypnosis*, pp. 203–206; *Uncommon Therapy*, pp. 164–169

Case #59

MENSTRUAL PROBLEMS

Case Summary: A woman in her thirties sought MHE's help for irregular and uncomfortable menstrual periods. She had severe headaches, vomiting, and gastrointestinal problems and had to take to her bed for five days each month. MHE induced a deep trance and told her that she would have a

dream on any Saturday night she chose. In that dream, time would be tele-
scoped so that the dream would seem to last five days. She should dream
that she had her period. Yet she would sleep soundly and awaken refreshed
the next morning. He also suggested that she develop amnesia for having
had the dream. Two weeks later she reported having an unusually pleasant
menstrual period. She was rather perplexed as to how and why it happened.
She had no more discomfort during periods after that.

Presenting Problem: Painful menstruation; irregular menstrual cycles

Age Group: Adult

Modality: Individual; outpatient

Problem Duration: (20 years, since menarche)

Treatment Length: One session

Result: Success. The woman had more comfortable menstrual periods following treatment.

Follow-up: Several years

Techniques: Hypnosis; time distortion; posthypnotic suggestion; amnesia

Sources: *Collected Papers II*, pp. 182–183; *Mind-Body Communication*,
pp. 8–9

Case #60

∿

Case Summary: A woman sought MHE's help because she had a late
menstrual period and was fearful about that. MHE suggested that she attend a swimming party that weekend. He then built up her recall of pleasant
childhood, adolescent, and adult memories of swimming. Then he suggested that she might start to fear that she would start her menstrual bleeding at
a time which would interfere with her pleasantly anticipated swimming
party. She did start her bleeding before the party and was unable to attend.
[MHE describes two identical cases here.]

Presenting Problem: Late menstrual period; fear of pregnancy

Age Group: Adult

Modality: Individual; outpatient

Problem Duration: NA

Treatment Length: One session

Result: Success. The woman had her menstrual period.

Follow-up: NA

Techniques: Symptom transformation (fear of not menstruating into fear of menstruating)

Sources: *Collected Papers II*, pp. 187–188; *Mind-Body Communication* pp. 17–18

Case #61

Case Summary: A 30-year-old woman who had painful and difficult menstrual periods asked MHE to hypnotize her to have no unpleasant symptoms for her next period. MHE tried to get her to let him work on all future periods, but she insisted he only deal with the next one. She returned two months later and reported that the next period she had was fine, but then the most recent one was even more miserable than previous ones had been. He asked her why she had not allowed him to give suggestions covering all future periods. She told him she had wanted to find out for herself whether the suggestions worked. She then allowed him to give her suggestions for all future periods being comfortable, except for those times when it would be useful for her to have severe discomfort. MHE told her that even if her menstrual cycle was interrupted by illness or pregnancy, that as soon as she started to menstruate again, the suggestions would hold.

She was able to carry out the suggestion. She worked for a doctor and when she wanted a raise because the doctor was paying her too little, she had another severely painful period that caused her to look miserable during a very busy time at the office. Her physician, who saw her during this time and worked in the same office building, recommended that her employer let her go home because she was so ill. The employer decided instead to give her a raise. Later she had a false pregnancy and missed two periods. The next period brought the old discomfort back for a short time and then it went away automatically.

Presenting Problem: Painful and uncomfortable menstrual periods

Age Group: Adult

Modality: Individual; outpatient

Problem Duration: NA

Treatment Length: (Two sessions)

Result: Success. The woman had few more painful periods and those she did have were for useful purposes.

Follow-up: At least one year.

Techniques: Hypnosis; posthypnotic suggestion; splitting (the symptoms could occur when it was useful)

Source: *Life Reframing*, pp. 3–6

Case #62

PAIN

Case Summary: A 37-year-old woman with four children was dying of cancer of the uterus. The severe pain she was having necessitated large doses of narcotics so that she could sleep and eat without vomiting. The woman resented spending her last days in a "narcotic semi-stupor" so her doctor called in MHE to do hypnosis. In one four-hour session MHE taught her "to go into a trance, to develop a numbness of her body, to absorb herself in a profound fatigue so that she could have physiological sleep despite the pain, and to enjoy food without gastric distress." MHE's hypnosis, reinforced by suggestions MHE had taught her family members to give her, allowed her to forego medication with the exception of one heavy hypodermic on Thursday evenings to give her additional relief so she could enjoy the weekends. Six weeks later, while talking to her daughter, she suddenly lapsed into a coma and died soon after.

Presenting Problem: Pain (from cancer)

Age Group: Adult

Modality: Individual; outpatient (home visit)

Problem Duration: NA

Treatment Length: One session, four hours

Result: Success. The woman was able to be more lucid with less pain medication so that she could enjoy her last days with her family.

Follow-up: She died six weeks later.

Techniques: Hypnosis; anesthesia

Sources: *Collected Papers I*, p. 284; *Collected Papers IV*, pp. 256–257; *Uncommon Therapy*, p. 299

Case #63

❧

Case Summary: An 80-year-old dentist who was dying of prostatic cancer complained of a constant heavy, dull, throbbing ache, as well as sharp agonizing pains that came five to 10 minutes apart. He wanted to spend his final days with his family without being in a drug-induced stupor, so he sought hypnosis from MHE. He went off pain medications for 12 hours in order to be able to have hypnosis.

MHE used confusion and interspersal in his induction, then suggested that the man should let his body feel sodden with a heavy fatigue. He could then let his body sleep while his mind was awake. To cope with the sharp pains, MHE had the man fix his eyes on the clock and await the next sharp pain. The period of waiting for the pain seemed very long to the patient and the occurrence of the pain became a relief. MHE taught him time distortion to lengthen the period in between pains and to shorten the time of the pain. The man was able to get the pains to last only five to 10 seconds and to stretch the time between them to 30 to 40 minutes. He would have a sharp pain and scream, go into a quick trance for a few seconds, then open his eyes looking bewildered and pick up speaking right where he left off.

MHE told him that pain consisted of anticipated and remembered pain, so he taught the man amnesia for the pain so that he did not look back or forward to the pains. MHE then told the man that in his dreams he could be in a car, a boat, a plane, or in the other room. Since his body was having the pain right here, why not feel himself somewhere else, just as he did in dreams? He then was able to learn to put all his pain into his left hand, which he guarded carefully from being bumped. The patient reported to him that, although he felt heavy, weak, and dull physically, the hypnosis had overcome his pain so that it rarely "broke through." Some weeks later he went into a coma and died.

Presenting Problem: Pain (from prostatic cancer)

Age Group: Adult

Modality: Individual; outpatient

Problem Duration: NA

Treatment Length: NA

Result: Success. The man experienced pain relief.

Follow-up: The man died some weeks after treatment.

Techniques: Hypnosis; alteration of sensations; splitting (past/remembered pain from present pain); body dissociation; time distortion (condensation of pain experiences, expansion of pain free times); confusion technique; anchoring the symptom

Sources: *Collected Papers I*, p. 284; *Collected Papers IV*, pp. 258–261; *Healing in Hypnosis*, pp. 222–230; *Hypnotherapy*, p. 101; *Life Reframing*, pp. 25–27 and pp. 156–165; *Uncommon Therapy*, p. 300

Case #64

Case Summary: When this woman entered MHE's office, he could see by the way that she moved and guarded the right side of her face that she suffered from severe trigeminal pain. He instructed her to answer his assessment questions sparsely, so as not to cause her unnecessary pain. He found out that she was pronounced incurable by neurologists and given only the risky options of alcohol injections or surgery, neither of which were guaranteed and which might make her problem worse. She was skeptical of hypnosis but sought MHE's help as a desperate measure.

MHE read her an article about hypnotizing resistant patients which contained an induction script. She went into trance listening to the induction being read. When she was aroused from the trance, MHE reoriented her to the moments before he started reading the article, thus inducing amnesia for the trance. The woman was astonished to find she could easily talk without pain and that an hour had gone by. She had thought that only five or 10 minutes had passed.

The next day she returned for another session and told MHE that she thought that just meeting a doctor who used hypnosis must have helped her, as she was feeling better already, talking and drinking easily. Another trance was induced and MHE gave her a series of indirect suggestions. For example, he told her that cracking a hard nut on the right side of her mouth (where her pain was) would be quite painful and not at all like eating. Another was that it was too bad that the first bite of steak would be so very painful, but that she could enjoy the rest of the steak. She was again aroused from trance with amnesia and was surprised that the hour was already over. MHE remarked casually that the lost time had gone to join the lost pain.

She returned the next day and reported that she had enjoyed a filet mignon after a painful first bite and had also discovered that she was losing the sensitivity of the spots in her face that used to cause severe pain when touched. At the end of four hour long daily sessions, her pain was gone. She told MHE that perhaps she should return to her home (she was visiting from out of state), but he told her she had not learned how to get over the recurrences of the pain yet. In response, she stiffened with a recurrence of the pain and then went into trance and lost it. He had her practice six more times.

He gave her one more appointment for the next day and at that session had her overcome any doubts she might have. MHE instructed her to slap herself hard on the right side of her face. She did and it didn't hurt, but MHE noticed that she slapped herself a bit lightly. He had her repeat the procedure without holding herself back. She slapped herself hard and experienced no trigeminal pain. He told her that some people really have to have understanding pounded into their heads.

They shared a laugh over this and he told her he had one more thing to tell her. She had the habit of whistling tunes as she was walking down the street or at work. MHE told her that she was to make up a tune and whistle it to herself to accompany the words, "I can have you anytime I want, but Baby, there ain't never gonna be a time when I want you." He then dismissed her by telling her to bring him one good tomorrow and then she could have all good tomorrows in the future.

She came for her final session and MHE told her that if she encountered any skepticism from others, she could respond with amusement. When she returned to her home, her neurologist told her that her pain relief was only temporary. She responded by being amused but not giving up her progress.

Presenting Problem: Trigeminal pain

Age Group: Adult

Modality: Individual; outpatient

Problem Duration: Five years (the woman had had trigeminal pain 30 to 40 months out of the past 60)

Treatment Length: Five days, five sessions, five hours.

Result: Success. The woman was free of the trigeminal pain and the disabilities it had produced in her daily life.

Follow-up: NA

Techniques: Hypnosis; amnesia; implication; indirect suggestion; splitting (painful biting of a hard nut from eating; first bite of a steak from the rest of the steak)

Source: *Collected Papers I*, pp. 320–326

Case #65

Case Summary: A man in his late sixties sought MHE's help for phantom limb pain and resultant pain drug dependency following a hemipelvectomy. Frank had been through all kinds of traditional and exotic treatment methods, but had yet to find relief from his pain. His doctor had advised him that he was rich enough and old enough to live the rest of his life on "dope." He told MHE when he met him that he was a stubborn, impossible subject since previous attempts to use hypnosis had failed. MHE talked to him casually and began to intersperse hypnotic and pain control suggestions into the conversation. It took two months to reduce the pain enough for Frank to get off medications. He returned for more treatment nine months later, after a severe flu attack. He returned once more over a year later, after an operation and resultant infection had again brought back severe pain.

MHE had noticed that Frank was scrupulously honest in all his transactions, almost compulsively so. While a visiting psychiatrist was observing one of Frank's sessions, MHE suggested that Frank remember vividly some situation from the past in which he was dishonest or broke the law and had forgotten about it due to shame. Frank remembered an incident in which an acquaintance had persuaded him to catch more than the legal limit of fish. Frank was astonished that MHE had been able to pick up on that as an issue and been able to persuade him to remember something he very much wanted to forget. After telling MHE about the incident, however, he found it did not bother him quite so much.

Presenting Problem: Phantom limb pain; drug dependency

Age Group: Adult

Modality: Individual; outpatient

Problem Duration: Six years

Treatment Length: Three different times; first treatment two months duration, at least three sessions, probably more, of which the first two were three hours in duration each; second treatment nine months later, at least four sessions, of which the first three were two hours in duration; third treatment took place over a year later.

Result: Pain control and freedom from drugs for periods of time, with intermittent recurrences of both problems; the phantom limb pain was never totally relieved.

Follow-up: Nearly a year after the third treatment, the patient was seen socially, no mention was made by MHE of relapse or recurrence in his account.

Techniques: Hypnosis; interspersal; hypermnesia

Source: *Collected Papers II*, pp. 131–136

Case #66

ॐ

Case Summary: A man sought MHE's help for his wife, who was dying from lung cancer. She was so drugged with narcotics that she had become comatose. She and her family resented not being able to relate during her final days. At MHE's request, she underwent 12 hours of painful withdrawal from the medications, in order to be lucid enough to benefit from the hypnosis. MHE induced a deep trance, made possible, he said, by her extreme motivation. In the trance, he suggested that each day the hypnotic anesthesia suggestions would be strengthened and renewed. She was able to forgo both the medication and the pain for her final weeks.

Presenting Problem: Pain (from lung cancer)

Age Group: Adult

Modality: Individual; outpatient

Problem Duration: NA

Treatment Length: NA

Result: Success. The woman was free of pain and off the narcotics.

Follow-up: The woman and her family enjoyed more than five weeks of pain and coma free time. She experienced no more than a slight ache and a feeling of heaviness in her chest.

Techniques: Hypnosis; anesthesia

Source: *Collected Papers IV*, p. 51

Case #67

Case Summary: A man was complaining about heart pains, but MHE knew they were imaginary because he described them as being in his chest wall. Heart pains, MHE knew, are not felt in the chest wall. So MHE started to quiz the man about exactly where the pain was. Was it on the right side of the sternum, or was it on the left side of the sternum? Gradually, through asking questions that subtly suggested that the pain was in slightly different locations, MHE was able to get the pain to migrate down the man's arm, where it dissipated. MHE said that there was still a lot of investigation of the underlying reasons for the pain, but that since the physical pain was now eliminated, that investigation could more easily proceed.

Presenting Problem: Heart pains

Age Group: Adult

Modality: Individual; outpatient

Problem Duration: NA

Treatment Length: NA

Result: Success. The heart pain was eliminated. Therapy proceeded to examine other potentially problematic areas such as the man's relationships and attitudes.

Follow-up: NA

Techniques: Implication; pattern intervention (changing the location of the pain)

Source: *Collected Papers IV*, p. 95

Case #68

꙳

Case Summary: MHE did hypnosis with a 35-year-old woman who was dying of cancer. She had four small children. She had been in a narcotic stupor for a month before MHE saw her and wanted to use hypnosis for the pain instead of such stupefying medications. She willingly did without drugs for the entire day to prepare for the hypnosis. MHE saw her at 6 p.m. and she was in a great deal of pain. It took him four hours to induce a light trance. He then had her take a small amount of pain medication, eat lightly, and sleep for an hour before continuing the hypnosis. He then spent the rest of the night teaching her many hypnotic skills. She proved to be an excellent somnambulistic subject and learned to experience positive and negative hallucination in the areas of sight, smell, taste, feeling, touch, deep sensation, kinesthesia, and sound. She also learned dissociation, body disorientation, glove and stocking anesthesia, and partial and general anesthesia. She was able to spend the last five weeks of her life much more alert and pain-free, only occasionally resorting to some aspirin and, more rarely, a small amount of morphine.

Presenting Problem: Pain (from cancer)

Age Group: Adult

Modality: Individual; outpatient

Problem Duration: NA

Treatment Length: One session, 11 hours

Result: Success. The woman was able to spend her last days relatively free of pain and drugs.

Follow-up: Five weeks after the hypnosis, the woman died.

Techniques: Hypnosis; anesthesia; dissociation; body disorientation; positive hallucination; negative hallucination.

Source: *Collected Papers IV*, pp. 257–258

Case #69

꙳

Case Summary: Joe was a florist and an enthusiastic businessman. He developed a growth on the side of his face which turned out to be a malignancy. After being told he had a month to live, he became distressed and developed severe pain. A relative asked MHE to do hypnosis with him. Joe had toxic reactions from excessive medication and disliked even the mention of the word hypnosis. Joe had had a tracheotomy because of the damage to his face and could only communicate through writing.

MHE used the "interspersal" technique of hypnosis with Joe. He gave a lengthy discussion about the joys of watching tomato plants grow, emphasizing words like "comfortable," "peaceful," and "satisfaction." He talked about the plants in a repetitive and soothing way that put Joe into a deep trance. Periodically Joe would have episodes of toxic behavior, but he was generally responsive to MHE.

A month later MHE wanted to see Joe again. Joe's wife told MHE that his reported success with Joe had resulted in many amateurish attempts at hypnosis by the hospital staff. Joe had been infuriated by these attempts but they had not detracted from MHE's work because they bore no resemblance to his technique.

MHE went to Joe's home, where Joe greeted him with pleasure. He was shown all the special things about Joe's home, especially Joe's garden, and had a steak from his barbecue. Joe was quite pleased when MHE commented on a rare variety of plant. After lunch MHE continued his hypnosis of Joe, using the same technique but discussing different topics. MHE's hypnosis improved Joe's physical condition but the malignancy progressed. Four months after the discovery of his condition he died quietly.

Presenting Problem: Pain (from cancer)

Age Group: Adult

Modality: Individual; inpatient and outpatient (home visit)

Problem Duration: One month

Treatment Length: Two sessions

Result: Success. The man had pain control and improvement in his condition.

Follow-up: Joe died three months later.

Techniques: Hypnosis; interspersal; indirect suggestion

Sources: *Collected Papers IV*, pp. 268–275; *Experiencing Erickson*, pp. 41–43; *Uncommon Therapy*, pp. 301–306

Case #70

Case Summary: A 70-year-old retired soldier came to MHE for therapy. At age 56 he had developed tic douloureux. He had a couple of operations and alcohol injections to the ganglia. Neither treatment was lastingly effective. As the man described his problem MHE watched his eyes. When the man talked about his pain his pupils would dilate and his breathing would catch, suggesting that his pain was indeed somatic in origin. MHE put the man in trance and explained that the pain was a "habitual misinterpretation, a rhythmical, habitual misinterpretation of the ordinary sensation of the face." MHE suggested he lose the pain. When the man died seven years later he was still free of the pain.

Presenting Problem: Pain (from tic douloureux)

Age Group: Adult

Modality: Individual; outpatient

Problem Duration: 14 years

Treatment Length: (One session)

Result: Success. The man stopped experiencing pain.

Follow-up: The man was free of pain until his death.

Techniques: Direct suggestion; reframing

Sources: *Conversations I*, p. 267; *Mind-Body Communication*, p. 83

Case #71

Case Summary: A physician in Phoenix referred a pain patient to MHE. The man came to see MHE and gave a textbook description of pain. The man told MHE that he was an engineer and knew where to retrieve some machinery that had been lost in an accident. If MHE could lend him $100, he could retrieve the machinery and make them both rich men. MHE asked if the physician who referred the man had also invested in the scheme. The man admitted that the doctor had already invested $1000 in the scheme. MHE accused the man of faking the pain to get drugs and money from the doctor. He told the man that he would inform the doctor of his opinion. The doctor was angry at MHE for his accusation and defended the man. Years later, the doctor, his wife, and their daughter came to see MHE because the man had swindled them out of their life savings.

Presenting Problem: Pain

Age Group: Adult

Modality: Individual; outpatient

Problem Duration: NA

Treatment Length: One session

Result: Dismissal. MHE accused the man of faking the pain and refused to treat him.

Follow-up: Years later MHE found out that his diagnosis of malingering and swindling was correct.

Techniques: NA

Source: *Experiencing Erickson*, pp. 117–118

Case #72

Case Summary: A chronic pain patient was referred to MHE from California. She was antagonistic towards hypnosis, as it had already been tried and had failed with her. MHE told her he would not use any treatment that was unnecessary and would use whatever was necessary. MHE then asked her to describe in minute detail her pain sensations and perceptions. Then he gave her a pseudo-scientific lecture on the nature of pain, in which he convinced her that people could develop callouses to pain. He used analogies of building up callouses on one's hands by working in the garden each day and by eating hot, spicy Mexican food each day until one became inured to the spiciness. After one two-hour session, the woman returned to California able to reduce and manage her pain.

Presenting Problem: Pain

Age Group: Adult

Modality: Individual; outpatient

Problem Duration: NA

Treatment Length: One session, two hours

Result: Success. The woman developed pain control.

Follow-up: NA

Techniques: Metaphor; analogy

Source: *Healing in Hypnosis*, pp. 110–113

Case #73

Case Summary: MHE made a house call to treat a 36-year-old woman with terminal cancer. Her doctor had asked MHE to do hypnosis with her for pain control because no medicine would reduce her pain. When he entered the house he heard chanting coming from the bedroom: "Don't hurt me, don't hurt me, don't scare me, don't scare me, don't hurt me. . ." MHE entered the room and tried to introduce himself but the woman continued to chant. MHE listened to her for 20 to 30 minutes to learn the rhythm and emphasis of what she was saying and then decided to join in, chanting, "I'm going to hurt you, I'm going to scare you. . ." "Why?" she asked and continued to chant. "I want to help you, I want to help you. . ." he chanted. "How?" she asked between chants. Still chanting, he requested that she turn over "mentally, not physically, mentally, not physically." She followed his instruction.

Then he chanted that she should feel a terrible mosquito bite in her foot. She chanted that her foot was numb so she couldn't feel it. He had the numbness spread throughout her body, although he regretted not being able to remove the mosquito bite feeling from her mastectomy incision. She chanted that she didn't mind and was just glad to be rid of the pain.

MHE also gave her time distortion so that his visits seemed very close together. In one of the visits, MHE suggested that she would regain her appetite by describing how good beefsteak was. She ate a steak and regained some of her lost weight after that session.

MHE's wife and daughter accompanied him on another of his visits. During that visit the wife complained of a new pain in her stomach. MHE put his wife and daughter into trance and had them hallucinate pain in their stomachs. He then had the pain go away and the woman found that her pain was relieved.

The woman's last request was to walk around her home one last time, to look at all the rooms, and to use the bathroom by herself. MHE consulted with her doctor. The doctor warned that she had metastases in her bones and that she would be risking two broken hips. MHE hypnotized the woman and told her that he was putting a girdle on her which she would feel getting tighter and tighter. (It was really the tightening of her muscles to support her bones.) He warned that she really wouldn't be able to move her thighs to walk so she would have to do it from the knees down. The woman was able to get up, walk around her house and use the restroom. She died soon after.

Presenting Problem: Pain (from cancer)

Age Group: Adult

Modality: Individual; outpatient

Problem Duration: Less than one year

Treatment Length: Four months, five sessions

Result: Success. The woman was substantially pain-free until she died.

Follow-up: NA

Techniques: Hypnosis; time distortion; anesthesia; parallel treatment (MHE's wife and daughter); positive hallucination; utilization (of chanting)

Sources: *Healing in Hypnosis*, pp. 168–174; *Hypnotherapy*, pp. 98–99 and pp. 133–138; *Mind-Body Communication*, pp. 67–71; *Teaching Seminar*, pp. 185–187

Case #74

Case Summary: A well-educated woman developed cancer of the uterus. She had inoperable metastasis in her bones and was unresponsive to cobalt therapy. She was in great pain, which narcotics didn't affect. She didn't believe in hypnosis but her doctor referred her to MHE anyway. MHE went to her home and found her in bed being nursed by her 18-year-old daughter. He told her that hypnosis could help her with her pain and that "seeing is believing."

He put her daughter into trance using an induction that involved focusing on a spot on the wall. He told her that her body was losing all sense of feeling. She could become unaware of all sensations in the same way that her body could become unaware of the bedclothes at night. He told her that they were alone in the room and that if he turned his head away from her and spoke she would not hear it. MHE lifted up the girl's skirt and slapped her hard on the thigh. She showed no recognition of the sensation. Her mother asked if she had felt it but she didn't answer her. MHE told the mother that the girl couldn't even hear him when he wasn't looking at her. MHE told her that when he awakened her she would tell her mother she was ready to go into trance and then would be surprised to find her skirt up. She would have to ask MHE to pull it down for her. MHE awakened her a second time giving her amnesia for the whole experience.

At the next session MHE hypnotized the daughter again and had her experience herself as being on the other side of the room. Having convinced the mother of the power of hypnosis, MHE taught the mother to leave her body and her pain in the bed and to go out in the living room to watch TV. She became very adept at hallucinating different locations. Her wishes were to live until June to see her son graduate and her daughter get married. The daughter got married in the bedroom and she hallucinated the son's graduation. Shortly afterwards she died.

Presenting Problem: Pain (from cancer)

Age Group: Adult

Modality: Individual; outpatient

Problem Duration: NA

Treatment Length: NA

Result: Success. MHE helped her reduce her pain and attain the goal she wished to complete before her death.

Follow-up: The woman died shortly after treatment.

Techniques: Parallel treatment (daughter losing pain under her skirt paralleled mother losing pain under her skirt); hypnosis; dissociation; positive hallucination; analogy; negative hallucination; amnesia

Sources: *Healing in Hypnosis*, pp. 231–233; *Hypnotherapy*, p. 140; *Teaching Seminar*, pp. 180–184; *Uncommon Therapy*, pp. 306–310

Case #75

Case Summary: A veteran who had had his back broken in Vietnam suffered severe pain and was confined to a wheelchair. He and his wife came to

see MHE, but they were hostile and skeptical. MHE had the wife stand before him and he gave the husband one of his (MHE's) canes. He instructed the husband to hit him over the head with the cane if he did anything improper. MHE then used his other cane to start pulling the upper part of the wife's dress apart, as if to expose her breasts. She went into trance to escape the unpleasant situation and MHE told her that when she awakened, she would sit down and that whatever MHE said would be true. She agreed to comply. When she awakened, he suggested a body dissociation, so that she could not get out of her chair. Next he suggested she slap her thigh hard to demonstrate that she could not feel the slap. She did so. MHE then pointed out to the husband that he had been watching this demonstration for 25 minutes without pain and the man was surprised to note that this was true. After this demonstration, the husband was convinced of the effectiveness of trance and MHE used it to help him develop pain control. MHE taught them to go into trance by looking at each other.

Presenting Problem: Pain (from spinal injury)

Age Group: Adult

Modality: Couple; outpatient

Problem Duration: NA

Treatment Length: A few sessions

Result: Success. The man was able to develop pain control.

Follow-up: A few months later, the man had to come back for a "booster shot" of hypnosis after he suffered a recurrence of the pain after a bout of flu.

Techniques: Hypnosis; parallel treatment (having the wife develop dissociation and anesthesia)

Sources: *Hypnotherapy*, pp. 123–129; *Teaching Seminar*, pp. 175–179

Case #76

Case Summary: A 52-year-old woman had cancer and was in great pain. She was very well-read and had a marvelous sense of humor. She was brought to MHE by ambulance. When she entered the room she said, "Sonny, do you really think that your hypnotic words will so alter my body when powerful chemicals have no effect on it?" (MHE was 70 years old at the time.) MHE told her that he could tell by the action of her pupils and her facial muscles that she was in great pain. "Now tell me, Madam, if you saw a lean, hungry tiger in the next room, slowly walking into the room and eyeing you hungrily and licking its chops, how much pain would you feel?" She said she wouldn't feel any under those circumstances and in fact she was surprised that her pain had stopped. She said that she would like to take that tiger with her back to the hospital. The nurses thought she was hallucinating because she kept refusing pain medications, saying she had a hungry tiger under her bed.

Presenting Problem: Pain (from cancer)

Age Group: Adult

Modality: Individual; outpatient

Problem Duration: NA

Treatment Length: NA

Result: Success. The woman's pain was diminished.

Follow-up: NA

Techniques: Redirecting attention; positive hallucination

Sources: *Hypnotherapy*, pp. 138–139; *Teaching Seminar*, pp. 188–189

Case #77

Case Summary: A man who had been paralyzed suffered chronic pain from cystitis and pyelitis. He had no capacity to understand puns and wordplays, so MHE had the nurses tell him "shaggy dog" stories (long, rambling stories with a wordplay in the punchline). The man would listen politely, trying to follow and understand the stories, but would fail in his attempts. The effort was enough to keep him from focusing on his pain. After a while, he would summon a nurse to tell him a story for a few minutes, enough to distract him from his pain when it was recurring.

Presenting Problem: Pain (from cystitis and pyelitis)

Age Group: Adult

Modality: Individual; inpatient

Problem Duration: NA

Treatment Length: NA

Result: Success. The man was able to control the pain without drugs.

Follow-up: NA

Techniques: Redirecting attention

Source: *Hypnotherapy*, p. 139

Case #78

Case Summary: A woman dying of cancer of the uterus suffered from extreme bladder urgency. She sat on the edge of her bed all night and would just doze off for five or 10 minutes at a time. Her family was exhausted from having to watch her all night so she would not fall off the bed. Her physician asked MHE to do hypnosis with her, although the physician was skeptical about its usefulness in this case. The woman was also skeptical, so MHE had the woman send her daughter to the library to look up hypnosis in the *Encyclopedia Britannica* and thereby gained her trust, since he had written the encyclopedia entry.

MHE then hypnotized the woman's 19-year-old daughter and had her develop an imaginary pain in her knee underneath her dress. Then he had her move the pain to the other knee. Then MHE had the daughter hallucinate such pain that it would bring tears to her eyes, although she could control the tears. Mother did not like seeing her daughter in pain, but MHE assured her it was part of her treatment and then took the daughter's pain away.

After that he used hypnosis with the woman to develop an anesthesia starting at her knees and her shoulders and meeting in between. After she developed that, MHE had her focus on and remember the feeling in various parts of her body (like the back of her hand and in the small of her back) while she was going to sleep. Then he suggested that she have a urinary frequency of every three hours during the night. Next he had her learn to develop a somnambulistic trance state and maintain it while she was walking and talking. He suggested that she be comfortable walking to the bathroom, have pain when she urinated (she was convinced she would have pain while urinating as a result of the cancer), then walk back to her room with comfort. She was able to use these suggestions successfully.

Presenting Problem: Urinary frequency; pain (from cancer); insomnia

Age Group: Adult

Modality: Individual/family; outpatient

Problem Duration: NA

Treatment Length: At least two sessions

Result: Success. The woman had less urinary frequency and pain and was able to sleep more.

Follow-up: NA

Techniques: Hypnosis; parallel treatment; redirecting attention; dissociation; anesthesia; anchoring the symptom (pain linked with urinating); splitting (walking to and from the bathroom from urinating); positive hallucination

Source: *Life Reframing*, pp. 27–31

Case #79

꙳

Case Summary: A woman who had been operated on for both cancer of the uterus and cancer of the colon had developed a contraction of the lower colon. Defecation was painful and she had to go to the doctor's office each day for slow, gradual dilatation. She was referred to MHE for hypnosis to forestall the necessity of another surgery. MHE induced a trance and told her that floating comfortably in her pool everyday would make the dilatation much less painful. Not only did the dilatation become easier, but eventually her colon healed.

Presenting Problem: Pain (with defecation)

Age Group: Adult

Modality: Individual; outpatient

Problem Duration: NA

Treatment Length: NA

Result: Success. The woman's pain was reduced and her colon healed.

Follow-up: NA

Techniques: Hypnosis; linking (floating in the pool with relaxation); post-hypnotic suggestion

Sources: *My Voice Will Go With You,* p. 54

Case #80

Case Summary: A construction worker fell 40 stories and was paralyzed except for his arms. He came to MHE for help. MHE told him there wasn't much that could be done. He could develop calluses on his pain nerves to reduce the pain, but otherwise he was stuck. MHE told him he'd have to find some way to amuse himself. He told the man to ask his friends to bring him cartoons and comic books and to ask the nurse to get him scissors and paste. He should then cut out cartoons, jokes and funny sayings and put them in scrapbooks. When one of his fellow construction workers got injured he should send a scrapbook to him. The man made hundreds of scrapbooks.

Presenting Problem: Pain (from injury)

Age Group: Adult

Modality: Individual; inpatient

Problem Duration: NA

Treatment Length: NA

Result: Partial success. The man's pain was reduced and he found a hobby to entertain himself and keep him busy.

Follow-up: NA

Techniques: Task assignment (behavioral and cognitive)

Source: *My Voice Will Go With You,* pp. 176–177

Case #81

Case Summary: A young woman from a New England family was brought by her mother to see MHE. She had been in a car accident when a friend was with her. She had sustained only minor injuries, but the accident had resulted in four different families' suing each other. She experienced pain with no physical cause and had been given two unnecessary operations. She had spent several months discussing her past with a psychiatrist before being referred to MHE. When the woman entered the office she appeared resigned to an existence as an invalid.

MHE talked to her as if they were visiting socially. He encouraged her to think critically about her parents, her sister, and the time she spent at college. He asked her if she wanted to dwell on the past or to think about what she wanted out of the next 50 years. He told that in her future there should be no quarrels with parents and no lawsuits. The woman talked about her parents' disapproval of her sister's marriage. MHE wondered why parents wouldn't approve of their daughter's growing up and getting married. He asked her if she'd ever heard of a New Englander enjoying swimming in the winter and encouraged her to go swimming at her motel.

After 19 hours of treatment the mother and daughter went back home. MHE advised the mother to settle the lawsuit out of court or drop it. MHE also saw the mother for six visits. He had her write down all the stupid things she had done in her life. They laughed about her list, especially the times she had not enjoyed herself.

Presenting Problem: Pain with no somatic origin

Age Group: Adult

Modality: Individual/family; outpatient

Problem Duration: NA

Treatment Length: 19 hours

Result: Success. The young woman's pain subsided and she began to lead an active life.

Follow-up: NA

Techniques: Reframing; redirecting attention; task assignment (behavioral); direct suggestion

Source: *Uncommon Therapy*, pp. 278–279

Case #82

Case Summary: A woman with a severe phobia for dentists was in an automobile accident that damaged her jaw and required dental surgery. She had previously been so frightened and tense during dental procedures that she had broken off headrests on her dentist's chairs. She had a sensitivity to chemical anesthetics, so they could not be used for the procedure. She asked her family optometrist, who had studied with MHE, to hypnotize her to prepare her for the dental work without chemical anesthesia. He referred her to MHE, because he was not that confident of his abilities.

MHE saw the woman that same day. He induced trance by using hand levitation and suggested that, instead of pain, she could feel pressure. All the pain would go out through her big toe. MHE did four sessions of hypnosis with the woman. When the woman saw the dentist, he was reluctant to do the work without using chemical anesthesia, but finally relented. She was aware and relaxed during the session and experienced no pain, only intense pressure. There was minimal bleeding, even though a partial plate of steel had been inserted. She experienced no soreness, swelling or complications and was completely healed in three days.

Since that time, she has been able to go to dentists and periodontists comfortably. A year later, she asked MHE to help her stop smoking. He did one session and it did not work. He occasionally used her as a demonstration subject in the years that followed.

Presenting Problem: Fear of dental procedure; sensitivity to chemical anesthesia; cigarette smoking

Age Group: Adult

Modality: Individual; outpatient

Problem Duration: NA

Treatment Length: Five sessions

Result: Success/failure. The woman was able to go through the dental procedure comfortably and heal quickly. MHE did not succeed in helping her stop smoking.

Follow-up: 15 years. The woman still had no fear of dental procedures.

Techniques: Hypnosis; arm levitation; analgesia; symptom displacement

Sources: Alice McAvoy, personal communication, 1989.

Case #83

HEADACHES

Case Summary: A 50-year-old woman was treated by MHE for migraine headaches. MHE described her as very demanding and dictatorial about treatment. She wanted no exploratory psychotherapy, just hypnotic treatment of the headaches. She demanded that therapy be accomplished within four sessions in intervals of two weeks. She also required that she be allowed to keep her headaches in some manner to suit her needs. She usually had up to 45 severe and incapacitating headaches per year and was often hospitalized for dehydration (from vomiting) as a result. The headaches were never shorter than three hours and might last up to three days.

She was hypnotized and told to resist any suggestion that was not in accord with her wishes and personality. In trance, MHE trained her in time distortion (condensation and expansion) and directed her to have two headaches during the next week. The first was to be of not more than three hours' duration and the next would seem like it lasted three hours but would last no more than five minutes clock or solar time. She was instructed to develop amnesia for the suggestions.

She complied with the suggestions, having one almost three-hour headache starting at 10 a.m. and one five-minute headache which started on another day at 10 a.m. In the next session, MHE suggested that, to take care of her personality needs for headaches during the next two weeks, she should have five-minute headaches each Monday at 10 a.m. that would subjectively seem to last three hours. She had premonitions of headaches coming on two times in the next two weeks and found, to her amazement, that while they seemed to last hours, they were only minutes long. MHE told her that, whenever she needed to have headaches, she could do so for an excruciatingly long and painful 60 or 90 seconds.

Two-year follow-up with the woman and after that with her physician indicated that she remained mainly free of incapacitating headaches and never again had to be hospitalized for the aftereffects of headaches. She continued to have 50-to-80-second headaches almost every Monday morning at 10 a.m. and occasionally at other times.

Presenting Problem: Migraine

Age Group: Adult

Modality: Individual; outpatient

Problem Duration: Many years

Treatment Length: Six weeks; three sessions

Result: Success. The woman had very short headaches that no longer interfered with her life.

Follow-up: Over two years

Techniques: Hypnosis; time distortion; amnesia; direct suggestion; utilization (of need to have headaches)

Sources: *Collected Papers II*, pp. 295–298; *Life Reframing*, p. 119

Case #84

❧

Case Summary: A woman with a history of 11 years of having right-side-only migraine headaches was asked about the sensation at a specific location on the left side of her head. As she puzzled over that, MHE suggested that she begin to notice pain in that location. In this way, he was able to induce a left-sided migraine. Since he could bring it on, he could conceivably eliminate it and this he did, with the help of her "body learnings."

Presenting Problem: Migraine

Age Group: Adult

Modality: Individual; outpatient

Problem Duration: 11 years [or five years]

Treatment Length: NA

Result: Success. The woman eventually eliminated her migraines.

Follow-up: NA

Techniques: Hypnosis; indirect suggestion

Sources: *Collected Papers II*, p. 322; *Mind-Body Communication* p. 91

Case #85

~∂~

Case Summary: An employee at the hospital in which MHE worked had been dismissed from her job due to the severe headaches accompanied by irritability and quarrelsomeness. She had been having them since she had left her parental home four years previously. Since they sometimes occurred as often as twice a week, they severely disrupted her work, as she had symptoms before, during, and after the headaches. She was finally fired and given the option of seeing MHE and finishing out six weeks of her job. Since she was short of money and would have to wire her parents for money, she grudgingly saw MHE.

MHE told her that hypnosis might be able to help, but that he needed to see her when she was having a headache first. He was summoned to her room two days later and observed the pattern he had heard about. She was pale and unresponsive while she was having the headache. When he saw her two hours later, after the headache had passed, she was talking in a shrill, high-pitched voice and berating those around her. Next she became depressed and socially withdrawn.

A few days later, she sought out MHE and requested hypnosis for the headaches only. He spent the next four weeks inducing 15 profound trances with her. In those trances he gave her the suggestions that she would go to sleep for at least 30 minutes whenever she felt the onset of a headache and that would abort the headache. Following that, she should berate those around her, giving free rein to her fantasies as she did so. At first, she would only be following the hypnotic suggestions when she did this, but after a while she would do this solely out of her sadistic desires. Then she should again sleep for another 30 minutes and awaken refreshed, having forgotten everything that happened.

She followed the instructions. During the fourth week, a new suggestion was given that she would develop a headache at a particular time and day. At first she was to fight against it, then to give in and follow the first set of suggestions for sleep. She complied and was observed to retire to her room for three hours and return refreshed. Next she was instructed to have the emotional outburst that presaged a headache but to try to resist it and hold her tongue. Then she should give in and go to her room and sleep it off. Again she complied and returned to work after three hours of sleep. The last session was spent consolidating the hypnotic suggestions and ensuring they would be followed in the future. She was seen again three months later and had had only two threatened headaches. She attributed the results to hypnosis.

Presenting Problem: Headaches

Age Group: Adult

Modality: Individual; outpatient

Problem Duration: Three years

Treatment Length: Six weeks

Result: Success. The woman was no longer troubled by headaches and the accompanying social problems disappeared.

Follow-up: MHE kept in touch with her over the years and had at least 15 years' follow-up which indicated no more job problems and only three headaches per year, which seemed different from the former headaches and which could be warded off by sleep.

Techniques: Hypnosis; pattern intervention; scheduling the symptom; posthypnotic suggestion

Source: *Collected Papers IV*, pp. 247–251

Case #86

Case Summary: MHE was lecturing to a class of medical students on hypnosis when one of the students began rudely to denounce hypnosis and demanded that MHE demonstrate hypnosis on him. Another student informed MHE not to take it personally. The student who was rude was known to suffer from severe migraine headaches that were preceded by such hostile outbursts. The emotional outbursts were followed inevitably by a flushing of the face and neck, then projectile vomiting, then a headache of one to four days' duration. The student soon apologized for his outburst and asked to be excused to go home as soon as the headache developed. MHE suggested that he try hypnosis while the student was still in class. The student was skeptical but assented.

MHE then began a lecture to the students on hypnosis that was really a disguised induction. The student had been instructed to sit in front of the class and to slowly rotate his chair in a complete circle. MHE explained that as the student rotated his chair he would become drowsy and that his eyes would close and he would stop moving the chair and go deeply into trance. The student went into trance. MHE then told him that he would awaken and declare that hypnosis made him sick to his stomach. He should then try to prove his statement by going to the window and trying to vomit out of it. The student was surprised when he found that he couldn't vomit. He said that usually by this time he would be losing the contents of his stomach. MHE continued his lecturing and disguised suggestions by saying that if a patterned behavior were interrupted, it could be stopped. Then the student was given the suggestion that he would no longer have any headaches.

Presenting Problem: Migraine headaches

Age Group: Adult

Modality: Individual; outpatient (lecture)

Problem Duration: NA

Treatment Length: One session

Result: Success. The student did not develop his usual headache.

Follow-up: NA

Techniques: Hypnosis; linking (chair movement to induction; vomiting with skepticism about hypnosis); indirect suggestion; posthypnotic suggestion; pattern intervention

Source: *Collected Papers IV*, pp. 252–254

Case #87

Case Summary: A woman had a headache three days of every week. In the first interview MHE explained to her that she had the headaches for a reason but that he wondered if that reason might not be satisfied by headaches of shorter duration or of lesser severity. Three weeks later she returned and told him that she had not had a headache for three weeks but that she was going to have one next week. MHE offered her several choices for the onset, the intensity, and the duration of the headache she would have. She chose to have her headache begin in the usual manner for the usual length of time. MHE agreed that that would be a sensible thing, because a month from now she might want to alter it. MHE instructed her to study this week's headache thoroughly and, by suggesting a time frame of one month, indirectly suggested that she would skip the next three weeks. She had no headaches for the next three weeks.

Presenting Problem: Headaches

Age Group: Adult

Modality: Individual; outpatient

Problem Duration: NA

Treatment Length: NA

Result: Partial success. The woman's headaches became less frequent.

Follow-up: NA

Techniques: Indirect suggestion; symptom prescription; task assignment (perceptual); implication

Source: *Conversations I*, pp. 63–64

Case #88

Case Summary: During World War II, a man had been granted a 60-day leave from the Army to take his wife to a psychiatrist. On the last day of the leave he finally got around to calling MHE, who worked with the draft board in Michigan, and requested an appointment for that evening. The woman entered his office and said, "I have a terrible headache and that mess on your secretary's desk made my headache worse. And you would think that a doctor could have more decent furniture. Anyone who reads medical books ought to be able to line them up properly on the shelf."

After hearing the woman's first three remarks, MHE told her that he didn't know anyone he hated enough to refer her to. Her response to that was to come to the hospital in which MHE taught on visiting days. She would come to MHE's office and talk to him about her children. He instructed his secretary to write down verbatim what the woman said, but not to talk to her. MHE would not talk to her either. Finally, one day MHE got a call from the admissions nurse telling him the woman was admitting herself to the hospital.

MHE sent one of his psychiatric residents down to greet her and to get her to write her life story. The woman wrote 37 pages on a hot afternoon. MHE had those pages typed up and locked away before the woman could revise them in any way. The resident was happy with the treatment at first, but after a short time he reported to MHE he had made a mistake that had set therapy back months. Then he made progress again, but again after a short time made another mistake. He kept repeating this sequence until he finally realized that she was always setting him up to fail.

Another doctor decided he could do better with the case and took it over. He decided the woman needed X-rays to diagnose her condition. She kept interfering with the X-rays by drinking water and vomiting the barium, until the man had her strapped down to give her X-rays. She then ran away from the hospital. Next she got herself committed to another hospital in which MHE worked so she would be under his care. She then ran away to New Mexico.

Fifteen years later, she contacted MHE in Phoenix, saying she still had headaches and telling MHE she was seeing a *good* doctor in Phoenix now. MHE called up the doctor and warned him about the woman, but the doctor was not impressed. The woman ran back to New Mexico and left the doctor to pay the hospital bill for her. MHE got another letter from her some years later and she was still complaining and negative.

Presenting Problem: Headaches

Age Group: Adult

Modality: Individual; inpatient

Problem Duration: NA

Treatment Length: NA

Result: Failure. The woman still had headaches.

Follow-up: 23 years. The woman was still critical and negative.

Techniques: Task assignment (behavioral)

Source: *Experiencing Erickson*, pp. 96–99; 110–115; 169–170

Case #89

§

Case Summary: A man came to MHE for help with his headaches. MHE determined that the man was extremely competitive. MHE elicited the history of the man's problem and then told him he was not going to work with him. All he would do was this: he told the man to place both hands on his knees and to see which hand reached his face first. The competition was so great that it took about a half an hour for one hand to win. MHE asked him why he should have the tension of muscle competition in his neck and shoulders and suggested that the man have muscle relaxation by letting his hands compete in relaxing. After this experience in relaxation, he remained headache-free.

Presenting Problem: Headaches

Age Group: Adult

Modality: Individual; outpatient

Problem Duration: NA

Treatment Length: NA

Result: Success. The man stopped having headaches.

Follow-up: Six years. The man was headache-free.

Techniques: Hypnosis; symptom transformation; utilization (of competitiveness)

Source: *My Voice Will Go With You*, p. 82

Case #90

Case Summary: A man came to MHE for his severe headache. He'd had it since he was seven years old. He also was concerned about his family difficulties and his addiction to cocaine and Percodan. MHE scolded the man for keeping a seven-year-old boy's headache. MHE said it was very dishonest of him to keep that headache. (The man prided himself on his honesty in business.) He left MHE's office angry, but at dinnertime he found he didn't have a headache. He kept expecting the headache to come back but it didn't.

Two months later he came to see MHE and admitted that MHE had been exactly right. The MHE asked him, "Tell me, what kind of misery did you inflict on your wife, what kind of miserable shrew did you make out of your wife, and how many of your six children have you damaged?" His oldest son was unmanageable, his daughter was overweight, his next son was 14 and couldn't read, and his fourth son had a harelip. The other two were too young to tell.

MHE did therapy with the mother, the daughter, and the son who couldn't read. His therapy with the mother began with his telling her in no uncertain terms what a shrew she was. She tried to defend herself and became very angry. On her way home she realized that MHE was absolutely right and decided to make another appointment.

MHE's therapy with the son began with an assignment. He told the boy to go home and copy 100 words out of the newspaper, each from different locations. The boy brought back a list of words that included capital letters and periods where appropriate. MHE believed that the boy's ability to recognize the beginnings and ends of sentences suggested that he really knew how to read but didn't realize it. MHE had the boy walk forwards, backwards, and sideways in his office. Having established that the boy could walk, MHE told him that he could graduate from the eighth grade. Each day he was to walk the 14 miles from his home to MHE's office, arriving at 9 a.m. He was to read or work until 4 p.m. and then walk back home. One day he said, "Can I stay another hour? Fractions are very interesting." The boy went on to high school.

MHE began therapy with the obese sister by telling her she looked like the "south end of a northbound horse." She was deeply offended and ran out of the office. Sometime later she got married. The marriage was stormy and she finally ran back to her mother. The mother brought her to see MHE. He told her mother to sit in the next room. "Don't close the door too tightly," he said. The young woman told MHE about her husband. She said he was wonderful and that she loved him very much. Their quarrels were only "momentary flashes of temper." Overhearing all this, the mother came in exasperated. The daughter had given her mother a completely different picture of the marriage. The mother insisted that the daughter resolve her difficulties on her own.

Once the father had a recurrence of his headache. MHE asked him how far it was to his office. "Eleven miles," he said. MHE replied, "Be sure you start early enough in the morning so that you can walk to your office; the fresh air will cure your headache."

Presenting Problem: Headaches; family problems; addiction to cocaine and Percodan

Age Group: Adult

Modality: Individual/family; outpatient

Problem Duration: Since age seven

Treatment Length: NA

Result: Success. The man's headaches stopped, he quit using cocaine and Percodan, his marriage improved, and his children became better adjusted.

Follow-up: NA

Techniques: Reframing; utilization (of the man's sense of honesty); task assignment (behavioral); linking (walking with getting rid of the headache); ordeal

Source: *Uncommon Therapy*, pp. 258–263

Case #91

Case Summary: A 38-year-old man with migraine headaches and depression saw MHE. He had been searching since he was 20 for a wife of the same religion (Catholic), in order to have Catholic children and a Catholic home. All of the hundreds of women he had dated through the years, however, had turned out to be Protestant. MHE told the man that he had proved thoroughly through those 18 years that he did not really want a Catholic wife and home. The man had also managed, despite his intelligence, to graduate in the lower 10% of his class in college. He had gotten fired from many jobs within a year and a half from starting them. He had see four psychiatrists before seeing MHE. MHE refused to treat him as he was convinced the man was intent on failing.

Presenting Problem: Migraine headaches; depression

Age Group: Adult

Modality: Individual; outpatient

Problem Duration: (18 years)

Treatment Length: NA

Result: Refusal. MHE refused to take the case.

Follow-up: NA

Techniques: NA

Source: "Double Binds"

Case #92

SKIN PROBLEMS

Case Summary: A young man had been tutored at home through most of grade school and high school because he had such severe neurodermatitis. MHE asked him how much he really needed to keep of his skin condition, since it was incurable. The young man settled on small patches on his forehead, neck, wrist, elbow, and thighs. When he got angry he would get another patch on his chest and when he got really angry he would get another patch on his abdomen. He was able to go through college and graduate with honors. He was also president of his fraternity.

Presenting Problem: Neurodermatitis

Age Group: (Adolescent)

Modality: Individual; outpatient

Problem Duration: At least six years

Treatment Length: NA

Result: Partial success. The young man was able to limit the amount of dermatitis so he could lead a normal life.

Follow-up: NA

Techniques: Implication (that some of the skin problem could go away); splitting (how much he needed to keep and how much could change)

Source: *Life Reframing*, pp. 128–129

Case #93

Case Summary: A woman in her sixties with neurodermatitis sought hypnosis from MHE. No physician had been able to cure her skin problem, so she was finally referred to a psychiatrist. After hearing from her that she married her husband for money and was just waiting for him to die, the psychiatrist suggested that she divorce the man and that would cure her skin condition. Since she was unwilling to divorce her husband, she sought treatment from two other psychiatrists, each of whom had offered the same opinion.

She told MHE that she had been honest with her husband and had been a good wife, though he was a rather unpleasant man who drank quite a bit. She was certain he would die soon and felt entitled to the money. MHE told her that she seemed resistant and asked her to use the resistance to deal with the difficult emotions being in such a difficult situation must entail. If she transferred her resistance to that area, she would be able to leave the skin problem unguarded for him to work with. He told her that she certainly had earned her money and she deserved it. Then he asked her to recall a time when her skin felt good and she remembered the warmth of the sun on her skin very vividly.

She paid him for the session and told him that she had paid enough of her well-earned money to him and did not intend to spend any more. A year later she returned and asked MHE to do another session with her because the previous one had resulted in the neurodermatitis clearing up until just recently. She had tried to recall what he had done with her to save spending any more of her hard-earned money on him, but had not been able to. MHE hypnotized her and then asked her to write him in six months to let him know how the treatment as working, as that was much less expensive than coming to see him.

Presenting Problem: Neurodermatitis

Age Group: Adult

Modality: Individual; outpatient

Problem Duration: NA

Treatment Length: Two sessions

Result: Success. The woman's skin problem cleared up.

Follow-up: Six months. The woman wrote MHE a letter and told him she was still free of the skin problem.

Techniques: Hypnosis; splitting (between emotions and skin problem); anchoring the resistance; reframing

Source: *Mind-Body Communication* pp. 151–153

Case #94

꘎

Case Summary: A doctor who lived in Massachusetts wrote MHE and asked him if he could treat her 18-year-old son's severe acne. He wrote back and told her that she did not need to bring the boy to see him. All she needed to do was to take her son to a cabin for her usual Christmas vacation ski trip. She was to see to it that the cabin had no mirrors and to keep him from seeing himself in a mirror for the entire trip. His acne cleared up in two weeks.

Presenting Problem: Acne

Age Group: Adolescent

Modality: Family; outpatient (by mail)

Problem Duration: NA

Treatment Length: NA

Result: Success. The boy's acne cleared up.

Follow-up: NA

Techniques: Task assignment (behavioral and perceptual); pattern intervention

Sources: *My Voice Will Go With You*, p. 87; *Phoenix*, p. 127

Case #95

꘎

Case Summary: A woman came to MHE for warts on her hands and knees and face. Knowing that warts are susceptible to changes in blood pressure, MHE assigned the woman to soak her feet in ice water, then in very hot water, then in ice water again. She was to do this three times a day. When the warts were gone she could forget about soaking her feet. Three years later the woman brought her son in for treatment of another issue. MHE asked her about her warts. "What warts?" she asked. She insisted that MHE was confusing her with somebody else.

Presenting Problem: Warts

Age Group: Adult

Modality: Individual; outpatient

Problem Duration: NA

Treatment Length: (One session)

Result: Success. The woman's warts cleared up.

Follow-up: Three years. The warts were gone and the woman did not remember that she had ever had them.

Techniques: Task assignment (behavioral)

Source: *My Voice Will Go With You*, pp. 87–88

Case #96

Case Summary: A woman came to MHE for her psoriasis. She wore long sleeves and high collars in the summer because she was so ashamed of her peeling skin. MHE asked her to roll back her sleeve so he could look at her psoriasis. He told her that she had only one-third the psoriasis she thought she had. What she had was a little psoriasis and a lot of emotions. The woman was angry so she paid him and said she wouldn't return. Two weeks later she called to apologize and to ask that he see her again. Her psoriasis had diminished to a few small patches.

Presenting Problem: Psoriasis

Age Group: Adult

Modality: Individual

Problem Duration: NA

Treatment Length: NA

Result: Success. The woman's psoriasis diminished.

Follow-up: NA

Techniques: Splitting (between emotions and psoriasis); linking (lots of emotion with little psoriasis); interpersonal evocation (of emotion, anger)

Source: *My Voice Will Go With You*, pp. 154–155

Case #97

BEDWETTING/ENURESIS/SOILING

Case Summary: An eight-year-old boy (10 in another version) wet the bed every night. His parents dragged him into MHE's office with the promise of a "hotel dinner" afterwards if he cooperated. MHE told the boy that he knew he was mad and that he also knew that the boy thought nothing could be done about his bedwetting. "Your parents brought you here," MHE said, "they made you come. Well, you can make them get out of the office. In fact, we both can—come on, let's tell them to go out." MHE signaled them to leave and they went, to the boy's satisfaction. MHE said, "But you're still mad, and so am I, because they ordered me to cure your bedwetting." MHE made "a slow elaborate, attention-compelling gesture towards the floor." "Look at those puppies right there. I like the brown one best, but I suppose you like the black and white one because its front paws are white." The child went into a somnambulistic trance and walked over to pet the imaginary puppies, petting one more than the other. MHE told him that if he kept his bed dry for a month he would get a puppy very much like the black-and-white one, even if he never said a word about it to his parents. MHE told the boy's parents of their agreement without the boy's knowledge. During the last month of school the boy got up each morning out of his dry bed and crossed off the day on the calendar. At the end of the month the boy got a black and white puppy.

Presenting Problem: Bedwetting (enuresis)

Age Group: Child

Modality: Individual; outpatient

Problem Duration: NA

Treatment Length: One session

Result: Success. The boy stopped wetting the bed.

Follow-up: 18 months later there had been no recurrence.

Techniques: Matching (the boy's anger with MHE's); positive hallucination; hypnosis

Sources: *Collected Papers I*, pp. 172–173; *Collected Papers IV*, pp. 144–145; *Hypnotherapy*, pp. 81–82; *Uncommon Therapy*, pp. 193–194

Case #98

Case Summary: A 12-year-old boy, 5′10″ and 170 lbs., named Joe was brought in by his parents for his bedwetting. The boy was described as sullen and rebellious. The parents had spanked, ridiculed, scolded, and deprived the boy in an effort to get him to stop wetting the bed. They had tried not letting him have any liquids after noon, but nothing had worked. MHE told the parents to treat Joe courteously, as if he were a model son. They were not to mention Joe's bedwetting to him again and should let the household maid check the bedsheets, since Joe was now MHE's patient and their involvement would be interfering with his treatment.

MHE informed Joe of his instructions to his parents. Then he began discussing with Joe how much energy his body had put into growing him that big and strong in just 12 years. Did he think he was going to be taller and bigger than his father? What kind of a man was he going to make? In this way he induced a light trance with Joe. He then told Joe that it was nobody's business when he stopped wetting the bed. It would be unrealistic to expect him to have permanent dry beds in one night or two nights or even this week. MHE expected him to have a wet bed on Monday of next week, but the thing that puzzled him, he said, was which night he would have a dry bed accidentally on Wednesday or Thursday of the next week or would he have to wait until Friday?

Joe was given another appointment for the next Friday. At that time he proudly told MHE that he was wrong. It wasn't Thursday or Friday he had dry beds; it was both Thursday and Friday. MHE responded that two consecutive dry beds did not prove anything, and that since January was almost half over, he would almost certainly not be able to have a permanent dry bed by the end of January and February was such a short month, so the question really was: Would Joe start having permanent dry beds beginning on St. Patrick's Day (March 17th) or April Fool's Day (April 1st)? MHE continued to see the boy and never again discussed the bedwetting, as he told Joe it was none of his or anybody else's business. Joe let him know sometime later that he no longer wet the bed. Joe's parents didn't find out he had been having all dry beds until June.

Presenting Problem: Bedwetting (enuresis)

Age Group: Child

Modality: Individual; family; outpatient

Problem Duration: 12 years

Treatment Length: At least two sessions

Result: Success. The boy stopped wetting the bed sometime between St. Patrick's Day and April Fool's Day.

Follow-up: The boy became a dentist and a friend of MHE's and occasionally referred bedwetters to him.

Techniques: Implication; task assignment (behavioral); hypnosis; time framing

Sources: *Collected Papers I*, pp. 416–417; *Collected Papers IV*, pp. 229–232; *Healing in Hypnosis*, pp. 175–177; *Teaching Seminar*, pp. 105–106

Case #99

Case Summary: MHE treated a couple who were both bedwetters. Neither knew that the other was a bedwetter and always assumed that the wet bed was solely his or her own doing. They had been married for about a year when one of them said that it was too bad they didn't have a baby to blame for the wet spot on the bed. This had led to the discovery that both of them had enuresis. They had both been afraid to tell their terrible secret to the other during their courtship and were grateful for the other person's amazing forbearance. They had only had sex once on the wedding night and had avoided it thereafter out of embarrassment.

They were students who had little money and lived some distance from MHE's office. MHE offered to take their unusual case for no fee if they followed his instructions absolutely and got results from the therapy. If they failed in either of those tasks, they would be charged in full for MHE's time. They agreed to the conditions. They were both very religious and inhibited. MHE got them to agree to kneel on the bed each night before they went to sleep and deliberately urinate on the sheets. They were to drink lots of fluids before sleeping and to lock the bathroom door two hours before bedtime. They were to carry out the task for two weeks and then take one night off. They were not to talk about the assignment or the results of the task. The next morning, if they awakened to find a wet bed, they should do the task for three more weeks. They were to have another appointment with MHE in five weeks, at which time they were to give him a full and amazing account. Then they were quickly dismissed.

Five weeks later they returned to tell MHE that they had followed his instructions and found that they had dry beds after the two weeks. He reminded them that they had been told to return and give an amazing account and this pleased them and MHE and they could continue to be pleased. He added casually that the next month was May and then bade them goodbye.

They dropped in for a casual visit in May and informed MHE that they were still having dry beds. A year later, they brought their infant son to visit MHE and told him that now they had a little spot on the bed that they didn't mind. They wondered whether he had used hypnosis, since they knew he practiced that method. He told them that the results were obtained from their honest and sincere efforts.

Presenting Problem: Bedwetting (enuresis)

Age Group: Adult

Modality: Marital; outpatient

Problem Duration: Lifelong

Treatment Length: Two sessions, five weeks

Result: Success. The couple stopped wetting the bed and started having sex.

Follow-up: One year. The couple had a child and still were not wetting the bed.

Techniques: Task assignment (behavioral); utilization (of religiosity, of bedwetting); indirect suggestion (implying success by telling them to return and give a full and amazing account)

Source: *Collected Papers IV*, pp. 99–102

Case #100

꩜

Case Summary: A woman told MHE that she could not tell him what her problem was. After taking a history, MHE could find no clues as to what the problem was. MHE put her in trance and suggested that she could start to experience whatever problem she had with increasing intensity, at the right time and the right place. After six sessions in which similar suggestions were given, the woman reported that she had discovered what her problem had been. She had discovered that she had been soiling herself since childhood and hiding that fact from herself. She had never used a pair of panties twice. She had always taken them off in the dark and thrown them away without looking at them after soiling herself. She had been sitting on the toilet recently when she felt the strong urge to have a bowel movement. It was then that she realized that she used the toilet very little. She started using the toilet for her bowel movements and also stopped compulsively bathing herself up to three times per day. She no longer had to throw away her panties after each use.

Presenting Problem: Soiling

Age Group: Adult

Modality: Individual; outpatient

Problem Duration: NA

Treatment Length: Six sessions

Result: Success. The woman stopped soiling herself, stopped spending so much on underwear, and stopped compulsively bathing.

Follow-up: NA

Techniques: Hypnosis; direct suggestion; pattern intervention (changing the intensity of the symptom)

Source: *Collected Papers IV*, p. 109

Case #101

꘎

Case Summary: A selectee for the draft asked MHE to help him overcome his lifelong bedwetting, which would prevent him from entering military service. He had never spent a night away from home for fear of wetting the bed. He wanted to visit his relatives before going into the service. The man had had all the medical treatments available but they were of no help. MHE told him that hypnosis would help him. MHE put the man in trance and told him to go to a motel for three days. The first day he should worry about the maid discovering a wet bed. After a few hours of worrying it should occur to him how ironic it would be if his bed were dry after all the worrying. Then he was to get very confused in his thinking and worry about the shame of having a dry bed. When the maid came to change his dry sheets he should look out the window to hide his distress. The second and third nights he should again fear a dry bed. After the third night he was to be consumed with anxiety over which grandparents to visit first, the maternal or paternal. Ten weeks later the man returned to report that his bedwetting had been cured thanks to the "amazing experience" he had at the hotel, in which he unwittingly followed MHE's instructions to the letter.

Presenting Problem: Bedwetting (enuresis)

Age Group: Adult

Modality: Individual; outpatient

Problem Duration: Lifelong

Treatment Length: One session

Result: Success. The young man stopped wetting the bed and was able to visit his relatives and enter military service.

Follow-up: NA

Techniques: Hypnosis; posthypnotic suggestion; amnesia; task assignment (behavioral and cognitive); symptom transformation (worry and shame about wet beds → worry and shame about dry beds → anxiety about which relatives to visit first)

Sources: *Collected Papers IV*, pp. 153–155; *Uncommon Therapy*, pp. 87–88

Case #102

Case Summary: A 29-year-old man had wet the bed every night for 29 years. He lived in the guest house behind his parents' home and never dared to spend the night anywhere else. By 12 or 12:30 the bed would be wet and he would get up, change the linen and go back to sleep. In taking the man's history MHE learned that the man hated to walk. Erickson instructed him to get an alarm clock and set it for midnight or half past twelve or for one o'clock. When the alarm rang, he was to get up and walk 40 blocks, regardless of whether the bed was wet or dry. The man told MHE he preferred a wet bed to this walking assignment and discontinued therapy. Months later the man returned and agreed to carry out the task for two weeks (three in another version). After the two weeks were over he would have another week of walking at midnight if he ever found the bed wet again. After two weeks the man reported a dry bed. He returned again and reported that he still had not had to complete the third week's walking and that he had received a promotion and a long-needed transfer in his job.

Presenting Problem: Bedwetting (enuresis)

Age Group: Adult

Modality: Individual; outpatient

Problem Duration: 29 years

Treatment Length: (Three or four sessions)

Result: Success. The man stopped wetting the bed.

Follow-up: The man received a promotion and a transfer in his job.

Techniques: Task assignment (behavioral); ordeal

Sources: *Conversations I*, pp. 55–56; *Healing in Hypnosis*, pp. 264–265

Case #103

Case Summary: A mother and her 12-year-old son came to MHE because the boy wet the bed every night. MHE told the boy he had a solution for him which he wouldn't like but that his mother would like even less. Each morning at four or 5 a.m. the mother was to awaken the boy and check his bed. If it was wet he would have to copy out of any book he chose until 7 a.m. in an effort to improve his handwriting. The mother had to sit with him and encourage him. The father came in for one session during the course of treatment. In a very loud voice he told MHE that he had wet the bed until he was 16 [19 in another version] and that it was perfectly normal. He also told MHE that a man of any common sense would support a certain political party. When the mother and son came in next they were clearly embarrassed by the father. [In another version the boy's father rejects him and refuses to come in to speak to MHE. When the boy stopped wetting the bed his father took him on a fishing trip.] In regard to the father's ideas, MHE said to the son, "I'm just going to forget them because it's the ideas that you and I and your mother have that are important." Then MHE turned to the mother and said, "It's the ideas that you and I have, and Johnny has, that are important." Johnny began wetting the bed less and less until he stopped wetting it altogether. He began developing friendships with kids his own age, his grades went up, and he was elected class president [captain of the baseball team, in another version].

Presenting Problem: Bedwetting (enuresis)

Age Group: Adult / child

Modality: Family; outpatient

Problem Duration: (12 years)

Treatment Length: NA

Result: Success. The boy stopped wetting the bed.

Follow-up: NA

Techniques: Task assignment (behavioral); implication (ideas they have are important for the treatment)

Sources: *Conversations III*, pp. 94–98; *Uncommon Therapy*, pp. 206–208; *Teaching Seminar*, pp. 106–109

Case #104

Case Summary: A boy wet the bed every night at midnight, laid in it until 2 a.m. and then went to his parents' room, where he would receive a spanking. The parents had tried every possible bribe and punishment to get him to stop wetting the bed. MHE wondered about the boy's need to punish himself. He suggested that the boy take charge of his own punishment. The boy had a collection of minerals and stones. MHE told the boy to spread them on a concrete floor and put a blanket over them. When he wet the bed at midnight he was to sleep on the stones for the rest of the night. After about a month he quit wetting the bed.

Presenting Problem: Bedwetting (enuresis)

Age Group: Child

Modality: Individual; outpatient

Problem Duration: NA

Treatment Length: (One month)

Result: Success. The boy stopped wetting the bed.

Follow-up: NA

Techniques: Task assignment (behavioral); ordeal; pattern intervention; symptom transformation (punishing himself by bedwetting → punishing himself by sleeping on rocks)

Sources: *Conversations III*, pp. 124–124

Case #105

Case Summary: A 10-year-old boy named Jimmy [Jerry in another version] wet the bed. His parents had gone to great lengths to get him to stop, including having him wear a sign around his neck that said "I'm a bedwetter" and having the congregation of their church pray aloud for Jimmy to stop wetting the bed. They told Jimmy that they were taking him to a nut doctor and literally dragged him into MHE's office. Jimmy laid on the floor and screamed. When he took a breath, MHE screamed. MHE told him that they would take turns screaming. Then MHE said he would rather use his turn to sit in a chair and the boy followed suit. MHE said that Jimmy's parents had ordered him to make Jimmy stop wetting the bed. "Who do they think they are?" he asked Jimmy. MHE told Jimmy that he didn't want to discuss bedwetting with him. MHE noticed the boy's build and speculated on his athletic ability and coordination. He talked about muscles and which sports require fine muscle control. He knew that Jimmy was good at baseball and archery. Then he talked about the way the circular muscle at the bottom of the stomach opens when it's time to let the food out, but stays closed the rest of the time. During the next two sessions they discussed Boy Scouts and other subjects that interested Jimmy. At the fourth session Jimmy came in wearing a great big smile. He said, "You know, my ma has been trying for years to break her habit, but she can't do it." (His mother was a smoker.) The boy's bed remained dry.

Presenting Problem: Bedwetting (enuresis)

Age Group: Child

Modality: Individual; outpatient

Problem Duration: (Several years)

Treatment Length: Four sessions

Result: Success. The boy stopped wetting the bed.

Follow-up: MHE kept in contact with the boy through high school and college and reported that there was no recurrence of the bedwetting.

Techniques: Metaphor; refocusing attention

Sources: *Conversations III*, pp. 128–130; *Uncommon Therapy*, pp. 199–201; *Teaching Seminar*, pp. 110–112

Case #106

Case Summary: An 11-year-old girl had been treated for recurring bladder infections throughout her childhood and her bladder and sphincter were so stretched that she had little bladder control. She had been free from the infection for four years and her parents thought she should have learned to control her bladder. Her sisters and schoolmates knew of her problem and she endured lots of ridicule for wetting her bed and occasionally her pants. MHE told her she already knew how to control her bladder, but she denied it. He told her he would ask her one simple question that would let her know that she knew how to do it. He dramatically told her that the question was what she would do if a strange man popped his head into the bathroom while she was urinating. She looked surprised and told him that she would freeze. He told her that when she froze, her muscles would freeze and that would stop her urination. All she had to do after she left was to remember that strange man and to stop and start urinating until she was sure she had developed that control. He told her that having dry beds was a very hard job. She might have one in the next two weeks, but he did not expect all dry beds before three months. He would be surprised if she did not have all dry beds before six months. She had her first dry bed within two weeks and within six months she could spend the night at friends' homes because she no longer wet the bed.

Presenting Problem: Bedwetting (enuresis)

Age Group: Child

Modality: Individual; outpatient

Problem Duration: 11 years

Treatment Length: One session, one and a half hours

Result: Success. The girl stopped wetting her bed and pants.

Follow-up: Six months

Techniques: Interpersonal evocation (of ability to change sphincter muscles); shock; linking (freezing to muscle control)

Sources: *My Voice Will Go With You*, pp. 113–116; *Phoenix*, 99–101; *Teaching Seminar*, pp. 79–84

Case #107

URINARY PROBLEMS

Case Summary: A woman in her mid-thirties was referred to MHE for treatment of psychogenic urinary retention. She had always considered herself too unattractive to be married, but had recently gotten married, a bit to her surprise. Soon after her honeymoon, she had developed a urinary tract infection, for which she was hospitalized. She was acutely embarrassed when she had to be catheterized several times during her treatment. Just before she was released from the hospital as cured, her husband received a military draft notice, much sooner than the couple had anticipated. After an initial reaction of grief, she composed herself, but soon discovered that she could not urinate. This led to more embarrassing catheterizations, twice per day for two weeks. She was even more embarrassed as she realized that her problem was psychological.

MHE first had her visit the lavatory to find out whether she really still needed treatment. This was done to introduce a seed of doubt about the symptom and to indicate the seriousness of a treatment that would only be undertaken if absolutely necessary. MHE then induced a light trance, then a deep trance, and elicited trance phenomena. He then instructed her to visit the lavatory once again, this time in trance, to have a bowel movement but not to urinate. However, he told her, she would probably not have a bowel movement since she did not have to at that time. This had two implications. One was that hypnosis could not induce bodily behavior for which there was no need, but it could only facilitate bodily functions for which there was a biological need. The other implication was that she was now complying with hypnotic suggestions when she did not urinate. Not urinating was now defined as a response to hypnotic suggestion and not a personal inability.

Then, in trance, the woman was encouraged to discuss her general life situation and to gain insight into her conflicts. Next MHE reminded her about how children played a game of holding their urination until the very last minute, then urgently rushing to relieve themselves. He then asked her in detail how long it would take her to get home from his office, exactly what route she would take, how much distance between the car and the front door and how far from the door to the nearest bathroom. Next MHE gave her a series of suggestions to the effect that she would begin to have a feeling of urgency for urination and a fear that she wouldn't make it home during the last 20 minutes of the drive. The last five minutes would be spent in a feverish anxiety about whether she would make it to the bathroom or would wet herself. As soon as she got to the toilet, she would feel comfortable and relaxed all over and would gain insight into her current conflicts. She was instructed to forget the suggestions given in trance.

Her husband, who had accompanied her to the session, was privately given instructions to drive home in a relaxed manner, commenting only on the beauty of the night and to speed up if his wife requested, but not to exceed the speed limit. Subsequent reports from the husband, the patient, and the referring physician indicated that she followed the suggestions and urinated when she arrived home. Thereafter she had no problem and was also able to accept her husband's military service much better.

Presenting Problem: Urinary retention

Age Group: Adult

Modality: Individual; outpatient

Problem Duration: 14 days

Treatment Length: Three hours, one session

Result: Success. The woman was able to urinate easily.

Follow-up: One year. The results persisted.

Techniques: Hypnosis; direct suggestion; amnesia; linking (failure to urinate with compliance to hypnotic suggestion); symptom transformation (anxiety about not being able to urinate transformed into anxiety about wetting herself); implication

Source: *Collected Papers IV*, pp. 23–26

Case #108

Case Summary: A man was selected for the draft who could only urinate through a wooden or metal tube that was between 8 and 10 inches long. In trance, MHE instructed him to make a bamboo tube of 12 inches and to urinate through that with his thumb and his forefinger holding the tube and his other three fingers holding his penis. He was to try to notice the flow of the urine through the bamboo. He then told the man that he might decide that in a day or two or a week or two that he could shorten the length of the tube by 1/4″, 1/2″ or even an entire inch, but that he need not be compelled to do so. MHE induced amnesia for the trance instructions.

The man gradually reduced the length of the tube until after several weeks he was able to discard the tube altogether. He remembered the trance all at once when he bought the bamboo and was surprised at how quickly he was able to reduce the length. Finally the man was able to realize that he always urinated through a tube—his penis. At his reexamination three months later, he was accepted into the service after demonstrating to MHE that he could urinate normally.

Presenting Problem: Inability to urinate except through a tube

Age Group: Adult

Modality: Individual; outpatient

Problem Duration: The problem developed when the young man was a small boy.

Treatment Length: One session, less than one hour

Result: Success. The man was able to discard the tube he had previously needed for urination and to enter military service as he desired.

Follow-up: NA

Techniques: Hypnosis; pattern intervention; task assignment (behavioral and perceptual); posthypnotic suggestion; implication

Sources: *Collected Papers IV*, pp. 155–158; *Conversations I*, p. 154

Case #109

Case Summary: A 62-year-old retired farmer suffered from frequent urinary urgency during his waking and sleeping hours. If he did not give in to the urge, he would urinate on himself. He carried extra underwear and trousers with him at all times in case of accidents. He had been medically treated and examined many times and the general conclusion was that his problem was psychosomatic. No one had been able to offer effective treatment for it. He had been to several lay hypnotists, who took his money but gave him no results. Finally he heard about MHE and came to see him.

MHE used an interspersal technique. In a general discussion about tomato plants, he interspersed phrases to suggest time distortion, improved bladder functioning, and amnesia for the trance experience and suggestions. MHE also suggested that the man take a nice leisurely walk home and gave him another appointment for the next week. The man returned and excitedly reported that he had been able to go home and wait four hours before urinating. As he was talking to MHE he suddenly remembered MHE telling him all about a tomato plant and realized that he must have been hypnotized at the previous session. He then realized that he had gone six hours last week without urinating and that he had been sleeping through the night and urinating less frequently during the day. The rest of the session was primarily a social chat and the man was never troubled with bladder problems again.

Presenting Problem: Urinary urgency and incontinence

Age Group: Adult

Modality: Individual; outpatient

Problem Duration: Two years

Treatment Length: One session

Result: Success. The man stopped having urinary urgency and incontinence.

Follow-up: Months later the problem had still not recurred.

Techniques: Hypnosis; interspersal; indirect suggestion; amnesia; time distortion; task assignment (behavioral)

Source: *Collected Papers IV*, pp. 263–266

Case #110

Case Summary: A woman had developed cystitis soon after she married and was not able to urinate. After she had gone daily to her physician to be catheterized to urinate, he referred her to MHE. MHE did hypnosis with her and implanted the idea of urinary urgency that would grow increasingly more urgent as she approached home. He instructed the husband to take her directly home, but they stopped on the way at her suggestion to buy some flowers for her mother and the therapy failed.

Presenting Problem: Urinary retention

Age Group: Adult

Modality: Individual; outpatient

Problem Duration: Two weeks

Treatment Length: (One session)

Result: Failure.

Follow-up: NA

Techniques: Hypnosis; posthypnotic suggestion

Source: *Life Reframing*, pp. 192–193

Case #111

Case Summary: Robert Dean, a graduate of the Naval Academy, was assigned to a destroyer during war time. He wanted a land-based assignment because he could only urinate in completely private surroundings. Whenever he heard anyone coming he would hear a clap of thunder and then he would freeze stiff. It could take him as much as an hour to unfreeze. Robert's father sought MHE's help for his son.

MHE agreed to speak with the father while on a visit to Philadelphia. Robert's father was extremely abusive to MHE when they met. He criticized MHE's choice of hotel and his clothing and he asked him questions like, "Do you suppose you could haul that gimpy carcass down the street or do I have to call a cab?" The two went out to dinner where the father canceled

MHE's order and ordered the worst thing on the menu for him. When the food arrived MHE told the waitress to give the bad order to the father and the father's order to himself. Then he insisted that Robert's father pay for the meal.

MHE agreed to see Robert. Like his father, Robert was belligerent to others, although not to the same degree. MHE had Jerry, a medical student, and an art professor sit in on the session. MHE put Jerry into trance and demonstrated every trance phenomenon he could. Then he put the professor into trance and told him not to hear or see Jerry. MHE played around with his two subjects for quite some time in an effort to impress Robert with the authenticity of trance phenomena.

The next evening MHE put Robert into a trance. He suggested that when Robert awakened he would draw a picture but would not realize it because he would also be talking to Jerry. Robert drew a very simplistic drawing of a man and labeled it "Father." He then tore off the sheet of paper and put it in his pocket. The next evening Robert blushed when he entered the office. MHE questioned him and Robert finally admitted that he had urinated on his drawing of the father and flushed it down the toilet.

Jerry was going away for the weekend so MHE gave Robert the opportunity to use his weekend as he pleased. Robert decided that he wanted to visit his mother. If it didn't rain, he would mow the lawn. While Robert was away MHE had Robert's father come in. Again the father was very abusive. MHE had the father pay the secretary, the art professor, and the medical student. Then MHE asked the father for a fee of $1,500. The father complained but paid the money. Then he had the father write a $1,000 pay-on-demand note for MHE. MHE told the father he would collect it if he so chose the next time the man got drunk. (Robert had told MHE that his father had a drinking problem.)

When Robert returned from his visit he blushed. MHE assumed the voice of a drill sergeant and marched Robert around the room. Then he gave him the command, "Take a deep drink at the water fountain and march to the lavatory and take a piss." When the exercise was completed MHE told Robert to stand at ease. Then he asked him what had happened at his mother's house. Robert had mown the lawn as planned. Once he finished he brought the mower to the garage and urinated on it. When he did that he suddenly remembered an incident that occurred when he was young. His mother caught him urinating on the new lawn mower, boxed his ears, and gave him a fearsome lecture. After relating the story, Robert said he didn't think he would have any more trouble.

Six months later MHE got a call from Robert's father. "I'm drunk as a hoot owl, so cash that damned pay-on-demand note." MHE told him he wouldn't cash it. After that Robert's father didn't get drunk again and began attending church more regularly. [In another version, MHE had the father post a $3,000 bond and told him he would cash it if the man ever had another drink. When the father stopped drinking, he became a reasonably nice man. The man stayed sober for some time but called MHE at Christmas and asked if he could have one beer, because he did not want the beer to cost $3,000. MHE asked the man how big a beer he planned to have and the man said he was afraid MHE would ask that. They finally agreed that the man could have one eight-ounce beer on Christmas and another on New Year's Day.]

Presenting Problem: Difficulty urinating

Age Group: Adult

Modality: Individual/family; outpatient

Problem Duration: Since childhood

Treatment Length: One week

Result: Success. He got over his urinating difficulty. MHE also helped his father with his alcohol abuse.

Follow-up: Robert served on a destroyer throughout the war. He died in 1949.

Techniques: Linking (the father's drinking with the son's urination problem; the father's drinking with money to be paid); automatic drawing; hypnosis; dissociation; utilization (of the son's military background)

Sources: *Ordeal Therapy*, p. 59; *Teaching Seminar*, pp. 256–268

Case #112

MISCELLANEOUS PHYSICAL PROBLEMS

Case Summary: A woman who had fainting spells with no organic basis sought therapy from MHE. Since the spells began shortly after she was married, MHE saw her with her husband. He thought they were ill-matched. The husband was very cold and distant. MHE confronted the husband, with no results. Then he suggested privately to the woman that she get a divorce. She refused. Then he suggested that she have children, but warned her that she would probably need therapy in her forties, when her children were grown. The fainting spells disappeared when she became pregnant, but returned when she was in her forties and her children were in college.

Presenting Problem: Fainting

Age Group: Adult

Modality: Individual/couple; outpatient

Problem Duration: NA

Treatment Length: NA

Result: Partial success. The fainting spells stopped for 20 years, but returned as MHE had predicted.

Follow-up: 20 years. Jeffrey Zeig, one of MHE's students, saw the woman when she sought therapy from MHE in her forties, because MHE had died by then.

Techniques: Task assignment (behavioral); redirecting attention

Source: *Experiencing Erickson,* pp. 82–83

Case #113

Case Summary: A woman with an allergy to the sun persisted in going out into the sun constantly. She would then develop a rash on her face, hands, and arms and scratch herself at night until she was covered with horrible scars. She told MHE he would probably tell her to stay out of the sun, as all the other doctors had advised her. MHE told her that would be unnecessary, since she had already said that herself, but that he was entitled to his own opinion in the matter. He told her that she should enjoy as much of the sunlight as she wished. He kept repeating this idea to her until she was in a medium trance and then told her to go home, lie down on her bed for an hour or two, and let her unconscious mind think about that. She said she did not need to think about it, since she consciously remembered what he had said. She went home and sat down to rest for an hour, then got up, put on a long-sleeve dress and a wide-brimmed hat and went out to work in her garden in the sun. The rash cleared up promptly. She resented paying MHE's fee, since he had done so little to help her, but referred 10 people to him.

Presenting Problem: Allergy to the sun; rash

Age Group: Adult

Modality: Individual; outpatient

Problem Duration: NA

Treatment Length: One session

Result: Success. The woman's rash cleared up.

Follow-up: NA

Techniques: Hypnosis; implication; redirecting attention

Source: *Experiencing Hypnosis*, pp. 12–13

Case #114

Case Summary: A professional harpist sought hypnotherapy from MHE for sweaty palms. Her hands would get so slippery from sweat that they would slip off the strings as she was playing. She had consulted numerous medical doctors and they offered little hope for treating her condition and were amazed at its severity. She could hold out her hands and make a puddle on the floor. MHE had her go into trance focusing on some music she enjoyed. He then induced hand levitation in both hands. He then induced a body dissociation and told her she couldn't stand up. Then he had her try to make a puddle with the sweat from her hands while still in trance. She failed to do so.

MHE then gave her a posthypnotic suggestion that she would not be able to sweat while playing the harp and that the suggestion could go into effect on the plane ride back to her home state. He then distinguished between having normal perspiration and excessive sweating. Next he had her unconscious mind signal by lifting one of her hands whether it would clear up the sweating or not. The hand signaled that the sweating would clear up, but the signal was ambiguous, because the other hand lifted a little as well.

MHE then told her a story about a bedwetter who changed gradually. Next he told her to go home and rest and let her unconscious mind think things through. She returned the next day and told him she was confused about the previous session. He reinduced a trance and gave her the posthypnotic suggestion that she would suddenly, upon being given a cue, tell him the date and place when she would approach the harp to play. He suggested that her hands would warm and they did. He had her awaken not seeing the others in the room (there were observers present). She reported knowing that others were present but that somehow they did not impinge.

He asked her to remember something good and something bad from the past. She was reluctant to have the bad memory. MHE kept preparing her and finally got her to commit to telling him the secret in 15 minutes. She revealed at that time that she never really wanted to play the harp professionally and experienced some insight into her family of origin's dynamics. She also got insight into her claustrophobia and fear of flying, which she related to being locked into a closet with a cat by her brother. When she came out of trance, MHE asked her to send him a Christmas card and she agreed. She sent him Christmas cards for the next three years. She was free of the symptom, playing music just for her own enjoyment and raising a family.

Presenting Problem: Sweating palms

Age Group: Adult

Modality: Individual; outpatient

Problem Duration: NA

Treatment Length: Two sessions

Result: Success. The woman stopped having sweaty palms.

Follow-up: Three years. The results persisted.

Techniques: Hypnosis; positive hallucination; hand levitation; posthypnotic suggestion

Source: *Hypnotherapy*, pp. 144–234

Case #115

Case Summary: A woman who had encephalitis with ensuing spastic paralysis sought hypnosis from MHE to reduce the spastic movements of her left arm and leg. She was a psychology student and was rather hostile and demanding during the first session. MHE decided to take a hostile approach

back to her and told her that her buttocks were so large she could sit on her left arm and keep it still. Then she could cross her large right leg over her left leg to keep it still. She went on to get a doctorate in psychology and had reduced her spastic movements so much that few people noticed she had them.

Presenting Problem: Spastic movements

Age Group: Adult

Modality: Individual; outpatient

Problem Duration: NA

Treatment Length: NA

Result: Success. The woman reduced her spastic movements quite a bit.

Follow-up: At least three years. She and MHE went out to eat and the waiter was solicitous of MHE, because he walked with a limp, but did not even notice the woman's handicap.

Techniques: Utilization (of hostility); task assignment (behavioral); redirecting attention

Sources: *Life Reframing*, pp. 35–37; "Double Binds"

Case #116

Case Summary: A 50-year-old woman with Raynaud's Disease (a decrease in circulation of the extremities) was suffering extreme pain and sleep deprivation from her disease. She had developed ulcerated fingers from lack of circulation to her hands and had already had one finger amputated. She was in such pain that she could only fall asleep for one to two hours at a time before the pain reawakened her. She was anticipating another finger amputation in the future. She asked MHE whether he could use hypnosis to help her.

He hypnotized her and told her that her body had years of experiential learnings and that she could spend the rest of the day sorting through and reorganizing those learnings at the unconscious level. At 10:45 p.m that night, her usual bedtime, she was to sit down in a chair and go into a deep trance similar to the one she had developed in MHE's office that morning. Then she was to review and consolidate all the learnings her unconscious mind had reorganized during the day. At 11:30 p.m., she was to call MHE and tell him what therapy her unconscious mind had decided to provide to ensure that she would have a good night's sleep. She told him that she had gone into trance and become extremely and painfully cold for about 10 minutes. Then her body had begun to warm up and got burning hot. After that she felt weak, so weak she could barely phone MHE. He asked her if the weak feeling was relaxed and she said it was. He suggested she use that relaxed feeling to get to sleep and to call him in the morning.

She slept through the night for the first time in 10 years and began to trust her unconscious to help with her pain and with healing the disease itself. After that, the ulcers on her fingers started healing and she routinely got six to eight hours of sleep per night.

Presenting Problem: Raynaud's Disease; circulatory problems; pain; insomnia

Age Group: Adult

Modality: Individual; outpatient

Problem Duration: 10 years

Treatment Length: NA

Result: Success. The disease was arrested and the woman had less pain and therefore more sleep.

Follow-up: NA

Techniques: Hypnosis; direct suggestion; task assignment (cognitive and behavioral)

Source: *Life Reframing*, pp. 229–231

Case #117

Case Summary: A 12-year-old girl had had infantile paralysis. She wanted MHE's help in regaining the use of her arms. When she came in to see MHE he noticed that she had very well-developed breasts for a 12-year-old, but that her right breast was under her arm. MHE asked her to practice drawing down the corner of both sides of her mouth while sitting topless in front of a mirror. She agreed but said that instead of looking at a mirror she would imagine a TV program. After practicing the facial expression her breast begin to migrate to its proper position.

Presenting Problem: Paralysis of the arms

Age Group: Adolescent

Modality: Individual; outpatient

Problem Duration: NA

Treatment Length: NA

Result: Success. She regained the use of her arms and her breast returned to its proper position.

Follow-up: At least 10 years. When she grew up she became a lawyer.

Techniques: Task assignment (behavioral)

Source: *My Voice Will Go With You*, pp. 133–134

Case #118

Case Summary: A woman had seen 26 doctors for physical examinations. Some had kept her in the hospital for as long as two weeks, running tests. None of them had found anything significant. The woman was sure something was wrong with her. She thought it might be syphilis or gonorrhea since she had been promiscuous. Finally one of the doctors suggested she see a psychiatrist so she went to see MHE. MHE took her history and then asked her what strange or weird thing she had done to interrupt each of the examinations. [In one version he first asked her if all the doctors palpitated her breasts.] She thought for a while and then answered that she had sneezed each time a doctor had begun to examine her right breast.

While the woman was still in his office, MHE called a gynecologist [a surgeon in another version] and told him that he had a woman there whom he believed had a lump in her right breast. MHE sent the woman to the gynecologist where she was examined. MHE had told the doctor that if he let her leave the office she probably wouldn't come back so he took her to the hospital immediately to remove the malignancy in her breast. [In another version, the woman knew she had a lump in her breast, but kept avoiding going to the hospital to get a biopsy. MHE gave her the choice of going to see the physician he recommended the next morning or that afternoon. She chose that afternoon. MHE advised the doctor to use the same method, giving her the choice of going into the hospital right after the examination or waiting until 4 p.m. that afternoon. She went to the hospital. A biopsy was done and a malignancy was discovered. With radiation therapy, the woman lived several years.]

Presenting Problem: Somatic complaints that physicians had been unable to diagnose; procrastination; avoidance of a medical procedure

Age Group: Adult

Modality: Individual; outpatient

Problem Duration: NA

Treatment Length: One session

Result: Success. MHE correctly identified her somatic problem as a tumor in her breast and got her correctly diagnosed and promptly treated.

Follow-up: NA

Techniques: NA

Sources: *My Voice Will Go With You*, pp. 190–191; *Phoenix*, pp. 116–117; "Double Binds"

Case #119

Case Summary: A medical technician had a very large rear end which MHE guessed she didn't like. He was curious about her and so he kept an eye on her. He noticed that on visiting days the woman would stand outside the hospital and offer to babysit the visitors' children. One day the woman developed a case of hiccups that the medical doctors could not cure. They all recommended psychiatric consultation, which meant seeing MHE. She refused to see him at first, but after her boss threatened to discontinue her free medical care she gave in. When MHE entered her room, he said, "Keep your mouth shut, don't say anything." He told her that her trouble was that she hadn't read the Song of Solomon, in which the pelvis is referred to as the cradle for children. He told her that he'd watched her for the past year, that he knew she liked children, and that he knew she thought no man would marry her because of her big rear end. He told her that the man who would want to marry her, the man who would fall in love with her, would look at that great big, fat fanny of hers and see only a cradle for children. He told her to read the Song of Solomon after he left. Then he told her to wait for a few hours to stop her hiccups so that nobody would know that he had stopped them. A few months later the woman showed MHE an engagement ring and a few months after that she brought in her fiancé. They had plans to build a house together with lots of bedrooms and a great big nursery.

Presenting Problem: Hiccups

Age Group: Adult

Modality: Individual; outpatient

Problem Duration: NA

Treatment Length: One session

Result: Success. The woman's hiccups were cured. She also got engaged to be married.

Follow-up: NA

Techniques: Reframing; direct suggestion; task assignment (behavioral and cognitive)

Sources: *Phoenix*, pp. 67–69; *Teaching Seminar*, pp. 164–165

Case #120

Case Summary: MHE saw a boy at age 14 and predicted to himself that the boy would develop ulcers. The boy did develop ulcers at age 21. He was a tense, obsessive person. MHE advised a radical change in his life. He advised the man to move to the hills, live like a hillbilly, and give up his obsessive, compulsive ambition. The young man followed his advice and enjoyed the physical life he led. He lost his ulcers.

Presenting Problem: Ulcers

Age Group: Child/adult

Modality: Individual; outpatient

Problem Duration: (Seven years)

Treatment Length: NA

Result: Success. The man's ulcers cleared up.

Follow-up: MHE planned to get the man to do some non-essential tasks, like growing a garden, to learn to please himself rather than others.

Techniques: Task assignment (behavioral)

Sources: "Double Binds"

Case #121

Case Summary: A dentist's wife had tempomandibular joint (TMJ) problems caused by the fact that she would chew only on the right side of her mouth. She insisted that chewing on the left side hurt, although no physical cause for the pain could be found. Her husband was disgusted at her for not changing this habit. MHE told her that she should continue chewing on the right side of her mouth and that if food should get on the left side, she should haul it back over to the right side. She soon started eating on both sides of her mouth.

Presenting Problem: Tempomandibular joint (TMJ) problems

Age Group: Adult

Modality: Individual; outpatient

Problem Duration: NA

Treatment Length: NA

Result: Success. The woman started eating on both sides of her mouth and presumably got rid of the TMJ problems.

Follow-up: NA

Techniques: Symptom prescription; implication (that food would get on the left side of her mouth)

Source: "Double Binds"

Case #122

3

Sexual Problems

IMPOTENCE

Case Summary: A college-educated young man came to MHE after his honeymoon. He was despondent over the fact that he had been unable to get an erection to consummate the marriage. The wife wanted an annulment. When the couple came to the office, MHE had the man look at his wife and re-experience the shame, humiliation and hopelessness he felt. As he did this he would want to do anything to escape that feeling. He would become unable to see anything but his wife. He would go into a deep hypnotic trance "in which he would have no control over his entire body." He would hallucinate his bride and himself naked. He would sense intimate physical contact that would be very exciting but he would be unable to control his physical response. However, there would be no completion of his physical response until his bride requested it. At the conclusion of the trance MHE told him that there was nothing he could do to keep from succeeding again and again. That night they readily consummated the marriage.

Presenting Problem: Impotence

Age Group: Adult

Modality: Marital; outpatient

Problem Duration: Two weeks

Treatment Length: Two sessions

Result: Success. The couple went home and consummated their marriage.

Follow-up: No further sexual problems. MHE acted as a family advisor for them for at least the next 10 years and saw them as happily married.

Techniques: Hypnosis; linking (shame/humiliation with going into trance; going into trance with lack of control over his body; hallucinating bride and self in the nude leading to sexual response); positive hallucination; posthypnotic suggestion

Sources: *Collected Papers I*, p. 172; *Uncommon Therapy*, p. 158

Case #123

Case Summary: A 42-year-old physician had been impotent since his first year in college, after his first failure with a prostitute. He had tried systematically and desperately through the years to cure his condition with no success. He had recently met a woman and they had fallen in love. He had confessed his problem to her and she had tried to help him overcome it, but again with no success. She was willing to marry him without the promise of intercourse, but he thought that she would grow dissatisfied with that. He sought MHE's help and wanted hypnosis.

MHE put the man into trance and suggested that he would go to bed next to his fiancée precisely at 11 p.m. each night and have an erection from 11 p.m. until midnight, when he would finally go to sleep and lose the erection. He was to arrange with colleagues to avoid any night or early morning calls or medical activities for the next three months, even if that meant taking three months off from his practice. He was not to engage in any sexual activity during the three months. He told the man that the months would seem intolerably long, but that one month could be just as intolerable as two or three. MHE gave him amnesia for the hypnotic instructions.

MHE separately instructed the fiancée in trance to avoid all sexual contact and any talk about his problem with the man. She should be ready to go to bed at 11 p.m. each night, when her fiancé would turn out the light. She agreed. Thirty days later the man appeared at MHE's office and introduced the former fiancée as his new wife. He had taken three months off from his practice and had enjoyed the time. The evenings were always over at exactly 11 p.m., when he and his fiancée would go to bed and turn out the light.

Each night he would have that hourlong erection and not lose it until he went to sleep until one night (27 days after the hypnosis) he realized that he couldn't lose the erection until he went to sleep. He immediately rolled over and had intercourse successfully with his fiancée. They were married the next morning. The success continued.

Presenting Problem: Impotence

Age Group: Adult

Modality: Individual / marital; outpatient

Problem Duration: Over 20 years

Treatment Length: Two sessions

Result: Success. The man was able to achieve consistent intravaginal erections and ejaculations.

Follow-up: Five years. The couple was happily married.

Techniques: Hypnosis; behavioral contract; posthypnotic suggestion; amnesia

Sources: *Collected Papers IV*, pp. 374–382; *My Voice Will Go With You*, pp. 157–158

Case #124

Case Summary: A medical student married a very beautiful girl. On their wedding night he could not produce an erection, despite the fact that he'd had plenty of past experience with other women. For two weeks he tried and failed to get an erection. When they returned from their honeymoon the wife wanted an annulment. MHE had the husband bring the wife in for therapy. He told the husband to wait in the other room while he talked to her. MHE proceeded to tell the woman what a compliment her husband had paid her. MHE said that her husband was so overwhelmed by her beauty that he couldn't perform. Then he sent the wife out and brought the man in to tell him what a compliment he'd paid his wife. On the way home, the couple almost stopped the car to have intercourse.

Presenting Problem: Impotence; marital problems

Age Group: Adult

Modality: Marital; outpatient

Problem Duration: Two weeks

Treatment Length: One session

Result: Success. The man was able to get an erection.

Follow-up: NA

Technique: Reframing

Sources: *Conversations II*, pp. 118–119; *Uncommon Therapy*, p. 157

Case #125

PREMATURE EJACULATION

Case Summary: A psychologist MHE knew sought his help for premature ejaculation. After he had described his worsening condition, MHE put him off by saying that he would have to consider the matter and advising that he seek help from another psychiatrist. In the meantime, he secured the man's participation in a hypnotic experiment. In trance, MHE convinced the man that he had had a traumatic experience involving accidentally breaking a treasured art piece made by a colleague's daughter by leaving a burning cigarette in it. This trauma was accepted as an actual memory so that after awakening from trance the man showed evidence of having developed a neurotic complex about things associated with the induced traumatic memory. When MHE led him to realize that it had been induced and not a real trauma, he was able to overcome it and use the painted ashtray in MHE's office comfortably for a satisfying smoke. Following this procedure, he discovered that he no longer ejaculated prematurely. At first he did not relate this to the hypnotic experiment, but MHE led him to make the connection. The problem recurred occasionally, but with none of the shame and persistence associated with it previously.

Presenting Problem: Premature ejaculation

Age Group: Adult

Modality: Individual; outpatient

Problem Duration: Three years

Treatment Length: One session

Result: Partial success. The man was able to last longer during intercourse and lost the sense of shame when he ejaculated quickly.

Follow-up: One year

Techniques: Hypnosis; induced memory of trauma; parallel communication

Source: *Collected Papers III*, pp. 320–331

Case #126

✑

Case Summary: A 30-year-old unmarried man sought MHE's help for premature ejaculation. He had his first sexual encounter at age 20 and that started his problem. He would always ejaculate before entering the woman's vagina. He could maintain an erection and continue intercourse, but he always found it unsatisfactory and felt compelled to withdraw to ejaculate. He had sought out many different kinds of women in his search for a satisfying sexual encounter, but had not yet found it. He had read MHE's article about the induction of an artificial problem to resolve premature ejaculation and had tried it on himself but it hadn't worked. He agreed to cooperate with any procedure MHE devised except the one he had already attempted and failed with.

Through six sessions he repeated details of his attempts to solve his problem and MHE repetitiously kept inquiring about the man's ability to maintain an erection. Each time the man would assure MHE that there was no question about it and seemed annoyed by MHE's repetition of the question. The next two sessions were spent in inducing trances with the man, who developed amnesia for much of the trance experience. At the next session, a trance was induced and MHE offered the man the suggestion that as soon as the man entered the courtyard of his current woman friend, he would get an erection and would maintain that erection until he left the courtyard. Then MHE offered a series of suggestions about how neurotic symptoms could change over time and how they could disappear as suddenly as they arose. It was added that premature ejaculation could turn into a frightening inability to ejaculate and if that happened to the man, he would really have something to worry about. Perhaps ejaculate would be delayed for as long as 30 minutes. MHE suggested further that for the next 10 days the man would feel an impending change coming. He was given an appointment for Sunday morning, strategically arranged after his Saturday night date with his woman friend. On Sunday he reported to MHE that during his date he had become distracted by the worry that he would not be able to ejaculate. His companion became aggressive sexually and he went along, all the while worried about not being able to ejaculate. He found himself wearing his wristwatch to bed and watching the minute hand. He was so distracted by his concern that he ejaculated in the woman's vagina after 20 minutes. He experienced a second intravaginal ejaculation that night and both were satisfying. The experience was repeated the next night and thereafter the man no longer had a problem with premature ejaculation.

Presenting Problem: Premature ejaculation

Age Group: Adult

Modality: Individual; outpatient

Problem Duration: 10 years

Treatment Length: (11 sessions)

Result: Success. The man was able to ejaculate intravaginally and not prematurely.

Follow-up: At least three months, probably years. At the time of writing, the man was engaged to be married.

Techniques: Hypnosis; parallel communication (getting an erection coming into the courtyard and not losing it until he left the courtyard parallels getting an erection when he entered the woman's vagina and not losing an erection until he left the vagina); symptom transformation (worry about prematurely ejaculating into worry about an inability to ejaculate); posthypnotic suggestion

Sources: *Collected Papers IV*, pp. 343–347; *Uncommon Therapy*, pp. 83–88

Case #127

Case Summary: A 38-year-old man had a history of premature ejaculation since he was 20. He had vainly tried prostitutes and proper women as well as numerous medical procedures, but he had not been able to overcome his problem. Finally he researched hypnosis and sought out MHE. The man wanted hypnosis but was certain it would fail like all his other efforts. He might at least, he reasoned, be able to give up his compulsive quest to find a cure. He was certain the premature ejaculation was organically based and therefore that there was no cure. He insisted upon telling MHE all the details of his failures and his efforts to find a cure.

MHE learned that the man usually brought women to his apartment for sex. MHE suggested in trance that the man start to wear a wristwatch that he could see with a nightlight every time he was in bed. He learned from the man and from visiting the apartment building where the man lived that there were wooden slatted steps and a slatted boardwalk leading to the man's door. After inducing trance, MHE suggested that the man would, on his way to his apartment on his next date, develop an obsession with counting the cracks in the sidewalk and in the boards on the way to his door. He would try to keep his mind on the conversation but would be counting the cracks under him. As soon as he reached the door of his apartment, he would start to become obsessed with his watch and would find himself worrying about failing to ejaculate for 27 and a half minutes.

The suggestions worked and he got over his problem. He had an amnesia for the trance suggestions and attributed his recovery to a spontaneous organic reversal of his problem that must have been brought about just by telling MHE all about it. Twenty-one months later he came to see MHE and recovered his memories of the hypnotherapy.

Presenting Problem: Premature ejaculation

Age Group: Adult

Modality: Individual; outpatient

Problem Duration: 18 years

Treatment Length: NA

Result: Success. The man was able to maintain an erection during intercourse.

Follow-up: Seven years. The man was happily married.

Techniques: Hypnosis; utilization (of the man's obsessions and compulsiveness); symptom transformation (worry about quick ejaculation into worry about not being able to ejaculate); parallel communication ("counting the cracks underneath him" is a parallel for all the vaginal cracks he had been obsessed with through the years); posthypnotic suggestion; amnesia

Source: *Collected Papers IV*, pp. 348–355

Case #128

Case Summary: A man came to MHE for premature ejaculation. MHE told the man that a premature ejaculation was rather nice because he could unload about a quarter of his sperm supply and cut down on his sensitivity. Then he could really enjoy foreplay. When the man returned for a later session he reported that he had gone to bed with a girl and had a premature ejaculation. After he ejaculated, he "really explored that girl," got another erection and really enjoyed it.

Presenting Problem: Premature ejaculation

Age Group: Adult

Modality: Individual; outpatient

Problem Duration: NA

Treatment Length: NA

Result: Success. The man learned to perform normally.

Follow-up: NA

Technique: Reframing

Source: *Conversations II*, pp. 114–115

Case #129

SEXUAL INHIBITIONS/RIGIDITY

Case Summary: A couple had been married for a week. Although the wife wanted to consummate the marriage she would go into a panic and cross her legs tightly whenever she was approached. MHE asked her if she was willing to be hypnotized. She said that she was, provided that she wouldn't be touched. MHE and the husband sat on one side of the room while she sat near the door. She was to leave if anyone tried to touch her. MHE had her lock her body in a stiff and rigid position with her ankles and arms crossed.

He then put her into trance and had her focus on her husband. Then she would start to panic and would go into a trance that would be directly correlated in depth with the amount of her panic. MHE then told her that she would begin to feel her husband caressing her body, although he would remain across the room. MHE told her the caressing would become even more intimate so the two men would turn their heads. She would feel very pleased and relaxed by the caressing. Five minutes later she announced that she was all right and wanted to leave. She asked MHE not to look at her because she was so embarrassed about her feelings. MHE instructed the husband to take the wife home and passively await any developments. Within two hours the couple had consummated the marriage.

Presenting Problem: Panic (when approached for sex)

Age Group: Adult

Modality: Marital; outpatient

Problem Duration: One week

Treatment Length: One session

Result: Success. The couple consummated their marriage.

Follow-up: 15 months later the couple brought their newborn infant to visit MHE.

Techniques: Hypnosis; linking (panic with going into trance); positive hallucination; utilization (of panic)

Sources: *Collected Papers I*, pp. 170–171; *Hypnotherapy*, pp. 79–81; *Uncommon Therapy*, pp. 159–161

Case #130

Case Summary: A man sought MHE's help after he lost 40 or 50 lbs. in the nine months following his wedding. His co-workers had teased him about the weight loss, attributing it to excessive sexual activity. Actually, he had lost weight due to being upset about not sexually consummating his marriage. Every time he would try to have sex with his wife, she would panic and beg him to wait until the next day, which had effectively prevented intercourse.

MHE saw the couple together, hypnotized the wife and told her she would become so absorbed with some meaningless but satisfying thought on the way home that things would happen so fast she would not have time to be afraid. The wife started her menstrual bleeding on the way home from MHE's office, some 17 days ahead of schedule. She had been extremely regular in her cycle from when she started having menstruation until then. When she returned to see MHE alone, he told her that he had made a mistake with her and now he knew that she should decide what night to consummate the marriage. He mentioned all the days of the week as possibilities, but kept stressing that *he* (MHE) preferred Friday. The woman waited until Thursday night and initiated sex with her husband. She woke him up again just before midnight to have intercourse again. She was laughing to herself on Friday morning and when her husband asked about it, she told him to make sure MHE got the message it wasn't Friday.

Presenting Problem: No intercourse/consummation of marriage; weight loss

Age Group: Adult

Modality: Marital/individual; outpatient

Problem Duration: Nine months

Treatment Length: (Three sessions)

Result: Success. The couple consummated their marriage.

Follow-up: At least six years. The couple went on to have three planned children at two-year intervals.

Techniques: Hypnosis; redirecting attention; implication; task assignment (behavioral); anchoring the resistance

Sources: *Collected Papers II*, pp. 185–186; *Collected Papers IV*, pp. 168–170; *Mind-Body Communication*, pp. 12–14; *Uncommon Therapy*, pp. 154–156

Case #131

Case Summary: A 23-year-old woman became suicidally depressed quite suddenly. Her roommate became worried about her and had to plead with her to eat. Her performance at work was deteriorating as she listlessly went about her duties. She had previously been an unusually capable worker. She

sobbed much of the time and when asked about her difficulties she was uncommunicative. Several psychiatrists diagnosed her as being manic-depressive in the depressed phase and recommended commitment. MHE and an analyst concluded, however, that it was an acute reactive depression that resulted from a recent trauma. Psychoanalysis was attempted for a month but the depression became more intense and disturbing. It was then decided that MHE would attempt to work with her indirectly with hypnosis. Accordingly, her roommate asked her to accompany her to hypnotic treatment with MHE as a chaperone.

Under the guise of working with the roommate, MHE indirectly hypnotized the woman and got her unconscious agreement to work on the problem. From others involved and from the patient herself under hypnosis MHE learned the background and event that led to the depression. The woman was the only daughter of a rather moralistic woman who had died when the patient was 13. They had been very close. The patient's only close friendship was with a neighbor girl of her own age. At the age of 20, the two young women had met a young man with whom they both fell in love. At first the young man had no favorite, but gradually he became closer to the patient's friend and subsequently married her. The patient was disappointed, but soon recovered. A year after the marriage, the wife died of pneumonia. The patient was grief-stricken. The husband moved away to another part of the country for a year. When he moved back, a chance meeting led to the development of a romance that culminated one night when the man told her he wanted to marry her and leaned over to kiss her. She responded by vomiting all over him. After that she had refused to see him or to discuss the matter. She maintained that he was not to blame, but that she was disgusting and dirty. It was then that her depression began. After that, she would become ill at the mention of the young man's name.

In trance, MHE reoriented her to an age somewhere between 10 and 13 and instructed her to recount everything she had learned about sex and specifically about menstruation. She responded by telling MHE that her mother had told her that good girls never let boys do anything to them. If they did they were disgusting. Having sex, she had been warned, would make the patient have nasty feelings and make her mother sick. MHE realized that he could not directly challenge her idealized deceased mother's instructions, so he started making suggestions that, since her mother had died when the patient was 13, she gave appropriate suggestions for the patient as a child. He wondered what instructions her mother would have given her if she had lived long enough to see her grow up to be a woman. Gradually the woman started to be less depressed and report shifts in her views of sex.

During the third hypnotic session, the woman promptly declared that she had just realized what had been wrong with her and became anxious to leave. MHE restrained her and she started asking him questions about what proper sexual morals were and what he thought of "kissing, necking and petting." MHE replied that people have to follow their own morals in accordance with their ideals and individual personality. She then asked MHE whether he thought it was okay to feel sexual feelings. He replied that it was natural for all living creatures to do so and the absence of those feelings in the appropriate situation was wrong. He added that if her mother were alive, she would undoubtedly agree with this. She reported to MHE the next day, with some embarrassment, that "kissing is great sport." At the next session, she told MHE that she had developed a new understanding of sex and that she had been so struck by it at the last session that she had felt like going to her man friend and offering him her virginity, but MHE's restraining had stopped her. She had since become engaged to the young man. She returned for some basic sex education before her wedding.

Presenting Problem: Depression; nausea

Age Group: Adult

Modality: Individual; outpatient

Problem Duration: (Two months)

Treatment Length: Four or five sessions

Result: Success. The woman was no longer depressed and had developed a good relationship and adjustment with the man whose actions precipitated the conflict and depression she had felt.

Follow-up: At one and two years. At two years, she was happily married with one child and with no depression.

Techniques: Hypnosis; age regression; splitting (what her mother told her as a child/what her mother would have told her as an adult)

Sources: *Collected Papers III*, pp. 122–142; *Uncommon Therapy*, pp. 75–82

Case #132

Case Summary: A physician brought his wife for hypnotherapy with MHE. He told MHE that he would have to tell MHE what the problem was because his wife would undoubtedly be unable to do so. They had been married for 12 years. His wife, a registered nurse, was exceedingly modest. She insisted that she undress for bed in the next room, where she put on pajamas covered by a nightgown. She would only enter the couple's bedroom if all the lights were off and the shades were drawn. At the start of their marriage, she would not have sex, but she finally allowed it (only in the dark) and they had a child. Her husband had to force her to see an obstetrician and she finally saw one when she was seven months pregnant. She required ether for the examination. The child was now five and the husband did not want the daughter to get the same inhibitions her mother had, so he had brought his wife for treatment.

The husband had precipitated a crisis two years previously when he had grown so disgusted at her inhibitions that he had ripped off her nightgown and pajamas and made her come to bed naked. She had gone into a panic, which ultimately resulted in her being hospitalized and given electric shock treatments. Her husband had apologized profusely and realized he had made a mistake, but she was not getting any better under the care of another psychiatrist. The other psychiatrist was advising more shock treatments, which the husband opposed.

MHE checked with the woman to find out whether her husband had been accurate in his account. She indicated that he had. MHE asked her if she wanted to become his patient and told her he didn't use shock treatments. She replied that she didn't want shock or hormone treatment, just help not being so afraid. MHE found out that she had done a lot of painting and dancing and had played the piano before her child was born. He instructed her to beat time with her upraised hand to a tune that she remembered dancing to while recalling a previous trance experience. [In another version he lifted her skirt up to expose her thigh to induce the trance.] The trance was then deepened and she was guided to experience negative hallucination for her husband and for the room she was in and to see before her a mirror. In the mirror she was to see herself ballet dancing and then discover that she was dancing in the nude. When she was doing a high kick she was to hear someone coming and be frozen in mid-air. She would see that it was her husband and that he was laughing and clapping because he liked her dancing. She would become unfrozen and then dance wildly until she collapsed into her husband's arms and was carried away.

At this point MHE had the mirror tactfully fade and left the woman on her own to finish the fantasy. When the woman indicated that she had followed his instructions, he told her that she should repeat the fantasy five more times and if she didn't he would have something much worse in mind for her. She complied. Then he induced an amnesia for what had occurred in trance and gave her a posthypnotic suggestion. The suggestion was that she would have an impending feeling that she was building up to something. She would catch glimpses of herself in various mirrors with a certain smile on her face. She would begin to itch all over with wonder. On Friday she would wonder why she sent her daughter to spend the weekend with friends and why she was preparing a wonderful meal. Then she would get ready for bed in the usual way except that when she looked down she would find that she hadn't put on her pajamas at all, but rather a pair of her husband's old ragged ones. On impulse she would tear them off and dance into the hall, where she would snap on the light, and then dance into her bedroom, where she would again snap on the light and watch her husband watch her in stunned, helpless wonder until. . . .

Her husband reported by phone that she was distracted all week and kept playing snatches of dance music on the piano and glancing in mirrors. Friday night played out exactly as MHE had suggested. They had a wonderful weekend, like a second honeymoon. The woman was greatly embarrassed when she came for the follow-up visit, but happy to be over her inhibition and fear. She continued to see MHE occasionally for relief of seasonal dermatitis. [In another version, MHE has her do the task gradually over six months and tells her that if she hasn't danced nude for her husband within that time, she will have to do the nude dance in front of him.]

Presenting Problem: Excessive modesty and anxiety

Age Group: Adult

Modality: Marital; outpatient

Problem Duration: 12 years

Treatment Length: Two sessions

Result: Success. The woman was able to dance nude into her bedroom with the lights on.

Follow-up: Five years

Techniques: Hypnosis; utilization (of compulsion, dancing, and piano playing); negative hallucination; positive hallucination; posthypnotic suggestion; task assignment; amnesia

Source: *Collected Papers IV*, pp. 356–365 and pp. 452–455

Case #133

Case Summary: Two women had been friends since high school. They both married their high school sweethearts. They confided most of their personal thoughts and feelings to one another. They had both decided they wanted divorces from their spouses. Each told the other that her husband had a perversion but was too embarrassed to tell what the perversion was. They decided that both should go see MHE. One day he saw one and she told him that her husband was a pervert because he liked to have sex with his legs outside of hers. She knew the proper way was to have sex with the man's legs between the woman's. The next day MHE saw the other friend. She told him that her husband was a pervert because he wanted to have intercourse with his legs between hers and she knew the right way to have sex was with the man's legs outside the woman's. MHE told them not to discuss the contents of their individual sessions with each other, but that they were both to attend the next session. When they came together, MHE explained that each was to repeat what she had told him. While one was talking the other was to sit in silence. After both were finished talking, MHE instructed them to ride home and wonder what was wrong with their friend. They each ended up trying both sexual positions and enjoying them.

Presenting Problem: Sexual concerns (worrying about the normalcy of sexual positions)

Age Group: Adult

Modality: Individual; outpatient

Problem Duration: NA

Treatment Length: Three sessions

Result: Success. Each woman gave up her idea that her husband's interest in a certain sexual position was perverted. They each tried and enjoyed different sexual positions after therapy.

Follow-up: NA

Technique: Reframing (by bringing two people with opposite views together)

Source: *Collected Papers IV*, pp. 455–456

Case #134

Case Summary: Ann came to MHE because she had choking and gasping spells. She feared that she could die at any moment. The spells tended to occur before bedtime and during lunchtime when her friends told risqué stories. MHE encouraged her to relate these stories and then acted surprised at their content. MHE asked her how various aspects of showering before bedtime affected her breathing. Next he asked her questions about the content of the bedroom. She named drapes and carpet but did not mention the bed. MHE found that she had her hope chest in the bedroom and pointed out that there must have been a lot of changes in that chest in 12 years of marriage.

Next MHE asked her about what she wore to bed. He talked about how often husbands and wives have different metabolism at night and require different amounts of clothing. Ann slept in a very long nightie and her husband slept in the nude. Before bed they didn't kiss goodnight because her husband liked to hug her and she couldn't take the pressure on her chest. MHE remarked that this inability to take pressure on her chest must interfere with intercourse. He asked her whether or not she planned her only child. Ann replied that the child was planned and that they wanted more but "It didn't seem to work."

MHE asked her to imagine "the most horrible thing" that she could do in relation to going to bed. He instructed her not to tell him what it was but she wanted to. She said it would be dancing naked in the bedroom because her husband would drop dead. He instructed her to come to bed dancing nude in the dark so that her husband couldn't see her, and then to put on her nightie and go to sleep. Ann followed his instruction and giggled herself to sleep. Next MHE asked her what the most horrible, amazing, ludicrous thing she could do would be. She said it would be to undress in front of her husband and to have red ribbons tied around her nipples. Ann tried this and her husband responded by saying, "I think you're beginning to get some sense." Finally MHE discussed sexual matters directly with Ann. Gradually she became very open and comfortable about sex. MHE asked her what she would now use her choking and gasping for. She replied that she would use it to get rid of unwanted guests.

Presenting Problem: Breathing difficulties; inhibition

Age Group: Adult

Modality: Individual; outpatient

Problem Duration: NA

Treatment Length: NA

Result: Success. The woman learned to control her breathing difficulties.

Follow-up: NA

Techniques: Task assignment (behavioral); parallel communication; re-framing

Sources: *Conversations I*, pp. 123–149; *Uncommon Therapy*, pp. 249–258

Case #135

Case Summary: A woman and a man came to MHE after a few weeks of marriage. The man wanted a divorce. MHE told him he thought he was a coward for not sticking through the first month at least. He then turned to the wife and asked for her side of things. Her complaint was about the way her husband made love: all the lights had to be on, she had to leave her nightie on, he didn't kiss her, and he wouldn't touch her breasts. MHE told the woman, in detail, all the things that he thought a proper husband would do to her in bed. Next MHE suggested that the man ought to make up pet names for her breasts, or "twins," as MHE called them. The man refused because he thought it was undignified. MHE decided that the names would have to rhyme and that if the man hadn't named them by the next session, MHE would name one and the man would be stuck with a name that would immediately pop into his head. At the next session the wife reported that the man's love making had improved considerably. However, he still refused to name the twins. MHE christened the woman's right breast "Kitty." Six months later MHE got a Christmas card from the couple signed with their names and "K. and T." The husband turned out to be a good lover and the couple had children.

Presenting Problem: Marital (disagreement about sexual behavior)

Age Group: Adult

Modality: Marital; outpatient

Problem Duration: One month

Treatment Length: (Two sessions)

Result: Success. The man changed his sexual behavior and the couple became happy.

Follow-up: Happy sex life; children.

Techniques: Utilization (of husband's obsessive thinking); implication (of the name of the other breast)

Sources: *Conversations II*, pp. 28–31; *Uncommon Therapy*, pp. 162–164

Case #136

ॐ

Case Summary: A woman was completely unresponsive sexually. Her lack of response resulted in a divorce from her first husband. She had since gone with a number of men and the relationships had been unsatisfactory. She was currently living with a man who was separated from his wife but had no intention of marrying her. The man gave her expensive presents, but did not treat her with respect. In a trance MHE explained to her how being in different stages of arousal feels to a male and how boys learn to recognize those stages. He told her all about boys' wet dreams. Then he said that half of a boy's ancestors are female and that what any boy can do, any girl can do. MHE suggested that she could have wet dreams. In fact, she could have them in the daytime when she saw a handsome man. The woman became unusually still and then she flushed. "Dr. Erickson," she said, "you've just given me my first orgasm. Thank you very much."

Presenting Problem: Sexual unresponsiveness

Age Group: Adult

Modality: Individual

Problem Duration: NA

Treatment Length: NA

Result: Success. The woman was able to have two or three orgasms during sex with her new boyfriend after treatment.

Follow-up: The woman and MHE kept up a correspondence after treatment. The woman got involved in a relationship with a man who was interested in marriage.

Techniques: Hypnosis; implication (she could have sexual responsiveness due to her biological heritage and from unconscious activity); direct suggestion; posthypnotic suggestion

Source: *My Voice Will Go With You*, pp. 83–84

Case #137

PROMISCUITY/SEXUAL DEVIANCE

Case Summary: A social service worker at the hospital in which MHE worked entered his office one evening without an appointment. She was dressed very provocatively and said, "I want something." MHE replied that that was obvious, since she was in a psychiatrist's office. She expressed some doubt about whether she really wanted psychotherapy and MHE told her that she would have to have an actual desire to get results. She thought it over and declared her intention to have psychotherapy. She confessed that for the past three years she had a compulsion to have sex with any man; she called it a "prostitution complex." She would take any man, singly or in groups, of any class and race. She wanted to stop it but couldn't.

MHE told her that if he took her as a patient she would have to agree to control her compulsion between then and the next session. She could only commit to a daily promise not to have sex. She visited MHE twice daily during the next three days and renewed her promise not to have sex. On the fourth day, she had a three-hour session with MHE and spent most of the time berating herself. MHE was able to gather a little history. She had grown up with a domineering, nasty mother and a nice, but ineffectual father. Father was successful in business, but mother totally ruled the house with nasty shrieking. She wanted to make her father stand up to her mother. They had taught her that sex was dirty and to be avoided.

She spent another three-hour session berating herself and then MHE took charge. He told her to shut up and listen obediently to all that he said. He induced a trance, instructed her to have amnesia for all trance experiences, and had her learn various trance phenomena (automatic handwriting, depersonalization, crystal gazing, etc.). Trance didn't help obtain any useful information, however, as all she would do was compulsively recount details of all her sexual encounters. Finally MHE told her that her unconscious knew the reason behind the sexual compulsion and that it would indicate it by underlying words or letters on one of his discarded manuscripts. She did so and immediately MHE took the sheet of paper and locked it in his drawer. He asked her unconscious mind to let him know when she was willing to know the reason.

She failed to give the usual promise about refraining from sex at that session. She failed to give her promise as usual the next morning, but showed up for a late afternoon appointment and told MHE that she wasn't sure she would continue with therapy. She felt the compulsion to tell him two words, though—"three weeks." MHE noted the date on his calendar and induced a trance in which she confirmed an appointment for three weeks hence. She again failed to give the promise.

She appeared at the appointed time but said she had no idea why she was there. MHE told her she had been a patient of his and perhaps had drifted away from therapy or perhaps not. He told her he had used hypnosis and that she had usually had three-hour long sessions. She could now, in trance or awake, tell him exactly when she would be ready to know the reason. She sat down, uncomprehending, and said "6:30." It was 5:00 and they waited in silence until 6:30, at which time MHE took the sheet of paper out of the locked drawer and handed it to her. She looked at it, turned pale and then told MHE she now knew the reason. The underlined letters and words spelled, "I want to fuck fauthor [sic]." She realized that she had been trying to have sex with not just any man in the world, but with *every* man, which would include her father. That was her way of trying to make him a man and free him from the domination of her mother. Once she realized this she was free from the compulsion.

Presenting Problem: Sexual compulsion; having sex with any man

Age Group: Adult

Modality: Individual; outpatient

Problem Duration: Three years

Treatment Length: One month, seven sessions, plus several times of checking in twice daily

Result: Success. The woman was freed from her compulsion to have sex with any man.

Follow-up: The woman completed her social service training and MHE heard several years later that she was happily married and had three children.

Techniques: Hypnosis; behavioral contract; amnesia; positive hallucination; depersonalization; automatic handwriting; direct suggestion; indirect suggestion

Source: *Collected Papers IV*, pp. 163–168

Case #138

Case Summary: A traveling salesman came to MHE for brief therapy because he was unhappy with his transvestism. On business trips the man would bring well-locked suitcases full of women's lingerie. Once arrived at a motel he would go to his room, lock the door, and put on a bra and panties. He would then study himself in the mirror. In the first session MHE told the man that when he looked in the mirror he was seeing neither himself nor the clothes. He instructed the man to leave the office, go to a restaurant and try to "discover how a woman wears her clothes" by observing the waitresses. MHE emphasized the idea that a woman's gestures are just as important as her clothing. His second assignment was to go home and examine his own women's clothing and try to imagine how a woman would really wear it, thinking about her movements as well as how she would feel in the garments. When the man returned he reported that his transvestism had been absurd. He had given the clothing to charity and was now finding his wife much more sexually attractive.

Presenting Problem: Transvestism (man wearing women's clothing)

Age Group: Adult

Modality: Individual; outpatient

Problem Duration: (Since puberty)

Treatment Length: Five hours

Result: Success. The man realized that he was no longer interested in being a transvestite.

Follow-up: NA

Techniques: Task assignment (perceptual); reframing; symptom transformation (interest in seeing himself in women's clothes → interest in observing women); redirecting attention

Source: *Conversations I*, pp. 28–30

Case #139

Case Summary: A man was discussing voyeurism with his analyst. After several weeks of discussing he went out and did it. Once out of jail he left the analyst and came to MHE. The man asked MHE's advice about voyeurism. MHE asked him what he would like to see. The man described his idea of a female body, including how she would dress and undress. MHE had the man repeat his description a dozen times and then asked the man if he would look for such a woman. The man replied that he now realized that such a woman was only in his mind.

Presenting Problem: Preoccupation with voyeurism

Age Group: Adult

Modality: Individual; outpatient

Problem Duration: NA

Treatment Length: (One session)

Result: (Success. The man got over his obsession with voyeurism.)

Follow-up: NA

Techniques: Reframing; splitting (fantasy from reality)

Source: *Conversations I*, p. 105

Case #140

Case Summary: A psychiatric resident in training was treating a male homosexual who was employed by the hospital. Despite his homosexuality, he wanted to marry for appearance's sake. At that time MHE was seeing a lesbian who worked for the hospital who also wanted to get married. MHE had the resident tell his patient to walk along the sidewalk behind the hospital at four o'clock, where he would meet a woman who would suit his needs. MHE gave his own patient similar instructions. The two met, married and lived respectably. They both got jobs with a hospital in another state. MHE called a physician at the other hospital and asked him to help them out with their cover.

Presenting Problem: Desire to find a mate for the sake of appearance

Age Group: Adult

Modality: Individual; outpatient

Problem Duration: NA

Treatment Length: NA

Result: Success. MHE found a suitable mate for the man.

Follow-up: The couple got a four-bedroom house and often entertained friends.

Techniques: Task assignment (behavioral and perceptual)

Source: *Uncommon Therapy*, pp. 169–170

Case #141

MISCELLANEOUS SEXUAL PROBLEMS

Case Summary: A couple who had decided that they never wanted children used contraception and had a good sex life. One day, a friend who was doing research on sperm asked the husband for a sample and, since he knew the couple's attitudes towards children, happily informed the husband that his sperm count was essentially zero. At first, both husband and wife were happy not to have to use contraception, but after a few months they became increasingly irritated with each other and their sex life became so unsatisfying that they had stopped having sex altogether. The husband consulted MHE and MHE found out that he somehow felt as if something was lacking since he did not have sperm. MHE saw the wife and she related much the same attitude. Next MHE saw them together and told them that the lack of sperm was probably the result of their own bodies' altering their gonadal functioning to provide a psychosomatic protection against possible pregnancy; therefore they should resume their original use of contraception and thereby restore their happy sex life. They listened raptly to his explanation and it made sense to them, even though it was really a bit specious. MHE gave them another appointment for the next month and they reported that they had done as he had suggested and that their sex life was back to normal.

Presenting Problem: Sexual dissatisfaction

Age Group: Adult

Modality: Individual/marital; outpatient

Problem Duration: Six months

Treatment Length: Four sessions

Result: Success. The couple's satisfactory sex life was restored.

Follow-up: Several years

Technique: Reframing

Source: *Collected Papers IV*, pp. 366–369

Case #142

Case Summary: A couple had been married for one year. The wife was furious with the husband because every time they entered the bedroom he immediately got an erection. She felt deprived of the right to exercise her "female power," that is, the ability to produce or reduce an erection. MHE told the man to masturbate three times before going to bed one night, without the wife's knowledge. The woman wriggled and squirmed against him for quite some time before he got an erection. The two of them were happy since then.

Presenting Problem: Marital problems (sexual dissatisfaction)

Age Group: Adult

Modality: Marital; outpatient

Problem Duration: One year

Treatment Length: (One session)

Result: Success. The couple's sexual relations improved.

Follow-up: The couple reportedly remained happy.

Technique: Task assignment (behavioral)

Sources: *Conversations II*, pp. 119–120; *Uncommon Therapy*, p. 159

Case #143

Case Summary: A college professor came to see MHE because he believed that he could not ejaculate. The man had two children and his wife viewed their sex life as satisfying. MHE asked him how long he had wet the bed. He said that he was 11 or 12 years old when he stopped wetting the bed. MHE told the man that he peed semen into his wife's vagina. The man replied, "Doesn't every male?" MHE instructed the man to go home and masturbate every day, trying not to pee semen for as long as possible. While masturbating he was to notice all the different parts of his penis and all the different sensations he could have. After about a month the man called MHE at 11 o'clock one night and excitedly told him that he'd ejaculated. He called MHE back at 1 a.m. and told him he'd done it again. The wife later told MHE that their sex life had gotten even better since then, but she didn't understand why.

Presenting Problem: Inability to ejaculate

Age Group: Adult

Modality: Individual/marital; outpatient

Problem Duration: Since puberty

Treatment Length: NA

Result: Success. The man learned to ejaculate and began to enjoy sex.

Follow-up: NA

Technique: Task assignment (behavioral and cognitive)

Sources: *Conversations II*, pp. 132–134; *Uncommon Therapy*, p. 161

Case #144

Case Summary: A doctor had been married for 13 years. He and his wife had a very unsatisfying sex life. Sex was an "unpleasant labor." MHE asked him how much he had masturbated as a child. He replied, "I masturbated twice and both times, thank goodness, my father caught me. I didn't complete it." MHE told the man to take a condom specimen to be analyzed. In all the man took 11 condom specimens. In some there were prostatic and urethral secretions, in some prostatic and seminiferous, but the seminiferous secretions were generally not present in normal amounts. MHE told the man that he should have masturbated to learn how to make the secretions in the proper order. MHE told him to masturbate every day. On the 23rd day he met his wife in the hall as he was heading to the bathroom to masturbate. He picked her up, took her to the bedroom and made love to her. They both enjoyed sex for the first time.

Presenting Problem: Lack of sexual enjoyment

Age Group: Adult

Modality: Individual; outpatient

Problem Duration: NA

Treatment Length: NA

Result: Success. The man practiced ejaculating and learned to enjoy sex.

Follow-up: NA

Techniques: Direct suggestion; task assignment (behavioral); reframing

Source: *Teaching Seminar*, p. 243

Case #145

4

Sleeping Problems

INSOMNIA

Case Summary: A 65-year-old man came to MHE for insomnia. Fifteen years prior to seeing MHE, his physician had prescribed sodium amytal for the mild insomnia the man was having. The barbiturates eliminated his insomnia so he continued to take them for the next 15 years. Having habituated to the drug, the man found that his insomnia returned with a vengeance when his wife died. Each night he would toss and turn for hours, getting only one and a half to two hours of sleep for all the time he spent in bed. MHE learned from the man that his house had hardwood floors which he hated to wax because he couldn't stand the smell of the floor wax. MHE told the man that he could cure his insomnia if he was willing to give up eight hours of sleep. Each night the man was to polish the floors from 8 p.m. to 7 a.m. MHE believed he would be cured in four nights. For the first two or three nights the man followed MHE's instructions. On the next night he told himself he would just lie down and rest for 30 minutes before he waxed the floors. He awoke at seven o'clock the next morning. On the succeeding night he told himself that he would lie down at 8 p.m. If he could read the clock at 8:15 he would get up and wax the floors. [In another version, MHE suggests the fifteen-minute contingency.] A year later he reported that he'd been sleeping every night. MHE mentioned that the man

151

knew he still owed him two nights' sleep and he would do anything to get out of waxing floors, even going to sleep.

Presenting Problem: Insomnia

Age Group: Adult

Modality: Individual; outpatient

Problem Duration: 15 years, severe for three months

Treatment Length: NA

Result: Success. The man stopped having insomnia and stopped using drugs to go to sleep.

Follow-up: The man was still sleeping regularly one year later.

Techniques: Task assignment (behavioral); ordeal

Sources: *Conversations I*, pp. 54–55; *Ordeal Therapy*, pp. 3–5; *Phoenix*, pp. 149–150; *Teaching Seminar*, p. 193

Case #146

Case Summary: A man came to MHE for insomnia. For 12 years he had never fallen to sleep before 2 a.m. and had always awakened at 4 a.m. The man was a busy doctor who worked erratic hours. MHE learned that since college the man had been promising himself that he would read certain books but his busy lifestyle had prevented him from attaining this goal. MHE tried to make the man feel guilty about his broken promises and then he offered the man a cure for his insomnia. MHE told the man to read from 10:30 p.m. to 5 a.m. each night. (In another version he told him to go to bed at 11 o'clock each night. If he was still awake at 11:30, he was to get out of bed and read [Dickens in one version] standing by the mantel for the rest of the night.) If he awakened during the night he would have to do the same thing. Later the man asked if he could read sitting down. Then he told MHE that he found himself reading one page and then falling asleep sitting up. MHE told him that he could go to bed and if he found himself awake 15 minutes later, then he should get up and read. One year later he reported that he was sleeping nights, that he was more successful in his practice, and that he was happier and healthier.

Presenting Problem: Insomnia

Age Group: Adult

Modality: Individual; outpatient

Problem Duration: 12 years

Treatment Length: NA

Result: Success. The man stopped having insomnia.

Follow-up: One year later the man was still sleeping nights and had an improved quality of life.

Techniques: Task assignment (behavioral); ordeal; utilization (of guilt)

Sources: *Conversations I*, p. 59; *Teaching Seminar*, p. 194; *Phoenix*, pp. 148–149

Case #147

5

*Phobias and
Emotional Problems*

ANXIETY/PANIC

Case Summary: A man who appeared regularly in a TV broadcast came to MHE because he had a panic reaction before each show. For 15 minutes he would pant and gasp and then when it was time for the broadcast, he would perform with ease. The length of the reaction had been increasing and he feared that they would eventually last an hour. MHE pointed out that panicking before each broadcast required quite a bit of energy. MHE suggested that each morning the man should do 25 deep squats, although he said he thought it might take 100 to use up the excess panting energy. The man's panic was eliminated. The man so enjoyed the deep squats that he began working out to eliminate his obesity.

Soon, however, as he got more fit, the panic reaction returned. MHE told the man that he needed his psychological energy used up as well. He assigned the man to get up each night after he'd been asleep four hours and do deep squats. He would use up physical energy on the squats and psychological energy on hating to wake up. This eliminated the panic reactions for a while.

The man once again had an excess of energy. MHE asked him what his lifelong ambition was. The man said it was to own a home. MHE told him to buy a home and mow the lawn to use up the excess energy he had. The man followed MHE's instructions and had no recurrence.

Presenting Problem: Panic (before television broadcast)

Age Group: Adult

Modality: Individual; outpatient

Problem Duration: A few months

Treatment Length: NA

Result: Success. The man stopped having his panic attacks.

Follow-up: No recurrence

Techniques: Reframing; task assignment (behavioral); symptom transformation (energy for panic attacks—energy for doing exercises and mowing the lawn)

Source: *Conversations I*, pp. 258–261

Case #148

&

Case Summary: A 40-year-old man came to see MHE because he had become fearful of going insane. He had had a slight physical problem that had been made to seem more serious because each time he went to see a doctor, the doctor had left on vacation or an emergency before giving the man a diagnosis. The man had always feared turning 40 and, when he had so much time to worry about what was wrong with him, he developed intense fears. MHE had to hypnotize him by having him pay vigilant attention to the clock and to the man's wife sitting next to him, because he was so anxious and vigilant about going into trance. After three sessions, the man was able to return to work free of his fears.

Presenting Problem: Fears and anxiety about health and sanity

Age Group: Adult

Modality: Individual (conjoint with wife); outpatient

Problem Duration: Two weeks

Treatment Length: Three sessions, six hours

Result: Success. The man lost his fears and was able to return to work.

Follow-up: NA

Techniques: Hypnosis; utilization (of vigilance)

Source: *Healing in Hypnosis*, pp. 68–72

Case #149

Case Summary: A woman continuously flunked her Ph.D. exam. She knew the material but she always panicked and blanked out when confronted with an exam. MHE put her into trance and told her the story of a lawyer he had helped with his bar exam. The woman returned home and passed her exam.

Presenting Problem: Panic (during Ph.D. exam)

Age Group: Adult

Modality: Individual; outpatient

Problem Duration: NA

Treatment Length: One session

Result: Success. The woman passed her exam.

Follow-up: NA

Techniques: Hypnosis; metaphor

Source: *Teaching Seminar*, pp. 63–64

Case #150

DEPRESSION

Case Summary: A 25-year-old student sought therapy from MHE when he became depressed, discouraged, and anxious upon learning that he would be fired from a weekend job he had playing music. Because he attended college and worked a regular job on the late shift, it was clear that he had no time to practice. Since the nightclub had hired him with the idea that he was promising as a singer and guitar player, but that he would improve, the boss there was disappointed when no improvement was heard. MHE trained the man in time distortion in hypnosis and suggested to him that during lulls at his evening job, he could hallucinate practicing music in a very brief span of time on the clock. He was given amnesia for the suggestion. He used the hallucinated practice times so well that his co-workers didn't notice and he improved so much on guitar and in his singing that he was able to keep his music job as well as get a raise. The student was mystified about how the change occurred.

Presenting Problem: Depression; anxiety

Age Group: Adult

Modality: Individual; outpatient

Problem Duration: NA

Treatment Length: NA (two sessions?)

Result: Success. The student improved in his musical abilities and was able to keep his job.

Follow-up: "Many months later."

Techniques: Hypnosis; time distortion; amnesia

Source: *Collected Papers II*, pp. 278–279

Case #151

Case Summary: A 24-year-old college student attended one of MHE's lectures on hypnosis in which MHE discussed automatic handwriting and the possibility of the completely separate functioning of the conscious and unconscious. She sought his assistance for a recent depression and the development of an uncomfortable habit of doodling nervously. He had her prepare for doing automatic drawing by having her unconscious work on the problem before the next session. She came in and proceeded to relate the story of a recent novel she had read while at the same time drawing two pictures, one that reproduced much of the recent type of doodling she had been doing and a second that combined elements of those pictures into a more coherent drawing.

It gradually unfolded that she had become more and more annoyed and distant from her close girlfriend and that she had some matches from a local hotel that somehow reminded her of the picture she had drawn and of her annoyance with her friend. Through MHE's questioning of her unconscious through automatic handwriting and through suggestions that her unconscious would give her the information she needed, she realized that her friend had been having an affair with the patient's father. She was angry and brought the friend in to see MHE and to confront her with the realization. Her friend admitted it and the patient forbad her to visit the house. She severed their friendship. She also realized that her father had been having affairs through the years, which was subsequently confirmed to MHE by the friend. The patient stopped her nervous doodling. The friend continued the affair with the father. The patient adjusted and was happily married at last contact with MHE.

Presenting Problem: Depression

Age Group: Adult

Modality: Individual; outpatient

Problem Duration: Several weeks

Treatment Length: (Six weeks; five sessions)

Result: Success. The depression and nervous doodling disappeared.

Follow-up: Several years.

Techniques: Hypnosis; automatic writing and drawing; splitting (unconscious/conscious)

Source: *Collected Papers III*, pp. 158–176

Case #152

Case Summary: Dottie, a 31-year-old Ph.D. student in psychology, had been paralyzed from the waist down for 10 years. She had no sense of feeling below the waist, was confined to a wheelchair, and was incontinent for both feces and urine. She had been engaged at the time of her accident, but her fiancé had asked to be released from the engagement. She sought therapy for one of two possible goals. She either wanted a philosophy of life that would make her want to live or an adequate justification for committing suicide. All she had ever wanted was to be a wife and mother. She believed that her condition made her dreams impossible. She was intelligent and asked MHE to speak about her problems in a frank manner so that she might feel he understood her situation and had genuine hope for her.

In the first session he put her in trance and had her hallucinate one orchestra playing the song about the toe bone being connected to the foot bone while another orchestra played "Doing What Comes Naturally." At the next session, which lasted four hours, MHE put her in trance and evoked images of all the different types of couples there are and all the types of women men find attractive: he mentioned the giraffe women of Siam (Burma in another version) and how their heads collapse when the rings are taken off because they've lost their neck muscles, and he mentioned the Ubanga duck-billed and steatopygous women of Africa, who are found attractive by the males in their cultures. He challenged her belief that just because she was incontinent no man would find her attractive.

Next he reminded her that as a psychology student she knew about displacement of symptoms. Someone could worry about money, a pocket-book ache, and end up with an ulcer, a bellyache. If people could spontaneously, unwittingly, displace one thing, they could displace other things. She had the idea that since she had lost the feeling below her waist she was useless. The genitals, however, were like the rest of her body. The toe bone is connected to the foot bone, the foot bone is connected to the ankle bone and so on until finally the neck bone is connected to the head bone. Likewise, MHE told her, her external genitalia were connected to her vagina, which is connected to her uterus, which is connected to the ovaries, which are connected to the adrenal, which is connected to the hormone system, which is connected to the breast, etc. Her kidneys weren't paralyzed (as indicated by her urinary incontinence) and they were connected to the adrenal. So the external genitalia might be lost, but she still had her internal genitalia. (In another version he emphasized the idea that women can have orgasms in places other than their genitals.) He also spoke to her about children and the look of expectancy they get on their faces when they anticipate a gift or an affectionate embrace.

Dottie married a doctor who specialized in research involving feces and urine. [In another version he was an expert in the biology and chemistry of the colon.] Follow-up of 10 years indicated a happy marriage, a satisfactory sexual life with orgasms, and four children. When Dottie met MHE again after so many years, she invited him out to lunch. She thought she only remembered him from a lecture he had given. She had developed an amnesia for the treatment. He found out about her orgasms by asking her to answer a series of questions on a piece of paper. She was somewhat taken aback but agreed. Her answers indicated that her orgasms were not genital. In a sealed envelope MHE had written the answers he expected her to give. After she answered the questions, he showed them to her. They correlated extremely well with her own answers. She still had amnesia for the treatment but became convinced it must have happened since MHE knew so much about her intimate life.

Presenting Problem: Depression; suicidal impulses

Age Group: Adult

Modality: Individual; outpatient

Problem Duration: (10 years)

Treatment Length: NA. "I did a lot of therapy on Dottie."

Result: Success. Her depression lifted. She got married and had a satisfying sex life.

Follow-up: 10 years

Techniques: Splitting (of sexual responsiveness from external genitalia); linking (connections that could lead to orgasm); reframing (what is attractive); analogy; parallel communication

Sources: *Conversations I*, pp. 24–27; *Hypnotherapy*, pp. 428–442

Case #153

Case Summary: In September 1956, MHE was to do a hypnosis demonstration as part of a large workshop at a Boston State Hospital. MHE told Dr. Leo Alexander, who was organizing the presentation, that he would need to find a demonstration subject. The doctor suggested that MHE select someone at the hospital. The woman MHE selected was a nurse named Janice Pond. The assistant superintendent of the hospital was upset at MHE's choice of Janice because she was known to be extremely depressed and possibly suicidal. Dr. Alexander warned MHE of the danger but MHE reassured him.

Janice was helping with the workshop and MHE asked if he could borrow her for a few minutes. He took her into another room and talked to her about going into trance. She was apprehensive about being a demonstration subject because she was afraid she might burst into tears in front of the audience or reveal her plans to commit suicide. MHE had her relax and suggested that she use her right hand to write her name as she had the first time she had been able to do that as a child and that she would feel the same gratification she had then. She explained that she could not do that, because she was naturally left-handed and though several of her teachers and her mother had tried and tried, she had never been able to use her right hand to do anything. MHE then asked her how she tied her shoes with only one hand. She got confused, but admitted that she must use her right hand and had not realized it. He then told her that if she wanted to volunteer for the demonstration, he had only two conditions. She must hear everything he said and she must sit where she could see him.

Later that day, she told Dr. Alexander that her right hand was aching and she could not use it. After giving a lecture and another demonstration, MHE asked the other person in the audience who was in trance to come to the front of the room. Janice got up and walked to the front of the room. MHE asked her to write her name. She wrote it with her right hand. MHE then asked her which hand she would like to use. She hesitated and put her hands to her forehead. MHE leaned forward and told her, "I'm your friend, not your teacher." At that, she rewrote her name with her left hand and seemed extremely pleased. After the session was over, she told MHE that she had been about to cry when she put her hands to her forehead. He told her he knew that and the fact that she had lived through that showed that she could live through her current problems.

Dr. Alexander remembered that MHE had told her that after the rain comes the sunshine and that no pain lasts forever. Janice had whispered in his ear that night at the banquet for the conference that she had planned to commit suicide that night, but that MHE's work with her had saved her. The depression lifted and she did well until she left the hospital to take another job.

[In MHE's version, which seems to be somewhat fictionalized and embellished, he worked with her for some time in the demonstration. He had her hallucinate going with him to various places in the city of Boston. At each place he talked about life cycles. For instance, when they went to the zoo, MHE talked about the baby kangaroos in the mother's pouch and when they went to the arboretum he talked about the turning of the trees. After the demonstration, according to MHE, Janice disappeared. In actuality, she stayed around for about a year and a half. MHE, however, said he was blamed for her suicide. Sixteen years later Janice called MHE and reported that she had served two enlistments as a nurse in the Navy, moved to Florida, married, and had four children.]

Presenting Problem: Depression; suicidal plans

Age Group: Adult

Modality: Individual; outpatient (demonstration)

Problem Duration: NA

Treatment Length: One session

Result: Success. Janice's depression lifted and she changed her life.

Follow-up: Twenty-four years. Jan (as she preferred to be called) spoke at the First International Erickson Congress about her recollections of MHE's work with her. Dr. Leo Alexander also recalled the demonstration. Their versions were each different from MHE's. They all agreed that Jan had been suicidal and depressed and that MHE's intervention had made a profound difference for her. She was married and had five children.

Techniques: Hypnosis; task assignment (behavioral); reframing

Sources: "Clinical Experiences"; *Ericksonian Approaches*, pp. 219–227; *Phoenix*, pp. 102–104; *Teaching Seminar*, pp. 148–152

Case #154

Case Summary: A woman who had been very depressed sought therapy from MHE. She had been raised by adoptive parents. Her adoptive father had been rather cold and distant. Her adoptive mother had gotten the idea that the girl had been bad and was constantly quizzing and accusing her on this point. Older siblings had moved away and visited infrequently, for which the patient was usually blamed, although she had done nothing to antagonize her brothers and sisters. The patient had escaped into her studies, doing brilliantly through high school, college and graduate school. Her parents insisted that she go to college in her hometown as she was too immature to leave home. When she finally rebelled and declared her intentions to move away, her parents severed their relationship with her. Her siblings refused to have anything to do with her for fear of angering the parents.

She eventually severed her ties to her family and moved to another city, where she obtained a job as a secretary. She failed to develop a social life, however, and became depressed. She sought psychiatric help, but the treatment always seemed to revolve around the subject of sex, which she found unacceptable. She had tried to flee from her problems by joining the army and learning three new languages. After several different transfers, however, she found herself still depressed. She had learned of hypnosis and wanted MHE to use it to blot out all thought of sex. She wanted nothing else, no questions, no psychiatry, just for MHE to get on with the hypnosis and fulfilling her request.

Given her tearful appearance, MHE objected to working without some information on her history and background. At this, she burst into tears and he used this as evidence that he needed to know a little about her to be able to work so as not to upset her. She gave the history recounted above. He agreed to do hypnosis and told her that it would require effort on her part and some time would be needed for her to learn hypnosis, as she well knew that it took effort to learn things. First he would have her learn hypnosis, which was rather like learning the feel of a new language. She liked that analogy and agreed.

MHE had her fix her gaze on a rock in his office and began an indirect induction involving her in her earliest memories. He took her through the years one by one, discussing how many good things a baby learns automatically and unconsciously through the years. He re-evoked various memories of learnings from her first six years of life in this manner.

At the next session, she came in and told MHE that she was so mad at him she could slap his face and she did not know a bad enough name to call him. He suggested that she start with calling him a stinking bastard of an S.O.B., since that was about the best she could probably do. She then called him that and burst out into an embarrassed laugh, saying that she did not know why, but saying that made her feel better. MHE asked her if she would like to repeat it since it made her feel better, but she replied that she only wanted to tell him that she had had normal bowel movements and her stomach did not ache when she ate since their last session. She told him she would have been too embarrassed to tell him that before. She now wanted more hypnosis.

He put her in trance and had her review her life learnings from ages six through 10. He called these the little learnings that grow into the language of life. He made certain that she would review only memories involving herself and would exclude others, so she wouldn't remember the traumatic memories of her family life. After she finished the review up to the age of 14, she told MHE that she had moved to a new apartment and was starting to like herself. She was no longer depressed. She had started to see her parents as sick. She talked freely to MHE during that session.

When she returned for the next session, they reviewed her high school and college years. At the next session, she asked whether MHE had anything to say about the day they just talked. He told her he had a great deal more to say than she wanted to hear about that. At that she became extremely enraged and started berating him again. He then induced another trance and had her bitterly criticize the "good girl" that she tried to be. She did so and MHE told her to go home and sleep and finish the job. She returned the next time and told MHE that she woke up still in her dress, soaked with perspiration and found she had torn her pillowcases. She got up, undressed, showered and lay back down on the bed and did a thorough life review. She told MHE that her life had been much more horrible than she had related to him. Following this life review, she was finally well-adjusted and over her depression and social withdrawal.

Presenting Problem: Depression; inhibition

Age Group: Adult

Modality: Individual; outpatient

Problem Duration: At least 15 years

Treatment Length: NA

Result: Success. The woman got over her depression and became less inhibited.

Follow-up: NA

Techniques: Hypnosis; task assignment (cognitive); utilization (of anger)

Source: *Hypnotherapy*, pp. 450–459

Case #155

Case Summary: The aunt of one of MHE's clients (Case #229) who lived in Milwaukee had been very depressed for nine months. All she ever did was go to church. When she was there she spoke to no one. At the request of her nephew MHE dropped by to see her one day when he was visiting the area. He demanded a tour of her house and saw a depressingly dingy, lonely house. In one room he saw three different colored African violets. MHE knew that African violets require an extraordinary amount of care. MHE told the woman that he was going to give her some medical orders. She was to go out and buy every type of African violet available. She was to take cuttings from some of those plants and nurture them into adult plants. For every engagement, christening, illness or death that occurred within her congregation she was to send an African violet. The woman followed his instructions and soon had as many as 200 African violets in her home at once. The woman made a lot of friends with her violets. When she died, she was mourned as "The African Violet Queen of Milwaukee," whose kindness and friendship would be missed by many.

Presenting Problem: Depression

Age Group: Adult

Modality: Individual; outpatient

Problem Duration: Nine months

Treatment Length: One visit

Result: (Success. Her depression lifted.)

Follow-up: 20 years, until her death

Techniques: Task assignment (behavioral)

Sources: *Phoenix*, pp. 18–19 and pp. 124–125; *Teaching Seminar*, pp. 285–286

Case #156

Case Summary: A retired man was depressed after building a house when he found out how much it had cost him to build it. He stopped working on it and spent his time moaning about his aches and pains and sitting in a rocking chair all day. He didn't have the energy to finish building a bookcase he had started and did not want to spend the money for lumber for it. So he started collecting used lumber and filled his backyard with the unsightly mess. Dr. Rogers sent him from Yuma, Arizona to Phoenix to MHE for treatment. MHE told the man he ought to convert the energy from the aches and pains into positive action. MHE had the man plant flower gardens for a few people. The man soon recovered from his depression. He went back home and sorted out the lumber in his back yard and made shelves for his house. He also returned to work and gave the rocking chair to a charity.

Presenting Problem: Depression

Age Group: Adult

Modality: Individual; outpatient

Problem Duration: NA

Treatment Length: NA

Result: Success. The man's depression lifted.

Follow-up: NA

Techniques: Reframing; symptom transformation (energy for aches and pains → energy to plant gardens); task assignment (behavioral)

Sources: *Phoenix*, pp. 128–129; *Teaching Seminar*, p. 251

Case #157

꘎

Case Summary: A woman with severe arthritis had been depressed and suicidal for nine months. She wanted to have a baby but all of her doctors advised against it because of her severe arthritis. MHE told her to get pregnant as soon as she could. When she did her arthritis improved and her depression lifted. She named the baby Cynthia and was very happy. Unfortunately the child died of crib death at six months. The woman's depression was worse than ever and she wanted to commit suicide. MHE told her that it was criminal of her to destroy the memories of her pregnancy and her child by killing herself. He told her to plant a eucalyptus tree in her backyard and to name it Cynthia. She was to watch Cynthia grow and to look forward to sitting in Cynthia's shade. A year later MHE visited her and found a tall sapling and a considerable flower garden growing in her backyard.

Presenting Problem: Depression

Age Group: Adult

Modality: Individual; outpatient

Problem Duration: Nine months

Treatment Length: NA

Result: Success. The woman's depression lifted.

Follow-up: NA

Techniques: Task assignment (behavioral and symbolic); direct suggestion

Source: *Teaching Seminar*, pp. 287–288

Case #158

Case Summary: A competent industrialist became depressed after the sudden loss of his fortune. He was admitted to Worcester State Hospital. He spent his time crying and moving his hands back and forth in a repetitive motion. MHE said to him, "You're a man who has had his ups and downs." Then he encouraged the man to move his hands up and down instead of side to side. The man complied with MHE's wishes. Then MHE took the man to the occupational therapist and had sandpaper attached to his hands and an upright piece of would placed between them. At first the man just listlessly moved his hands up and down next to the wood, but soon he got interested in sanding it. In time he made carved chess sets and other wooden crafts which he was able to sell. The first year after he was discharged he made $10,000 (a great deal of money for the time) in real estate.

Presenting Problem: Depression; compulsive arm movements

Age Group: Adult

Modality: Individual; inpatient

Problem Duration: NA

Treatment Length: NA

Result: Success. The man's depression lifted and he was able to begin working again after his discharge.

Follow-up: NA

Techniques: Utilization (of the hand movements); metaphor; pattern intervention; redirecting attention

Source: *Uncommon Therapy*, p. 28

Case #159

ANXIETY/PANIC

Case Summary: A 30-year-old man sought MHE's help for an elevator phobia. He had to ride to the seventh floor on one as part of his job. He typically fainted as he approached or rode on the elevator. He insisted he wanted no psychiatric treatment, so MHE agreed to treat him purely as a hypnotist. MHE put him in trance and had him describe the feelings he had when he was riding down on the elevator. He had never fainted on the way down and reported feeling relief and good feelings in the knowledge that he was leaving the situation. MHE told him that he would be unable to think of anything except those pleasant feelings of going down in the elevator the next time he approached it. He never fainted again and got over his elevator phobia.

Presenting Problem: Elevator phobia; fainting

Age Group: Adult

Modality: Individual; outpatient

Problem Duration: NA

Treatment Length: NA

Result: Success. The man was able to ride elevators without fainting and overcame his phobia.

Follow-up: NA

Techniques: Hypnosis; redirection of attention; posthypnotic suggestion; evocation of feelings

Sources: *Collected Papers II*, pp. 188–189; *Mind-Body Communication*, pp. 18–19

Case #160

Case Summary: Bob came from a disturbed family. Two of his siblings had committed suicide while in the state mental hospital. Bob could only drive on certain streets. If he tried to drive on others past the city limits of Phoenix, he would vomit and faint. Even if he tried to walk or had others drive him, he would still vomit and faint. Although he had many other personal problems, he shopped around for a therapist who would agree to treat only the driving/fainting problem. MHE was the only psychiatrist to agree to work on only the driving phobia.

MHE got Bob to agree unconditionally to follow the prescription he would be given to cure his phobia. MHE then told Bob to dress up in his best suit and drive to the city limits on a certain deserted highway at 3 a.m. Once he had arrived, he was to stop his car at the farthest telephone pole he felt he could make it to. Then he was to begin to drive to the next telephone pole, switching off the ignition so that when he fainted the car would stop on the shoulder. He was then to get out of his car and lie in the ditch by the side of the road until the fainting spell passed. He was to have pinned on his clothes an envelope explaining to any interested person who found him that he was MHE's patient and following medical orders and that he would probably awaken in the next few minutes.

Bob thought that this was ridiculous, but MHE reminded him that, since he had made a promise, he must carry it out. The man used this technique to drive 20 miles. He only fainted a few dozen times because he was able to go longer and longer distances. He got so mad at MHE that he drove all the way to Flagstaff (quite a distance) through mountain roads. He returned to Phoenix and drove all around on roads he had previously been unable to take. MHE mentions that Bob still had self-defeating patterns.

Presenting Problem: Agoraphobia (fear of driving on certain streets); fainting

Age Group: Adult

Modality: Individual; outpatient

Problem Duration: NA

Treatment Length: (Two sessions)

Result: Success. The man was able to drive on previously difficult roads and eventually took a trip throughout the South.

Follow-up: 13 years.

Techniques: Utilization (of fainting); task assignment (behavioral)

Sources: *Collected Papers IV*, pp. 134–138; *Conversations I*, pp. 118–120; *Uncommon Therapy*, pp. 69–70

Case #161

Case Summary: A 19-year-old student nurse was used as a demonstration subject for MHE because she was intrigued by hypnosis. After MHE hypnotized her he realized that she really needed therapy. He had learned from one of his students who had hypnotized her that she had indicated that she had a fear of water that she really wasn't very consciously aware of. In trance she remembered long forgotten traumas. She had been punished for letting her infant sister fall into a bucket of water until she had almost drowned and was falsely accused of having deliberately pushed her sister into the bucket. Another time she accidentally tipped over her sister's highchair and, though her arm had been hurt by the chair, her father had punished her for moving the chair when she had been told not to. It was the first time her father had ever punished her.

She had then developed a fear of swimming and had another trauma when a neighbor had tried to force her into the water and she had bitten him, kicked and screamed. Her mother had punished her for this behavior. She had later gone swimming with her sister in very cold water, and her sister had refused to leave the water even though she was blue from the cold. The sister's blue skin had subconsciously reminded the patient of the time her sister had fallen into the bucket and turned blue.

These experiences had become woven into a pattern that resulted in a fear of water and a negative attitude toward marriage. She would go out to a movie or date and sneak out without her date before the evening was over. In hypnosis, MHE became "The February Man," a friendly adult figure who visited her throughout her childhood right after her birthday. He helped her remember the traumas and develop more adult understandings of the traumatic scenes. She developed amnesia for each session, but as the sessions went on she developed more and more conscious awareness of the problems of the past.

Between the second and third sessions, MHE told her not to go swimming. In the third session, he had her future project and tell him about some swimming that she had done during the summer. She described several comfortable swimming experiences and having bought a new swimming suit. He then gave her a pack of cigarettes with a note he had written inside that said, "Just afterwards," and asked her to keep it until just after she went swimming.

At the last session, she remembered that MHE had her age project in the last trance. She reported on her vacation during which she enjoyed swimming and had suddenly remembered the cigarettes MHE had given her. She smoked them and saw MHE's note. She had also lost her fear of driving across bridges, which she had never mentioned to MHE, when she had lost her fear of swimming.

[In the condensed version of this case, MHE seems to have fabricated or changed many of the details, as evidenced by the complete transcript. For example, he details how the woman got over her fear of taking baths and the transcript indicates that he tried to attribute that problem to her but she denied she had such a problem.]

Later the woman's mother was seen and, while hypnotized, verified some of the patient's recollections.

Presenting Problem: Fear of swimming and water

Age Group: Adult

Modality: Individual; outpatient

Problem Duration: NA

Treatment Length: Four sessions

Result: Success. The woman was able to go swimming and enjoy it.

Follow-up: At least several years. MHE mentions that she had two children.

Techniques: Hypnosis; age regression; age projection; amnesia

Sources: *Collected Papers IV*, pp. 413–420; This case is transcribed in *The February Man*.

Case #162

Case Summary: A man named Bill, age 30, had served in the Marine Corps in World War II. When he returned home he moved in with his parents and worked as a secondhand car salesman. His parents told him what to eat, what to wear, and what to read. He followed their suggestions because he was trying to be a good son. Bill was fearful about entering many places, particularly a restaurant called the Golden Drumstick. The man fainted when he tried to go in. He was also afraid of crossing Van Buren Street on foot and of socializing with women.

MHE gave him a choice of several types of women and asked him to select most frightening one. He chose an attractive divorcée. He then told the man that he would have to take MHE, Mrs. Erickson, and a friend of MHE's out to the Golden Drumstick. Of course, the friend was an attractive divorcée. When they arrived at the Golden Drumstick. MHE pointed out places where the man might faint, but the man made it inside. The four of them sat at a table very far from the door; MHE and the two women made jokes that were over the man's head. Then MHE started a fight with the waitress and the manager of the restaurant. When it was time to order, the divorcée, named Keech, ordered all of Bill's food for him; then she supervised him as he ate, telling him when to take a bite of this or that. Keech also told Bill that he ought to pay for the dinner and she told him the amount for the tip. After dinner the four of them went back to the Erickson's house. Keech said she would like to dance. Bill said that he didn't know how so Keech insisted on teaching him. Then she insisted that Bill take her dancing. They stayed out till 3 a.m.

The next morning Bill told his mother exactly what he wanted for breakfast and told his father that he didn't agree with his reading tastes. He also told his parents that he was moving out. The next night he was able to take a friend out to dinner. But still the man could not cross Van Buren. MHE put him in a trance and reminded him that his unconscious knew that he could cross Van Buren without his conscious mind knowing it. Soon he was able to cross Van Buren, finding that afterwards he had no recollection of it.

Bill dated Keech for about three months and then broke up with her. Finally he began dating a young woman. She was very much like him: she lived with her parents, was afraid to go out, and was afraid of men. Bill asked MHE to see to it that the woman went with him to a party he wanted to go to. MHE told the woman that she would do well at the party because she would be the only good listener in a room full of talkers. She went to the party. Eventually she and Bill married.

Presenting Problem: Phobia (fear of certain restaurants, streets and women); avoidance of certain situations and people

Age Group: Adult

Modality: Individual; outpatient

Problem Duration: NA

Treatment Length: NA

Result: Success. The man's phobias diminished and ceased to control his behavior.

Follow-up: NA

Techniques: Task assignment (behavioral); ordeal; direct suggestion

Sources: *Conversations I*, pp. 154–158; *Uncommon Therapy*, pp. 67–69; *Teaching Seminar*, pp. 97–102

Case #163

Case Summary: A man came to live in Phoenix to get therapy from MHE for his fear of tall buildings. He was particularly troubled by three-story houses. MHE assigned him the task of going out with a pencil and notebook to record the addresses of every three-story house he found in order to be certain he could avoid them. Of course, in the Phoenix area, houses over one story are rare. So MHE told him he'd help him out by giving him the location of the nearest one he knew about. It was in a suburb about 20 miles away.

Presenting Problem: Phobia (fear of tall buildings)

Age Group: Adult

Modality: Individual; outpatient

Problem Duration: NA

Treatment Length: NA

Result: (Partial success. The man realized that there were very few tall buildings in Phoenix to fear, although his fear was not eliminated.)

Follow-up: NA

Techniques: Task assignment (behavioral and perceptual); utilization (of fear)

Source: *Conversations II*, p. 12

Case #164

Case Summary: A man with a fear of flying came to see MHE and asked to be hypnotized to get over his problem. He had to fly to Boston for his job in two weeks and he had been so fearful that he hadn't flown in five years. MHE put him in trance and did some work with him. After the trance, the man complained and claimed he hadn't really been in a trance since he could hear traffic noises the whole time MHE was talking to him. MHE, however, thought the man had been in a sufficient trance and told him that he did not need to come back. The man persisted and asked MHE to see him for another session of hypnotherapy. MHE finally agreed, but extracted a promise from the man that he would do nothing to correct his problem as he saw it. The man returned for the second session and considered it a failure like the first one. He went to Boston, however. MHE had decided that the man did not really have a fear of flying, but had a fear of boarding planes and getting on elevators. The man later reported that he had inexplicably ridden an elevator, something he had previously avoided, before taking the plane ride.

Presenting Problem: Fear of flying

Age Group: Adult

Modality: Individual; outpatient

Problem Duration: Five years

Treatment Length: Two sessions

Result: Success. The man was able to fly in a plane to Boston and back.

Follow-up: MHE had the man return for a visit with some students and a woman who had also overcome a fear of flying. During that visit, the man realized that MHE had gotten him over his fear of elevators as well as his fear of flying.

Techniques: Hypnosis; indirect suggestion

Source: *Experiencing Erickson*, pp. 122–126

Case #165

Case Summary: A woman came to MHE because she had an airplane phobia. Her boss had told her that she had to fly to Dallas for a business trip or else she would lose her job. Ten years previously she had been on an airplane that crashed. Nobody on the plane was hurt. Over the next five years she began to feel more and more fearful whenever she flew. She was fine when she entered the plane and when the plane was taxiing, but the moment the plane took off she was gripped with fear. She would shudder, be unable to hear and would perspire profusely. Once the plane touched down she was able to relax.

The woman wanted MHE to use hypnosis with her. MHE reminded her that she was a "rather beautiful woman" and he was a man, the degree of whose handicap she did not know. Bearing that in mind, MHE wanted her to promise to do everything, good or bad, that he suggested. She promised that she would. He had her make the same promise in a trance. "Now I can treat you for your airplane phobia," MHE said. He put her into a second trance and had her hallucinate being 35,000 feet up in an airplane. She was shuddering violently. "And now", MHE said, "I want you to have the plane descend and by the time it reaches the ground, all your fears and phobias, anxiety and devils of torture will slide off your body and into the seat beside you." When she awakened she leapt out of the chair and ran to the other side of the room. "They are there! They are there!" she said pointing to the chair. MHE called his wife in and asked her to sit in the chair. The woman physically restrained Mrs. Erickson from doing so.

MHE told her that her therapy was complete. She was to call him from the airport to tell him how much she enjoyed her flights. MHE had his daughter take three photos of the chair: one underexposed, one properly exposed and one overexposed. The first he labeled, "The eternal resting place of your fears, wholly dissipating into outer space." He labeled the second, "The eternal resting place of your phobias, fears and anxieties." And he labeled the third picture, "The eternal resting place of your phobias, fears, anxieties and devils of torture slowly descending into the oblivion of eternal gloom." He sent her the photos; she received them before leaving for her trip. She called from the airport to report that her trip had been wonderful.

MHE had her come to his office to tell her story to a group of Ph.D. students and to sit in the chair where her fears resided. MHE put her in trance and had her experience a plane trip to San Francisco. Once there, she was to go to the middle of the Golden Gate Bridge and look down. MHE told her a story about a workman who had caught seagulls from the bridge and painted their heads red. Then he had her hallucinate returning home. When she awakened she told the students all about the trip she had taken. After she told the story it dawned on her that she had been in trance when she did it.

MHE asked her what other phobia she got over on her trip to Dallas. She didn't know what he meant. MHE told her he would ask her a simple question and she would know what he meant. Later he asked the question, "What was the first thing you did in Dallas?" "Oh that? I went to that 40-story building and rode the elevator from the ground floor clear to the top." In the past she had gotten to the top of a building by switching elevators at each floor. MHE told the students that she had been afraid of closed spaces with no visible means of support. He also told her that she had had a fear of suspension bridges, which she confirmed.

Presenting Problem: Phobia (fear) of flying

Age Group: Adult

Modality: Individual; outpatient

Problem Duration: 10 years

Treatment Length: (Two sessions)

Result: Success. She got over her fear of airplane travel, as well of her fear of high places with no visible means of support.

Follow-up: Two years. She came back to serve as a demonstration subject for MHE.

Techniques: Hypnosis; anchoring the symptom; positive hallucination; implication (she was to call and tell MHE how much she *enjoyed* the flights)

Sources: *Experiencing Erickson,* pp. 122–125; *Hypnotherapy,* pp. 314–347; *Teaching Seminar,* pp. 64–70

Case #166

Case Summary: A 32-year-old woman came to see MHE for a fear of flying. She had married a man from Germany who was living in Arizona for a time to get training. When the time came to go to Germany with him, she was afraid to fly. MHE had her take a flight to Tucson from Phoenix. She was terrified the whole time there and back on the plane. When she returned, she asked MHE where he was going to have her fly next. He told her that she did not really have a fear of flying, but that she had never been weaned from her parents. She was able to fly to Germany.

Presenting Problem: Fear of flying

Age Group: Adult

Modality: Individual; outpatient

Problem Duration: NA

Treatment Length: NA

Result: Success. The woman was able to fly to Germany.

Follow-up: She sent MHE a card that said, in German, "from our home to your house." He considered this an indication that she had been weaned from her parents, because she now had a home in Germany, rather than just a house.

Techniques: Task assignment (behavioral); reframing

Source: *Experiencing Erickson*, pp. 131–132

Case #167

Case Summary: A woman told MHE that she was extremely fearful when at the dentist's office. He immediately asked her if she had done the same thing as a child. Before she had a chance to answer, he asked her what her favorite activity had been when she was a child. After she had described her favorite childhood activity, which was playing in the leaves, MHE suggested that after she wriggled around and got comfortably seated in the dentist's chair, she would have an overwhelming recollection of playing in the leaves. She was able to do that and became a most cooperative dental patient.

Presenting Problem: Fear of dental procedures

Age Group: Adult

Modality: Individual; outpatient

Problem Duration: NA

Treatment Length: NA

Result: Success. The woman was able to be comfortable during dental procedures.

Follow-up: NA

Techniques: Linking (pleasurable childhood memory to sitting in a dentist's chair); symptom transformation (childhood anxiety into childhood pleasure); redirecting attention

Sources: *Healing in Hypnosis*, pp. 127–128; *Hypnotherapy*, pp. 130–131

Case #168

☙

Case Summary: A woman whose great-grandmother, grandmother, and mother had all died at the age of 22 from heart disease came to MHE two months before her 22nd birthday. She also had heart disease and was afraid she was going to die on her birthday. MHE found out that she had put all her affairs in order in preparation for dying. She was a very fastidious woman who had made certain that all her bills were paid so that she could die in peace. She agreed while in trance that if her mother or grandmother had lived to be 23, they probably would have survived until a ripe old age. MHE then led her astray into a long discussion in which she agreed that all businesses had the right to set the date at which they were to be paid. He then told her that he expected payment from her for his services exactly on her 23rd birthday. She visited MHE on her 23rd birthday and paid him.

Presenting Problem: Fear of dying; belief that she would die at 22

Age Group: Adult

Modality: Individual; outpatient

Problem Duration: NA

Treatment Length: NA

Result: Success. The woman survived past 22 and decided she would probably live a long life.

Follow-up: 14 months

Techniques: Hypnosis; implication; task assignment (behavioral and cognitive); utilization (of the woman's commitment not to leave behind unpaid bills)

Source: *Healing in Hypnosis*, pp. 270–271

Case #169

☙

Case Summary: A woman came to MHE for claustrophobia. When she was a child her mother had punished her by locking her in the cellar and clicking her heels on the sidewalk so that it would sound as if she was going far away. MHE treated the woman by having her sit in his closet while he gradually closed the door until she was able to remain calm with the door closed if she looked through the keyhole.

Presenting Problem: Claustrophobia

Age Group: Adult

Modality: Individual; outpatient

Problem Duration: NA

Treatment Length: NA

Result: (Partial success. The woman became more tolerant of enclosed spaces.)

Follow-up: NA

Technique: Task assignment (behavioral)

Source: *My Voice Will Go With You*, p. 135

Case #170

Case Summary: An astronomer had been picked by the government to go to Borneo to photograph a solar eclipse. He was claustrophobic and feared he could not endure the planes and trains and cars he would have to ride in on his journey. When he entered MHE's office he opened all the windows and doors. MHE had him imagine the doors were closed under hypnosis. He was able to make his trip.

Presenting Problem: Claustrophobia

Age Group: Adult

Modality: Individual; outpatient

Problem Duration: NA

Treatment Length: NA

Result: Success. The man was able to make the trip.

Follow-up: NA

Techniques: Hypnosis; positive hallucination

Source: *My Voice Will Go With You*, pp. 136–137

Case #171

Case Summary: A young man traveled by back streets and alleys and had a fear of certain buildings. He worked at a job that was beneath his abilities. MHE believed that the man had an intense fear of women but he did not mention this to the man. The man lived with his dominating mother. MHE talked with the man about his physique. They talked about what sort of an apartment a man with his musculature, strength, and brains should have. The man moved into his own apartment. As MHE talked about his physique, the man's body-image improved and his phobias stopped troubling him.

Presenting Problem: Phobia (of main streets, of certain buildings)

Age Group: Adult

Modality: Individual; outpatient

Problem Duration: NA

Treatment Length: NA

Result: Success. The man got over his phobias.

Follow-up: The man got married.

Techniques: Redirecting attention; reframing; implication

Source: *Uncommon Therapy*, p. 67

Case #172

Case Summary: An elderly gentlemen had a fear of elevators. All his life he had worked in the top floor of a building. To avoid the elevator, he had always taken the stairs. Now that he was older the walk was getting to be too much. The elevators in his building were operated by young girls. MHE made arrangements with one of them in advance. At a time that wasn't very busy MHE had the man practice getting in and out of the elevator. Then he had the girl take them up. She took him up one story and then stopped the elevator in between floors. "What's wrong!" the man shouted. "The elevator operator wants to *kiss* you," said MHE. "But I'm a married man!" The girl approached to kiss him. "You start the elevator," he demanded. At about the fourth floor she stopped the elevator again and tried to kiss him. He insisted that she start the elevator again. The third time she stopped the elevator she made him promise to always take her elevator on his way home from work. He agreed and they continued to go up. His fear of elevators was cured.

Presenting Problem: Phobia (of elevators)

Age Group: Adult

Modality: Individual; outpatient

Problem Duration: Lifelong

Treatment Length: (One to two sessions)

Result: Success. The man's fear of elevators ceased.

Follow-up: NA

Techniques: Redirecting attention; interpersonal evocation (of embarrassment and fear)

Source: *Uncommon Therapy*, pp. 297–299

Case #173

Case Summary: A man with a fear of riding elevators was hypnotized by MHE and told to go to a certain address. While he was traveling back and forth to the address MHE gave him, he was to be fascinated by the sensations of the soles of his feet. When the man returned home after visiting the address, he realized he had ridden an elevator to get to the place he visited. Having ridden an elevator once, he could do it again.

Presenting Problem: Fear of riding elevators

Age Group: Adult

Modality: Individual; outpatient

Problem Duration: NA

Treatment Length: NA

Result: (Success. The man was able to ride elevators.)

Follow-up: NA

Techniques: Hypnosis; redirecting attention; task assignment (behavioral and perceptual)

Source: *Strategies of Psychotherapy*, p. 60

Case #174

Case Summary: A construction worker had a fear of heights and sought MHE's help after his wife had seen MHE for fear of dental procedures (Case #84). There were deep holes in the construction site where the man was currently working and he was afraid he would have to quit his job due to the fear. MHE had him come in on the weekend so as not to interfere with his job. He put him in trance and told a lot of stories. One story was about a tribe of American Indians who had no fear of heights. Another was about the time MHE's son had broken his leg and found as he recovered that he was afraid to get off the couch. The son had finally gotten off the couch by gradually getting his feet closer and closer to the floor. Another story was all about the experiments MHE had done investigating psychological and physical changes in people in trance when he changed the locus and movement of his voice.

MHE then told the man that our fear of heights is a natural thing and one of the least recognized components is that our unconscious minds recognize the slight differences in the echo of sounds in holes and at heights. He recommended the man investigate this at the holes at his construction site to find out for himself. The man thought the stories were not helpful to him, but he found himself intrigued by MHE's idea about sound differences. He started investigating by making sounds at different distances from the holes and discovered it was true. By doing this he got over his fear of heights and was able to keep his job.

Later the man sought MHE's help for his impotence. He had developed impotence after having a flu and a long fever. MHE saw him once, told him a number of stories and dismissed him, telling him, "I'm sure you'll work it out." The impotence never improved.

Presenting Problem: Fear of heights; impotence

Age Group: Adult

Modality: Individual; outpatient

Problem Duration: NA

Treatment Length: Two sessions

Result: Success/failure. The man got over his fear of heights, but not his impotence.

Follow-up: 13 years

Techniques: Metaphor; task assignment (behavioral and perceptual); implication (MHE told him he did not want anything to interfere with his job, so he gave him an appointment on Saturday)

Source: Philip McAvoy, personal communication, 1989.

Case #175

AVOIDANCE/NEGATIVE REACTIONS

Case Summary: A woman in her early twenties whom MHE used as a hypnotic demonstration subject had developed an intolerance of oranges, the source of what used to be her favorite drink, orange juice. She had developed a gastrointestinal illness and got a prescription for castor oil to treat it. When she mentioned to the druggist that she always got sick after drinking castor oil, he had mixed it with orange juice to disguise its taste and casually gotten her to drink it. When he informed her, she felt nauseous. After that, much to her chagrin, she found she could no longer drink orange juice or even have oranges or orange things around.

MHE heard about this from a doctor friend of hers and arranged to have himself maneuvered into doing a demonstration of hypnosis during a social gathering that the woman was also attending. She was maneuvered into being the demonstration subject and MHE induced age regression to two years previously [to the age of three in another version], a time before she had developed her reaction to oranges. He then had the host bring some oranges and fresh squeeze two glasses full of orange juice and offer one to MHE. The woman asked for a glass and drank it with enjoyment.

After arranging that no one at the party reveal to her what had transpired or even that she had gone into a trance, MHE brought her out. She was observed moving her tongue around in her mouth afterwards, trying to identify the familiar but elusive aftertaste of oranges. Within the next few days, she spontaneously discovered that she no longer had the intolerance of oranges and went back to drinking orange juice regularly. She later decided that she had unconditioned herself spontaneously. [In another version, she is a regular demonstration subject of MHE's and asks him several times to help her, but he tells her she should solve it on her own.]

Presenting Problem: Food intolerance (oranges); nausea; color avoidance (orange)

Age Group: Adult

Modality: Individual; outpatient

Problem Duration: At least seven weeks (probably two months)

Treatment Length: One session

Result: Success. The woman was able to tolerate orange juice and the color orange.

Follow-up: NA

Techniques: Hypnosis; age regression; amnesia

Sources: *Collected Papers II*, pp. 170–174; *My Voice Will Go With You*, pp. 77–78

Case #176

Case Summary: A 19-year-old dental assistant fainted or became extremely nauseated and distressed every time she saw blood. The dentist referred her to MHE. She insisted that he treat her in one session and not psychiatrically, but only hypnotically, for the fainting. She brought a chaperone, but once she was in trance she allowed the chaperone to leave. MHE put her in a deep, somnambulistic trance and asked her if she would mind if he smoked while she was in trance. She assented. He then told her that during the time it took him to smoke the cigarette, she would review all the traumatic incidents in her life and anything connected with blood or fear or fainting.

When she awakened, they just chatted about various things unrelated to the problem.

MHE then concluded the interview, but she protested that he should have done something for her problem if he was to charge her a fee. He agreed and continued to emphasize the idea that he should have really done something for her to have charged such a fee. She left perplexed and was surprised to find that the next day and thereafter she no longer fainted at the sight of blood. Her employer called and reported the dramatic change he observed the next day. He said that she had observed and handled bloody teeth and dental procedures all day without the slightest sign of discomfort. In fact, she did not seem to even notice the change. She returned for a follow-up interview in a month and took some time to pay the fee.

Presenting Problem: Fainting at the sight of blood

Age Group: Adult

Modality: Individual; outpatient

Problem Duration: NA

Treatment Length: One session; 10 minutes or 50 minutes

Result: Success. The woman stopped fainting at the sight of blood.

Follow-up: One month

Techniques: Hypnosis; time distortion; direct suggestion

Sources: *Collected Papers II*, pp. 189–190, pp. 279–282; *Mind-Body Communication* pp. 19–22

Case #177

Case Summary: A 45-year-old man was unable to wear his dentures due to gagging, retching, and choking when they were placed in his mouth. He had developed an intolerance of anything placed in his mouth when he was 10 years old. Systematic desensitization had been attempted at that time, but it had only made the problem much worse. The young man had been unable to brush his teeth for years, which resulted in the deterioration of his teeth. Finally, at age 23, he had to have all his teeth removed and was fitted for dentures. All the examinations and extractions had to be done while he was under general anesthesia due to his gagging. He even had the gagging when he tried to kiss his wife. He was discharged from military service because he couldn't wear his dentures or eat with implements. He had to take employment that was below his capabilities because he wouldn't wear dentures.

MHE saw the man in a demonstration. In trance, he was instructed to put in his dentures and then to forget that he had them in until he smiled or looked in a mirror. He was given amnesia for the suggestion. When he came out of trance he was asked if his dentures were still in their case and he asserted they were. He was quite startled to find, when handed a mirror, that they were in his mouth. He was able to eat a steak several times that day and when he went back home he was able to wear the dentures comfortably for a few months. He was given a raise and a better position at work. He was able to kiss his wife and children. He expressed his appreciation to his dentist, who had arranged the demonstration, and to MHE, for the treatment.

Then one day he announced to his wife at breakfast that he thought he would leave his dentures at home that day. When his wife protested he simply shrugged and told her he thought it was a good idea. Thereafter, even when his dentist induced a trance, the man simply matter-of-factly refused to wear his dentures. He had decided that his life was just as happy one way as the other. He could give no other explanation, but was unmoved by the pleas and exhortations of others.

Presenting Problem: Gagging and retching at any insertion into the mouth

Age Group: Adult

Modality: Individual; outpatient (demonstration)

Problem Duration: 35 years

Treatment Length: One session

Result: Failure. The man at first was able to wear dentures comfortably, but after some months abandoned them with no good explanation.

Follow-up: Two years. No change indicated.

Techniques: Hypnosis; amnesia

Source: *Collected Papers IV*, pp. 139–143

Case #178

Case Summary: A doctor who had a history since high school of an unreasoning fear of oral examinations sought MHE's help. He had always been able to get out of oral examinations by convincing those who gave them of his fear. He was an excellent student and an unassuming man, so he had been given special consideration in those situations that usually would have required oral exams. He was now facing a situation in which he could not get special consideration. An old medical school colleague who hated MHE's patient was presiding over the four-hour oral exam required for certification in the patient's specialty. He knew of the patient's fear of oral exams and was unwilling to make an exception. The patient declared himself helpless and willing to do anything MHE suggested to get through the exam.

MHE had the man objectively recount every symptom he had experienced in relation to facing oral exams. The man described nausea, tremors, perspiration, bladder and bowel incontinence, dizziness, and physical collapse. He noted that the severity of the symptoms did not seem to be related to how important the exam was. He would experience the symptoms any time he recognized the situation as one involving an oral examination. He told MHE that even on driver's license exams, he had to bring a pad of paper and write his answer, then read it to the clerk.

MHE used the patient for hypnotic experiments he was conducting and gave him extensive experience in using all the trance phenomena. Then MHE gave the man suggestions to develop amnesia for the hypnotic suggestions and to go take the examination in a trance. He was to travel to the distant city to take the exam and not to realize he was in an oral exam. He complied and while in the exam he saw the oral questions as if they were typewritten and saw textbooks with the appropriate pages with the answers written on them as if they were in front of him. His enemy disappeared from his view. At times he saw the situation as if he were in back of the man reading the question over the man's shoulder. At times he saw patients in front of him and imagined he was giving a lecture to students in response to the questions asked. He passed the exam by answering every question correctly and traveled home in a trance; later he recalled everything in detail.

Presenting Problem: Fear of oral examinations

Age Group: Adult

Modality: Individual; outpatient

Problem Duration: NA

Treatment Length: NA

Result: Success. The man passed his oral examination and got his specialty certification.

Follow-up: NA

Techniques: Hypnosis; amnesia; positive hallucination; negative hallucination; dissociation; utilization (of writing down answers and reading them as a coping strategy); posthypnotic suggestion

Source: *Collected Papers IV*, pp. 193–206

Case #179

Case Summary: A medical student in one of MHE's study groups on hypnosis had always avoided dermatology classes. He would either become sick or go to sleep during lectures and demonstration of dermatology. The dean had warned him that he would flunk out of medical school unless he finished his dermatology studies. He volunteered one night at the study group to remember some long forgotten memory by going into trance, even though he had previously avoided anything personal in trance. He spent several hours in trance and finally came across a traumatic memory of having accidentally stabbed his cousin in a boyhood fight. While the student was in trance remembering, he spent an hour or so shaking, fearful, and feeling sick to his stomach. The cousin had developed anaphylactic shock and had turned green. The medical student's father had turned him over his knee and spanked him in sight of a scummy, green-algae-filled horse trough. The doctor had come and almost had to perform an emergency tracheotomy, which had looked to the young medical student as if his cousin was going to be butchered. After recovering the memory, he forgot it after he emerged from trance. MHE gave him the opportunity to recover it consciously, which he did. After remembering, the student began to take an interest in dermatology and drifted away from his primary focus on psychiatry.

Presenting Problem: Avoidance of dermatology studies

Age Group: Adult

Modality: Individual; outpatient (study group)

Problem Duration: NA

Treatment Length: One session, three hours

Result: Success. The student no longer avoided dermatology classes and study.

Follow-up: Several years. The student completed medical school and a residency and was in private practice when the case was reported.

Techniques: Hypnosis; direct suggestion

Sources: *Collected Papers IV*, pp. 428–436; *Hypnotherapy*, pp. 348–352

Case #180

Case Summary: A doctor who had used hypnosis stopped using it after the tragic death of his eldest son, who had been his first hypnotic subject. After seven years, he tried to use it again, but found that he would stumble over his words and become confused when he tried to do hypnosis. He traveled a long distance to be treated by MHE, but was certain that he couldn't be hypnotized. MHE knew that the man would be resistant when at the beginning of the session the man gave him a check and said that it was for his *time*. MHE got the message that the payment was not for results. After MHE spent a number of hours failing to hypnotize him, he told the man that he was sorry, but that he couldn't be hypnotized. The man seemed content with the outcome. On the way out of the office, MHE asked the man to stop and meet MHE's wife. After he did, MHE shook his hand in farewell and induced catalepsy with a handshake induction (which involves ambiguous holding and movement of the hand). The man was then escorted back into the office, where he spent an hour working on his problem while in trance, with little interference from MHE. After that trance, the doctor was able to resume the use of hypnosis in his practice.

Presenting Problem: Block in using hypnosis

Age Group: Adult

Modality: Individual; outpatient

Problem Duration: NA

Treatment Length: One session, three hours

Result: Success. The man was able to use hypnosis after the session.

Follow-up: Seven years. MHE kept in touch by mail and found that the man was an enthusiastic practitioner of trance in the ensuing years.

Techniques: Hypnosis; anchoring the resistance (to the office); catalepsy

Sources: *Collected Papers IV*, pp. 437–438; *Experiencing Hypnosis*, pp. 15–16

Case #181

Case Summary: Ann, a 24-year-old woman from a traditional Mexican-American family was engaged to be married to a man in the Air Force. She lived in her mother's home and had been overprotected by her mother and her two maiden aunts as she was growing up. She was scheduled to marry the man in December but each time the wedding drew near she postponed it for six months. It had been postponed a total of 48 months. In the meantime, she developed intense phobias of various modes of transportation and reported hearing voices.

MHE used trance with her. To begin treatment he insisted that the young woman move out of her mother's home and told her that she should come to the next session alone, without her mother and aunts. He gave her several instructions and told her that she could violate one of them. She came to the next session with only her mother accompanying her. He developed a good relationship with her. Next he instructed her to back into a bus with her eyes closed and then to do the same with a train. He told her to sit in the back seat of a car and look out the window from Yuma, where she lived, to Tucson to Phoenix and back. MHE told her that she was to move from Yuma to Phoenix and to get a job there within the next month and that she was to spend the last part of the session whimpering and crying in fear of the move. She started to protest and brought up her voices. MHE told her that both he and she knew that the voices were just a charade to cover up her real problem. She made the move.

MHE found that when the subject of sex came up she appeared to become deaf. MHE told her that the next time she came in she was to bring the shortest pair of shorts she could find. She brought the shorts and MHE gave her a choice. The next time she came in she could either have the shorts on when she came in or she could put them on in front of him. She chose to wear them in and was surprised when MHE did not comment on them.

Finally, her fiancé wrote and told her that if she did not marry him the next month, he would break off the engagement. Next MHE told her that if she didn't listen to him when he discussed sex she would have to take the shorts off and put them on again. Ann listened. After MHE ascertained that

Ann really did want to marry the man, he told her that she was to marry her fiancé within the next 17 days. To prepare Ann for the marriage, MHE called his wife in to his office as an observer. He then instructed Ann to undress, showing him and touching various parts of her body such as her breasts, her buttocks, and her genitals. Then she was to point out where she would like her husband to kiss her. He suggested that she could avoid another session like that if she visited her fiancé in the distant state where he lived. After that Ann was able to go through with the marriage. She defied her family and insisted on a smaller wedding than they had planned for her. The couple had three or four children.

Presenting Problem: Phobias; postponing wedding

Age Group: Adult

Modality: Individual; outpatient

Problem Duration: Four years

Treatment Length: At least three visits

Result: Success. The woman was able to leave home and get married to her fiancé.

Follow-up: Seven years. MHE briefly saw the woman's husband for some adjustment problems when they moved to Arizona seven years later.

Techniques: Hypnosis; pattern intervention; desensitization; task assignment (behavioral)

Sources: *Collected Papers IV*, pp. 450–452; *Conversations II*, pp. 126–128; *Healing in Hypnosis*, pp. 206–208; *Hypnotherapy*, pp. 442–450; *Uncommon Therapy*, pp. 73–74

Case #182

Case Summary: A concert pianist came to MHE because he could not bring himself to play in the concert hall. He only had four hours available for therapy. The man was a professor at a college and was told by the administration that he would lose his position if he did not perform. MHE helped the man in three sessions. In the first session the pianist was "complacently cooperative." MHE put him into trance and the man followed all his instructions as they were given. MHE noted that he was "actually capable of learning." In the second session MHE put the man into trance and discussed metaphors of fluidity as they relate to music. MHE told the man that he had completed therapy. There was one more session scheduled, however. In the final session MHE put the man into trance and summarized what he'd talked about so far. He suggested that the man lay out various colored towels on the stage on the way to the piano and then he would have the choice of which color towel to faint on. Then he concluded by telling the man that his rigid refusal to do a concert would have to stop. In music "there's no room for rigidity." The man returned to the college and gave a phenomenal concert.

Presenting Problem: Fear (of performance)

Age Group: Adult

Modality: Individual; outpatient

Problem Duration: 15 years

Treatment Length: Three or four hours

Result: Success. The man conquered his fear of performance.

Follow-up: NA

Techniques: Utilization (of understanding of music); reframing; analogy; task assignment (behavioral and perceptual); redirecting attention

Sources: *Conversations I*, pp. 277–279; *Mind-Body Communication*, pp. 75–77; *Phoenix*, pp. 139–140

Case #183

Case Summary: A man in Detroit who had been in the construction business had lost his business and gone bankrupt because he developed a fear of tall buildings falling on him. He then had to avoid going any route where tall buildings existed. MHE had him calculate the size of all the buildings in downtown Detroit and figure out how far away from them he would have to walk to be safe. In doing this calculation, the man had to go near the buildings he had previously avoided. He and MHE calculated the safe distance and the man started enjoying walks down safe routes. Next MHE reminded him that he would see the building start to fall so he would have some time to move away. In this way, the man was able to walk much closer to buildings and go more places.

Presenting Problem: Fear of tall buildings collapsing; avoidance of certain areas

Age Group: Adult

Modality: Individual; outpatient

Problem Duration: NA

Treatment Length: NA

Result: Partial success. The man was able to walk many places he had previously avoided.

Follow-up: NA

Techniques: Redirecting attention; task assignment (behavioral)

Sources: *Healing in Hypnosis*, pp. 197–198

Case #184

6

Cognitive and Communication Problems

STUTTERING

Case Summary: During MHE's senior year in medical school another student sought hypnotherapy for stuttering. He was found to speak fluently while in trance but was not able to speak fluently out of trance at first. He was given a suggestion that he forget having been in trance and to come and visit MHE socially for the next two weeks. When he entered the room with MHE he was to develop a deep trance. He complied and at the next social visit he reported while in trance that he had not been stuttering in his daily life since he had developed an amnesia for his hypnotic experiences. Since the student was leaving the area, he and MHE agreed that the amnesia should remain in force and that the next time he met MHE he would instantly develop a deep trance. Nine years later MHE met him at a newspaper office where the former student worked as a writer. As they shook hands, the man developed a deep trance and MHE was able to determine that the amnesia had continued for the whole time and also that the stuttering had remained absent for those nine years. A check with the managing editor revealed that the man was a competent reporter and had never stuttered.

Presenting Problem: Stuttering

Age Group: Adult

Modality: Individual; outpatient

Problem Duration: NA

Treatment Length: (Four sessions; about one month)

Result: Success. The man stopped stuttering.

Follow-up: Nine years. The stuttering had remained cured.

Techniques: Hypnosis; amnesia; posthypnotic suggestion

Sources: *Collected Papers III*, pp. 67–68

Case #185

Case Summary: A fellow medical student asked MHE to hypnotize him to correct his stuttering. The stutterer had undergone some years of speech therapy but that had only made the problem worse. MHE was reluctant to take the case since he was due to move out of state in two weeks. When the man insisted, MHE hypnotized him and found that the stutterer was able to speak clearly in deep trance and that he manifested a spontaneous amnesia for the trance experience. MHE suggested that the man spend the summer transferring his ability for fluent speech from his unconscious mind to his waking state and putting the stutter into his unconscious mind. Thirty years later MHE met the man at a conference. The man was now a psychoanalyst and showed no recollection of the hypnotic therapy he had received; however, he did recall seeking MHE's help for stuttering. He reported that the stutter had spontaneously disappeared during the summer after he sought MHE's help. He had tried to deal with the issue during his own personal analysis, but had always found it elusive.

Presenting Problem: Stuttering

Age Group: Adult

Modality: Individual; outpatient

Problem Duration: NA

Treatment Length: Two weeks

Result: Success. The man stopped stuttering.

Follow-up: 30 years

Techniques: Hypnosis; amnesia; splitting (unconscious/conscious); linking (stuttering linked with unconscious, fluent speech linked with conscious)

Source: *Collected Papers III*, pp. 68–70

Case #186

Case Summary: A physician who stuttered came to MHE for treatment. MHE agreed to treat the man, but warned him that the treatment would be rather unpleasant. MHE put the man into trance and interviewed him about how he felt about his stuttering and about people in general. Gradually, MHE got the man to be quite angry at him; when the man thoroughly hated MHE, his stutter vanished. They cordially agreed that hating MHE was a good solution and would dissipate the general aggression and anger the man had towards others. Every year, the man would send MHE a nasty Christmas card telling him how much he hated him; at the same time, he would send gifts for Erickson's children.

Presenting Problem: Stuttering

Age Group: Adult

Modality: Individual; outpatient

Problem Duration: NA

Treatment Length: NA

Result: Success. The man stopped stuttering.

Follow-up: Through Christmas cards and personal contact, MHE ascertained that the stutter was gone for some years after treatment.

Techniques: Hypnosis; evocation (of emotion); symptom transformation (aggressive energy went from stuttering to hating MHE)

Source: *Collected Papers IV*, p. 92

Case #187

Case Summary: A man had been in psychoanalysis for 5 years to try to get rid of his stammer. MHE treated him and gave him a fixed hatred for any tree that was less than 18 inches from the sidewalk. The man channeled the hostility that used to be expressed through stammering into this harmless hatred. His analyst tried to rid him of the hatred, but when the man's stammer started to reappear, he decided to keep the harmless hatred and avoid the stammering.

Presenting Problem: Stuttering

Age Group: Adult

Modality: Individual; outpatient

Problem Duration: NA

Treatment Length: NA

Result: Success. The man's stammer disappeared.

Follow-up: NA

Technique: Symptom transformation (displacing hostility onto trees closer than 18 inches from the sidewalk)

Source: *Collected Papers IV*, pp. 92–93

Case #188

Case Summary: MHE agreed to see a 17-year-old from Massachusetts for one hour. The boy, named Rick, had had a severe stuttering problem all of his life. The boy came to the office with his mother. MHE could not understand the boy so he took a family history from the mother. The parents were Lebanese immigrants. Rick had two older sisters. MHE knew how strong the father's role is in a traditional Lebanese family and he knew that the father must have been disgusted by having his two first-born children be girls. MHE sent Rick and his mother to sightsee. He also sent Rick to a Lebanese flower shop where a woman would give him the dirtiest work possible.

MHE agreed to take on the case and sent Rick's mother home. MHE gave Rick an assignment. He told him to write the numbers from one to ten, the alphabet, and a two-page composition on any subject he chose. MHE told Rick this would prove he didn't stutter. Rick completed the assignment. He wrote the numbers and the alphabet backwards. In his composition he reversed the last two or three letters of every other word. MHE told Rick his problem was not that he stuttered but that he didn't communicate. He also explained to Rick that he misspelled words because of his older sisters. Rick was trying to symbolically reverse his two sisters with himself.

MHE told Rick to read a book out loud backwards so he could practice saying words without communicating. MHE told Rick that he was an American, not a Lebanese boy, and he should start behaving like an American, which meant thinking for himself. He told Rick to read a book beginning with the last chapter and then speculate on what happened in the previous chapter. This would teach him to think in a new direction.

MHE sent Rick home. He told him to tell his sisters that they were American women and they could do as they pleased. Rick's stuttering improved 90% in a couple of days and eventually vanished all together.

Presenting Problem: Stuttering

Age Group: Adolescent

Modality: Individual; outpatient

Problem Duration: 17 years

Treatment Length: 20 hours

Result: Success. Rick's stuttering went away and he became more assertive.

Follow-up: Four years. Rick went to college and separated himself from his father's influence. MHE saw him during one of Rick's vacations from college. He had defied his father's wishes and dropped out of college for a little while to work. His sisters had gone to college and both became professionals as well.

Techniques: Reframing; task assignment (behavioral and cognitive); direct suggestion

Source: *Teaching Seminar*, pp. 121–132

Case #189

Case Summary: A man with a stutter called MHE and said, "Ba, ba, ba, ba, ba, ba, . . . " MHE said, "Write to me," and hung up. He received a letter from the man which described all of the therapies he'd undergone, all of the failures he'd had, and his hope for MHE's help. MHE wrote him a letter in response which expressed great doubts as to the man's sincerity. The two continued to correspond but MHE never accepted him as a patient because he believed he was a hopeless case.

Presenting Problem: Stuttering

Age Group: Adult

Modality: NA

Problem Duration: Since age four

Treatment Length: NA

Result: Refusal. MHE refused to take the case.

Follow-up: NA

Techniques: NA

Source: *Teaching Seminar*, pp. 202–209

Case #190

SPEECH/COMMUNICATION PROBLEMS

Case Summary: A woman was sitting at church with her family one day and suddenly developed Tourette's syndrome, feeling a violent and irresistible urge to swear, grimace, and gesture involuntarily. She managed to cover her mouth with a handkerchief and induce retching by sticking her finger down her throat and escaped to the bathroom, where she proceeded to swear, grimace, and gesture for 30 minutes, covering up the sounds with running water and flushing toilets. After she realized that the symptoms weren't abating, she ran out of church, drove herself home, and locked herself in her room. When her family came home, she kept them away by saying that she was all right but needed to be left alone.

When she woke up the next morning, she still had the symptoms, so she called MHE, whom she had met socially. He made a house call and she demanded hypnosis. MHE told her that she must agree to go along with whatever he might ask of her and he gave her some outrageous examples of his techniques to let her know what she was agreeing to. She agreed to his conditions for treatment. He proceeded to hypnotize her by using a trance induction interspersed by swearing that was far cruder than what she was saying. This had the effect of fixating her attention and inducing a deep trance.

MHE regressed her to two years before the present. When he reoriented her in the age regressed state, she was free of symptoms. Her husband was then called in and the situation and the syndrome were explained to him. The woman, while still in an age regressed somnambulistic trance, was told of her situation. Her agreement was secured in following all of MHE's suggestions and she was told not to expect a miracle cure, but rather gradual improvement and modification of her symptoms. She was also taught 10 cues that could be used to instantly reinduce trance. She was given suggestions that she could modify the expression of the symptoms, whispering instead of shouting the obscenities and covering the gesturing with natural gestures. She was reminded that she would have to eat, drink and sleep and that these activities would interfere with the expression of her symptoms and that there undoubtedly would be other symptom-free times.

The family arranged to go on a two-week vacation to give her an opportunity to practice her symptom modification skills. She visited MHE weekly at first, turning the car radio on loudly to cover her shouts so she could get it all out of her system before the interview. At first she found that if she didn't have a session of unrestrained shouting at least once a week she would burst out yelling in the middle of the night. Gradually, however, the need for these relief sessions disappeared. After a year of therapy, the symptoms disappeared. The reason for their onset was never discovered.

Presenting Problem: Giles de la Tourette syndrome; compulsive swearing, gesturing, grimacing

Age Group: Adult

Modality: Individual; marital; outpatient

Problem Duration: One day

Treatment Length: Two years (at first weekly, then monthly intervals)

Result: Success. She was completely free of the symptoms after one year of therapy. The woman wanted to continue therapy, even though it was mostly social visits after the symptoms abated.

Follow-up: Five years. No recurrence of the symptoms.

Techniques: Hypnosis; age regression; posthypnotic suggestion; matching (swearing); pattern intervention

Source: *Collected Papers IV*, pp. 123–130

Case #191

Case Summary: A man on his way to church suddenly developed the compulsive urge to swear, grind his teeth, and shake his fists. This compulsion could be triggered by the sight of a church at first, then by the sight of anyone in religious garb, then by hearing anyone use obscenities. He began avoiding streets which had churches on them and had to resign his position in an exclusive bar as bartender. He took a job at a rough bar for much less income and became known as "The Cussing Bartender" when his episodes were triggered by someone using obscenity in his hearing. He had managed to hide his affliction from his wife, but one day she swore at him regarding their drop in income and she had a chance to witness his problem. She brought him to MHE for treatment.

MHE trained him in trance and in being able to selectively tune out parts of his sensory field. Then MHE had the man systematically learn to tune out parts of what used to be triggers for his episodes. Churches were to be perceived only as white buildings, nuns as women dressed in ridiculous black and white dresses, and obscenities as meaningless nonsense syllables. Any religious thoughts that came to his mind could be transformed into nonsense syllables. Shortly after this, his wife unthinkingly said grace at the beginning of a meal and the man immediately became confused, developed a headache, and went to bed.

With these interventions, the man was gradually able to lose his symptoms. He lost his job as "The Cussing Bartender" and regained his old one. He was seen at decreasing intervals and therapy was finally discontinued. The symptoms never recurred.

Presenting Problem: Giles de la Tourette syndrome; compulsive swearing, grinding teeth, and gesturing

Age Group: Adult

Modality: Individual; outpatient

Problem Duration: NA

Treatment Length: Two and a half years

Result: Success. The man stopped having the symptoms and regained his former job. He was eventually able to go to church with no problems.

Follow-up: Two years. One follow-up interview was done a year after the end of treatment when the man came in to ask why he had been in treatment with MHE. Following the recovery of the memory of his symptoms and treatment, the man was able to go to church without a recurrence of his symptoms.

Techniques: Hypnosis; negative hallucination; splitting (of religious meanings from religious objects, ideas and people)

Source: *Collected Papers IV*, pp. 130–132

Case #192

Case Summary: A state hospital patient who came under MHE's care spoke only "schizophrenese" or "word salad." The man spoke English, but uttered only meaningless (to others) phrases like " . . . bucket of sand, bucket of lard, fat's in the fire, had a flat tire. . . . " He had been in the hospital for over nine years, and although he seemed to be attempting to communicate with others, no one had as yet been able to understand him. He had arrived at the hospital without identification, no history had been elicited, and no therapy had been provided.

When MHE inherited the case, he sent a stenographer to sit at a desk near the man and surreptitiously record the man's utterances. After these were transcribed, MHE studied them closely but could discern no meaningful communications in them. He decided, therefore, that he would learn to speak "word salad" and communicate to the man in his own language. He introduced himself to the man, and when the man uttered some word salad in response, MHE responded with some word salad, uttered in a sincere tone. At first the patient seemed skeptical, but he soon began carrying on long conversations with MHE in word salad. He even started interspersing more everyday utterances in his word salad, and over time the percentage of sensible communications increased.

Gradually MHE obtained a history, provided therapy, and facilitated the man's release from the hospital. He received a postcard from the man some years later, with a bit of word salad on it, followed by the sentence, "It's nice to have a bit of nonsense in life, isn't it, Doc?"

Presenting Problem: Communication difficulties; word salad

Age Group: Adult

Modality: Individual; inpatient

Problem Duration: At least nine years

Treatment Length: Less than one year

Result: Success. The man started to communicate in understandable sentences and eventually was released from the hospital.

Follow-up: Three years

Techniques: Matching (of patient's language); utilization (of patient's language)

Sources: *Collected Papers IV*, pp. 213–215; *Conversations I*, pp. 223–224; *Phoenix*, pp. 49–50

Case #193

Case Summary: A 38-year-old woman developed an aneurysm and resulting aphasia (inability to speak), alexia (inability to spell), partial paralysis, and severe pain. MHE saw her first a year after her vascular accident and by then she had become quite depressed and discouraged about her condition. MHE decided to use the woman's frustration and despair as motivating factors in the treatment. He obtained her promise to cooperate with treatment regardless of how difficult. Next he had a relative accompany her to the sessions and enlisted the relative as a cohort.

The first joint session consisted of MHE's asking the patient a series of information-gathering questions. Before she got a chance to answer—it could take her as long as five minutes to utter a phrase—her companion would answer for her, sometimes with deliberately erroneous or slightly wrong answers. By the end of the session, MHE casually said to the patient that she was probably mad as a wet hen by then. Her companion quickly replied that the woman was not at all angry. When MHE guessed that she probably did not want to return, she was able to utter, "I promised." The patient left the office walking more steadily than she had entered it. The same procedure was repeated the next day and again the patient showed a marked improvement in her walk as she left furious.

Next MHE arranged for the relative to get the patient to follow a schedule of activities. MHE instructed the patient to follow the relative's instructions without question. Sometimes the relative would deliberately make a mistake in the schedule, such as insisting that it was time to go to bed because it was 10 p.m., even though the clock clearly read 9 p.m. After the relative made a number of these errors, including fixing and ordering the wrong food for the patient, the patient started to talk and correct the relative, a little at first and then more frequently and articulately. Nursery rhymes were used to both frustrate her and elicit corrections and to revivify early abilities.

Gradually the patient told MHE that she was angry at him and at her relative but she realized that it was helping. She was warned that the worst was yet to come and replied, "I'm game." Rhythms and music were used to help the patient restore her movement and coordination. When she had improved enough, MHE let her reverse positions and take the relative out to eat and order her all the wrong food. The relative eventually had to leave and was replaced by four other people in sequence, each contributing different things to the patient's improvement. She gradually regained near normal speech and much of her ability to move and read. She still had some pain that could be controlled by medication.

She was seen again seven years later when she regressed seriously upon learning of the assassination of President Kennedy in 1963. MHE's interview elicited little interest in any topic except a slightly positive response to recollections about one of her companions for whom she felt protective and maternal. MHE capitalized on this and led the woman from a discussion of Kennedy's assassination to her son's poor eating habits. This seemed to awaken her maternal feelings and she left MHE's much improved.

Presenting Problem: Aphasia (lack of speech ability); alexia (lack of ability to read); motor impairment and pain

Age Group: Adult

Modality: Individual; conjoint (with companions and husband on occasion); outpatient

Problem Duration: One year

Treatment Length: At least eight months

Result: Partial success. The woman was able to regain much of her speech, reading, and movement ability and had less pain.

Follow-up: Seven years. The woman moved from her home state, where she did not do too well in the cold weather, to Tucson, Arizona, to be somewhat but not too near MHE.

Techniques: Task assignment (behavioral); behavioral contract; interpersonal evocation of motivation; utilization (of frustration and anger)

Sources: *Collected Papers IV*, pp. 283–314; "Advanced Techniques I"

Case #194

Case Summary: A 70-year-old woman had arteriosclerosis that had affected her brain and caused a Parkinsonian-like problem in her face and interfered with her speech. She had become despondent and withdrawn due to her condition. MHE used hypnosis with her and instructed her to practice talking to her image in the mirror three times a day. She was to move her jaw up and down and right and left then back to the midline. Then she was to make baby noises, like "goo" and "gaa." She complied and within some months was almost completely normal and had returned to her active life. She reduced her practice to once a day since she was much better, but soon had a relapse of her symptoms. She returned to MHE for another session and he got her to continue to practice and restored her recovery within a month. She was gradually able to skip practice several days a week.

Presenting Problem: Speech difficulties; facial muscle problems

Age Group: Adult

Modality: Individual and conjoint (with her husband); outpatient

Problem Duration: NA

Treatment Length: (Two sessions, some months apart)

Result: Success. The woman regained normal speech and control of her facial muscles.

Follow-up: Almost 10 years. MHE reported that she was as active as a 40-year-old even though she was nearly 80.

Techniques: Hypnosis; task assignment (behavioral)

Source: *Collected Papers IV*, pp. 315–316

Case #195

$\sim$

Case Summary: A woman in her mid-sixties had been diagnosed with Parkinson's disease, which at first she refused to accept. Finally, after three doctors confirmed the diagnosis, she accepted it, but was not prepared to accept what they all said was an atypical symptom, that of talking with a harsh, grating deep voice. She sought hypnosis from MHE for relief of that symptom. He informed her that she couldn't be hypnotized since he deemed her resistant. Instead he asked her to come for another session. She seemed relieved. At the next session he used an indirect induction and instructed her that she was to practice reciting the alphabet and nursery rhymes backwards while reading them forwards with her eyes. MHE helped her practice in trance at each session. In less than two months she was saying less than two words in 10 in the formerly rasping way.

Presenting Problem: Speech difficulty

Age Group: Adult

Modality: Individual; outpatient

Problem Duration: NA

Treatment Length: 10 sessions over two months

Result: Success. The woman was able to finally lose the speech peculiarity.

Follow-up: NA

Techniques: Hypnosis; indirect suggestion; task assignment (behavioral)

Source: *Collected Papers IV*, pp. 317–320

Case #196

$\sim$

Case Summary: A woman brought her husband to see MHE. He had been totally paralyzed by a stroke and could not talk or move but could hear and understand everything said to him. The man was a very proud Prussian German. He had spent the last year in a teaching hospital as the model "hopeless patient" while he learned that, due to his illness, the business he had built had been destroyed and his family had to go on public assistance. His wife heard about MHE's work with paralyzed and aphasic people and brought her husband to Arizona in hopes that he could be rehabilitated. The man's eyes and his vocal grunts showed anger at his situation and impatience at the history MHE was laboriously taking. The wife warned MHE that her husband always liked to be in charge. MHE got the wife to agree that she would support him in whatever treatment he did, no matter how shocking. She assented.

Much to the man's disgust, MHE did not begin treatment at the first session. He refused to leave MHE's office and signified his intention of staying in MHE's office until he began working with him. MHE had his two sons carry the man out of his house. The man was furious all night and the next morning. His wife was sure that he would not return to see MHE, but when she brought the car around to take him to the appointment, she was surprised to see that he had somehow managed to walk to the door alone.

When MHE had the man in his office, he told him that he was going to give him a description of how the treatment would be. When the man indicated that he would like to skip the description and begin working right away, MHE threatened to end the session right then and send him back home. The man finally agreed to sit and listen. MHE told him that hypnosis was to be used and that he should obey all MHE's instructions without question. Then the man's wife was told that if the man tried to communicate to her by using grunts and gestures, she was to tell him to shut up and that she was following doctor's orders. The man walked almost all the way from MHE's office to his car using his wife only for balance.

In the next session, MHE began to berate Prussian Germans as animal-like, stupid, conceited Nazis. MHE also criticized him harshly for accepting charity and lying around for a year. MHE said that he couldn't think of all the horrible things he ought to say about him but he'd work on it for the rest of the day. "And you're going to come back, aren't you!" "No!" shouted the man. "So for a year you haven't talked. Now all I had to do was call you a dirty Nazi pig, and you start talking. You're going to come back here tomorrow and get the *real* description of yourself." "No, no, no!" he said and began staggering towards the door. He got all the way to the car by himself.

MHE told the wife to take her husband home, put him to bed and tell him he had an appointment with MHE the next day. In the morning she was to tell him that it was time to go, get the car and race the engine. She was to assist him as soon as she saw the doorknob turn. When he got to MHE's house he walked with his wife's assistance into the office. MHE told the man he'd rather not insult him again. He told the man that he could answer "yes" or "no" to pleasant questions, as well as insults. The man struggled and got out a "yes." MHE was supportive to the man while using hypnosis and continued to insult him when he was out of trance. He ordered the man to start walking every day.

When the man walked 15 miles one day and stopped to tell MHE about his accomplishment, MHE just insulted him and accused him of laziness. With MHE's help, the man returned to a satisfactory level of functioning and was able to return to work and supporting his family. His wife was shocked when near the end of treatment she heard her husband tell MHE that he loved him as a brother. He lived 10 years happily and then had another stroke. The wife asked for MHE's help but he told her that given her husband's advanced age and his inability to even get angry anymore, there was nothing he could do for him.

Presenting Problem: Paralysis and aphasia (inability to speak) due to stroke

Age Group: Adult

Modality: Individual

Problem Duration: One year

Treatment Length: Two months

Result: Success. The man regained speech and movement.

Follow-up: The results lasted for 10 years.

Techniques: Utilization (of anger); interpersonal evocation of motivation and emotion; hypnosis; task assignment (behavioral); behavioral contract

Source: *Collected Papers IV*, pp. 321–327; *Uncommon Therapy*, pp. 310–313

Case #197

Case Summary: Phillip had been in the hospital 10 years. In that time he had not spoken a single word. MHE sat down next to Phillip and told him he was going to take his history. He would write questions and he would

write down answers even if Phillip wouldn't give them. "Now your name is Phillip Jones. Let's see, Phillip is spelled 'Y-t-u-w-x-z'." MHE continued writing nonsense of this sort until Phillip finally grabbed the pad and pencil from him and said, "Don't write any more nonsense." MHE and Phillip became close friends and talked about many things.

Presenting Problem: Mutism

Age Group: Adult

Modality: Individual; inpatient

Problem Duration: At least 10 years

Treatment Length: NA

Result: Success. Phillip began to communicate.

Follow-up: NA

Technique: Interpersonal evocation (of correcting)

Source: *Conversations I*, pp. 225–226

Case #198

᠃

Case Summary: A woman who had a cerebral accident came to MHE for aphasia. MHE instructed her husband to buy a 15-gallon fish tank and stock it with tropical fish. The woman hated aquariums. Each night the two were to sit and look at the fish for 30 minutes without talking. After about a month of this fish watching her talking improved.

Presenting Problem: Aphasia

Age Group: Adult

Modality: Individual/marital; outpatient

Problem Duration: NA

Treatment Length: NA

Result: Success. The woman's speech improved.

Follow-up: They both learned to like fish. They now go to aquariums for pleasure.

Techniques: Task assignment (behavioral); evocation (of desire to talk)

Source: *Conversations II*, pp. 55–57

Case #199

Case Summary: A woman who worked in an office could not write with her right hand and refused to write with her left hand. MHE confused her so much by talking to her using puns that she did not know which hand was the *right* one to use and which one was *left* to use after the right one wasn't right. It took her a year to get her left hand distinguished from her right hand after that and by then she had become ambidextrous.

Presenting Problem: Inability to write

Age Group: Adult

Modality: Individual; outpatient

Problem Duration: NA

Treatment Length: NA

Result: Success. The woman was able to write after her work with MHE.

Follow-up: One year. She had learned to write with both hands.

Technique: Confusion technique

Source: *Healing in Hypnosis*, p. 235

Case #200

READING PROBLEMS

Case Summary: A woman called "Maw" [or Mother Kincannon or Ma Kate] had not been allowed to learn to read or write as a youngster, because her father considered that inappropriate and unnecessary for females. At age

16, she resolved to learn, but found herself blocked and unable to learn. At the age of 20, she hit upon the idea of taking in teachers as boarders and having them teach her to read and write. Her boarders and later her children all tried to teach her, to no avail. She would become frightened and go blank when anyone tried to explain reading and writing to her.

When Maw was 70, still unable to read or write, MHE became one of her boarders and took on the challenge of teaching her to read and write. MHE induced a trance and promised her that she would be reading and writing within three weeks and that he would ask her to do nothing that she did not already know how to do. She was skeptical and intrigued. First he asked her to pick up a pencil and hold it in any way, like a baby would. Next he asked her to make some marks on a paper, any scribbling marks like a baby that can't write would. Next he asked her to make some straight lines, like she would do on a board when she wanted to saw or like she would in a garden when she wanted to plant a straight row. She could make the lines up and down or across or sideways. Then she was to draw some donut holes and then draw the two halves of a donut when it is broken in half. Then she was to draw the two sides of a gable roof. He continued to instruct her to make these marks and to practice them. She practiced diligently, although she did not see the relevance of it.

At the next session, MHE told her that the only difference between a pile of lumber and a house was that the latter was merely put together. She agreed to this, but again failed to see the relevance. With MHE's guidance, she put the marks she had been making together to make all the letters of the alphabet. Only then did MHE let her in on the fact that she had just learned how to write the alphabet. Spelling words was merely a matter of putting the letter together. MHE then told her that like all the farm animals had names, all these word critters had names. He taught her the name for various words and gradually maneuvered her into writing her first sentence. The sentence read, "Get going Maw and put some grub on the table," a sentence that her late husband had often used. When she said this aloud, she realized that it was just like talking. The transition into reading was then easily made within the three-week period.

Presenting Problem: Inability to read

Age Group: Adult

Modality: Individual; outpatient

Problem Duration: Lifelong

Treatment Length: Three weeks

Result: Success. Maw was reading and writing within three weeks.

Follow-up: She died at age 80, having been for the last 10 years a prolific reader and a frequent correspondent with her children and grandchildren.

Techniques: Hypnosis; linking (previous life experiences, e.g., gardening, sawing, naming animals, with making marks); task assignment (behavioral)

Sources: *Collected Papers I*, pp. 197–201; *Conversations I*, pp. 243–245

Case #201

Case Summary: An 11-year-old boy blocked completely on reading. His parents had hired tutors but none could teach the boy to read. When he came to MHE, MHE told him that his parents thought that he should be treated, but MHE thought the parents should be treated because they had mismanaged the situation. They started to talk about the boy's interests and MHE found that the boy liked to travel. During one of their discussions, they had an argument about distances. MHE told the boy that it was 750 miles to L.A. and 350 miles to Spokane. The boy knew this was wrong and told MHE so. MHE got out a map to try to prove his point. He started looking on the map for Spokane in the vicinity of Salt Lake City. The boy found Spokane on the map and showed MHE.

MHE said, "Well, maybe I'm stupid on distance, but I can tell you a lot of things about Salt Lake City," and he proceeded to give correct facts about that city and several others. MHE and the boy would examine (not read) maps in each session. MHE would always make mistakes and the boy would always correct him, gradually learning to read with the effort.

That summer the boy's father took him on a trip. The father joined AAA (an automobile club) and had the kid use all the maps and pamphlets he got to read up on all the places they could visit. The boy planned out their entire trip. The boy enjoyed the trip and started back to school in the fall. When he returned to school, he asked the teacher to give him all the readers from 1st grade to 5th grade and he read them. Then the boy got out a newspaper clipping about the trip he and his father had taken and read it for the teacher. He was placed in the proper grade.

Presenting Problem: Inability to read

Age Group: Child

Modality: Individual; outpatient

Problem Duration: NA

Treatment Length: NA

Result: Success. The boy began reading and returned to school in the proper grade.

Follow-up: NA

Techniques: Interpersonal evocation (of corrections to MHE's mistakes that would involve reading)

Sources: *Conversations III*, pp. 126–127; *Life Reframing*, pp. 182–184; *Uncommon Therapy*, pp. 204–205

Case #202

ACADEMIC PROBLEMS

Case Summary: A nine-year-old girl was failing in her schoolwork and was becoming withdrawn socially. Her parents became concerned and asked MHE to see her in therapy. MHE learned that she had previously done well academically, but since her social adjustment had worsened, her grades had dropped. She refused to come to MHE's office, so he visited her at her home each evening. She informed MHE that she didn't like some of the other girls at school because they were always playing jacks, roller skating or jumping rope. Although the girl dismissed these activities as things that weren't fun, she admitted that she was not very good at them. MHE immediately challenged her to a game of jacks, explaining that since his right arm had been paralyzed, he thought he could play more terribly than she could. She accepted the challenge and they started playing jacks each night, with intense competition. Within three weeks, she got much better at playing jacks. They developed such rapport that MHE was able to induce trance with her and they played games with the girl both in and out of trance.

Next, MHE told her he thought that he could roller skate worse than she could. They spent two weeks roller skating before she got good enough to beat him consistently. Her parents were upset because they were only concerned about her academic performance and couldn't see the relevance of these activities. It took her only one week to master rope jumping. Finally, MHE challenged her to a bicycle race. She knew that MHE was a good bicyclist, as she had seen him ride. She owned a bicycle, but had barely ridden it. She agreed to the race and practiced hard, but made MHE promise to try his best to make it a fair race. She didn't know that if MHE pedaled with both legs, he was actually much slower than if he let his good leg do most of the work. They raced and she could see MHE pedaling hard with both legs, so she felt quite triumphant when she won the race.

That was the last session. She went on to become the school champion of jacks and rope jumping. Her grades improved dramatically. She later told MHE that her victory in the bicycle race gave her the confidence that she could do anything.

Presenting Problem: Academic difficulties; social withdrawal

Age Group: Child

Modality: Individual; outpatient

Problem Duration: NA

Treatment Length: (Two months)

Result: Success. The girl's academic and social adjustment was much improved.

Follow-up: She went on to marry and have a child.

Techniques: Hypnosis; skill building; matching (MHE could play worse than she could)

Sources: *Collected Papers I*, pp. 201–203; *Conversations III*, pp. 138–140; *Uncommon Therapy*, pp. 203–204

Case #203

Case Summary: A junior in college came to MHE because he could not pass a final exam. He performed adequately on mid-terms and other tests, but always failed finals. He said that just once he'd like to get an "A" on a final. MHE told him that for the rest of his junior year he should try to give "D" answers on his finals. He should write the exam happily. The man got "A's" on all of his exams.

Presenting Problem: Anxiety (about tests)

Age Group: Adult

Modality: Individual; outpatient

Problem Duration: Two-three years

Treatment Length: Two hours

Result: Success. The man's test performance improved from failing grades to "A's."

Follow-up: NA

Techniques: Redirecting attention; symptom prescription

Source: *Conversations I,* pp. 273–274

Case #204

ᔒ

Case Summary: A lawyer wanted to move from Wisconsin, where he currently practiced, to Arizona. He had, however, failed the Arizona bar examination five times. The next day he was to take the examination once more and he wanted MHE's help to pass it. MHE induced a trance with him and instructed him to enjoy the ride from Phoenix to Tucson looking at the scenery on both sides of the road and thinking what nice scenery he would be living in the future. He was to drive randomly around Tucson and park in a random parking lot, where he would find a building. He could walk into the building wondering what building it was. He would then notice some people, who wouldn't interest him. Next he would pick up an examination book and read the questions. They wouldn't make sense to him. Then he would read the first question again and it would start to make sense to him. A little trickle of information would come out of his pen onto the page. After that trickle dried up, another would start and dry up. This procedure would happen again with question after question. Then he would go eat a nice dinner, have a relaxing evening, and wake up refreshed to repeat the previous day's performance for as many days as the examination lasted. Follow-up indicated he was successful in passing the bar.

A couple of years later the man came to MHE again he said that his back had begun to ache and it worried him because the men in his family had a history of chronic backaches. MHE put the man in trance and told him that if his backache was psychological he did not need to have it but if it was organic in origin it would not go away without treatment. The man's backache went away. Nine years later, the lawyer returned again saying that his backache had returned. MHE sent him to a physician who gave him exercises for his back. A year later his back was better and his health had improved.

Presenting Problem: Multiple test failures (Arizona bar exam); backache

Age Group: Adult

Modality: Individual; outpatient

Problem Duration: NA

Treatment Length: One session

Result: Success. He passed the exam.

Follow-up: At least 11 years. He had no children when he first came to see MHE. After the birth of his third child, he returned to MHE for successful hypnotherapy for back pain.

Techniques: Hypnosis; amnesia; dissociation; posthypnotic suggestion

Sources: *Experiencing Erickson*, pp. 151–152; *Teaching Seminar*, pp. 58–60

Case #205

Case Summary: A doctor used his son as a hypnotic subject and was proud of him because he was such a skilled and responsive hypnotic subject. When the boy came home with bad grades one time, the man tried to hypnotize him to better his grades. The boy refused to go into trance. The man brought him to MHE, who told the boy that he probably did not feel too bad about getting D grades as they were not too important. He probably did not feel too badly about the C grades he got, MHE suggested, because they were average. MHE thought the boy really enjoyed getting B grades, however. With this new orientation, the boy started getting better grades.

Presenting Problem: Poor academic performance; poor grades

Age Group: Child

Modality: Individual; outpatient

Problem Duration: NA

Treatment Length: NA

Result: Success. The boy's grades improved.

Follow-up: NA

Techniques: Redirecting attention; linking (good feelings with good grades)

Source: *Life Reframing*, pp. 112–123

Case #206

MEMORY PROBLEMS

Case Summary: A 30-year-old woman kept having amnesic episodes during which she would forget her identity, not recognize her children or her husband and think it was 1934, even though it was in actuality 1952. She was often hospitalized during these episodes and would spontaneously recover her memory after varying lengths of time with amnesia. The Phoenix police asked MHE to help her. He initially observed that she had a negative reaction to hearing the policeman tell her his name. He had the policeman repeat his name until he observed that she was reacting to the "Eric" part of Erickson. She also showed a reaction to his cane, his mustache, and his gray hair.

She was at first reluctant to have therapy and hypnosis, but decided after one amnesiac episode that she was interested. MHE tried various hypnotic techniques with her (he lists them as age regression, automatic writing and drawing, crystal gazing, dream activity, mirror writing, free association, depersonalization, disorientation, identification with others, and dissociation techniques), all of which failed to help her recover any traumatic memories or stop having amnesiac episodes. Finally, MHE noticed that she developed an amnesia after seeing a Borden's milk truck through a window. Thereafter, he was able to trigger amnesiac episodes deliberately by exposing the woman to Borden's advertisements. Other things could also trigger an episode.

MHE developed an age progression technique of seeing a calendar with the monthly pages being torn off from 1934 to 1952. With that technique, she could rapidly be brought back to the present and full memories. After some time she was able to readily accomplish this in five minutes of clock time. He finally taught her time distortion and instructed her to experience her entire life to the present from childhood in 20 seconds of clock time. After she did this, she was able to recognize, remember, and report to MHE the source and triggers for the amnesiac episodes. She had witnessed the death of her father by heart failure at three years old when he was bending down to kiss her, and she had been tied and raped by a man named Eric Borden (who had gray hair and a mustache and used a cane) for three days and bore a stillborn child as a result of that rape. There were other traumas and any reminders of them had been enough to trigger an episode of amnesia. After recalling and discussing all the traumas, she only had a few more relatively brief amnesiac episodes, but functioned well at social, personal, and business levels.

Presenting Problem: Amnesia; disorientation in time; loss of identity

Age Group: Adult

Modality: Individual; inpatient and outpatient

Problem Duration: Eight years

Treatment Length: At least three months

Result: Partial success. She was able to shorten the periods of amnesia and regression.

Follow-up: Two years

Techniques: Hypnosis; time distortion

Sources: *Collected Papers II*, pp. 272–278; *Collected Papers IV*, pp. 79–80

Case #207

Case Summary: A doctoral student in psychology sought MHE's help after forgetting the identity of a gift she had given to the man she intended to marry. It had been about 10 months since she had given him the gift and she had been trying for two weeks to remember. MHE tried various means of

helping her remember, such as free association, direct questioning while she was in hypnosis, and a posthypnotic suggestion to spontaneously say the name of the forgotten object. All of these failed to induce the memory. Next automatic handwriting was used, which initially did not produce anything definitive.

Then MHE suggested that, in addition to her having a conscious mind and a subconscious, she could develop a third level of consciousness that would write the information. She wrote, "The painted cigarette box on the table," in a jagged manner. She complained of feeling funny while she wrote it, but it gave her no clue as to the identity of the gift. MHE then had her see a crystal ball while in hypnosis. She was able to see herself going into a store and buying something but her view of the object was always blocked.

She was then instructed to have a dream that night in which she would realize the identity of the gift but not know it verbally. When she woke up in the morning she was to remember the dream and the object. Instead she woke up during the night having remembered the object in her dream but then forgot it when she awoke the next morning. Instead she remembered that she had a letter in her possession that identified the gift.

She located the letter and finally remembered that she had given her man friend a box of paints. It turned out that she had met a man during the past month to whom she was greatly attracted, but who was the opposite of the man she was planning to marry. The man she was attracted to possessed a painted cigarette box that reminded her of the box of paints. This came to symbolize the conflict she felt about which man to choose.

Even after she found the letter, she would still forget the dream and the identity of the gift. She also found that she had a writing block when she sat down to write the man she intended to marry. Once she understood the connection, she was able to write the letter and commit herself to the long-time man friend.

Presenting Problem: Specific amnesia (forgetting the identity of a gift)

Age Group: Adult

Modality: Individual; outpatient

Problem Duration: Two months

Treatment Length: NA

Result: Success. The woman remembered the identity of the gift.

Follow-up: NA

Techniques: Free association; hypnosis; posthypnotic suggestion; automatic handwriting

Source: *Collected Papers III*, pp. 38–44

Case #208

꿈

Case Summary: A woman had no memory of her father. Her mother would only tell her that she had divorced the father when the child was less than one year old, that she had lost contact with him and had severed her ties to her friends and family at the time. The woman was now a 20-year-old student nurse. Since age 18, she had made a determined effort to find out about her father, an effort her mother discouraged. She had sought hypnosis from several psychiatrists who used hypnosis, but had always dismissed their efforts as futile because she was certain that they would lead her to fabricate memories.

When she sought MHE's help, he refused to treat her, but invited her to learn hypnosis as an experimental subject. She quickly became proficient in hypnosis, but refused all direct and indirect efforts to secure an age regression. MHE oriented her to the future and had her report events of the next two months as if they were memories. He then told her that she had probably forgotten a task he had given her. She had remembered various memories of her father when she was an infant. She was to now, still in her future projection, describe those memories and how she discovered them.

She told him that she had seen a series of crystal balls with her being progressively younger in each. She reported remembering a long-forgotten incident when she was six which resulted in a scar on the back of her knee. Then she reported seeing her father as he was holding her in his arms. He was tall, had a funny-looking front tooth, curly yellowish hair and blue eyes.

When the woman told her mother of the details, her mother became frightened that she had found the father. Reassured that they were hypnotically retrieved memories, the mother gave the daughter all the details she knew about the father and then asked the daughter to drop the subject for good. The daughter, with her curiosity now satisfied, complied.

Presenting Problem: No memory of father

Age Group: Adult

Modality: Individual; outpatient

Problem Duration: Two years

Treatment Length: NA

Result: Success. The woman remembered her father and got her mother to tell her about the father.

Follow-up: NA

Techniques: Hypnosis; age progression; positive hallucination; paradoxical intervention

Source: *Collected Papers IV*, pp. 407–410

Case #209

Case Summary: A psychiatrist who was blind sought hypnosis from MHE to help her recover some early visual memories from a time when she could still see. MHE hypnotized her and worked on deepening trance and hand/arm levitation, but the woman never recovered the memories. She did report that she was walking more easily after the session, however.

Presenting Problem: Desire to recall early memories

Age Group: Adult

Modality: Individual; outpatient

Problem Duration: NA

Treatment Length: One session

Result: Failure. The woman failed to recover the memories she sought.

Follow-up: NA

Techniques: Hypnosis; hand levitation

Source: *Experiencing Hypnosis*, pp. 64–108

Case #210

INDECISION

Case Summary: A doctor who worked at the same hospital as MHE had suddenly become very neurotic. She lost weight, developed an ulcer, and only felt comfortable in the company of patients. She approached MHE one day and told him she had an issue she needed to resolve and wanted him to come to her apartment at his convenience to hypnotize her. She gave him a set of explicit and detailed instructions for what to tell her to do in trance. When MHE talked to her on subsequent days, it became apparent that she had forgotten her request. When MHE showed up at her apartment several days after the initial request, she seemed surprised to see him, but was gracious. She complained about her recent insomnia and MHE seized upon that as an opening for using hypnosis. She assented and went into trance on her couch.

MHE left for 30 minutes to allow her to go deeply into trance. When he returned he told her the things she had told him to tell her to do in trance. She then told him that it was something she had to work out by herself and that he was to leave and return in an hour. When he returned, she told him she was almost done and to leave again and return in 30 minutes. When he returned she told him that she had solved her dilemma and that he should instruct her to remember the answer after she aroused from trance.

She showed evidence of forgetting that she had been in trance and seemed anxious for MHE to leave after she came out of trance. As he was leaving he told her that it was all right for her to know the answer. She suddenly grew agitated and told him that she had just realized something and that he should leave so she could be alone to think it through. Again she showed evidence of having forgotten the incident in subsequent days.

A month afterwards she showed MHE an engagement ring. She had surprised a number of her friends and colleagues by her marital choice. The man in question had been known to be interested in her, but she hadn't shown the same interest in him. They were rather different in their styles and social bearing. They were subsequently married and moved to a different city.

Three months later the woman came back to visit MHE, having just remembered the trance from four months before. She told MHE the whole story of how she had been undecided about marrying John and how in trance she had examined a long manuscript filled with two columns of pros and cons for marrying him. When the pro column won, she knew she had decided and had since been very happy in her decision and her marriage.

In 1956, after MHE had done a lecture at Boston State Hospital, a gray-haired woman approached him and asked MHE if he remembered her. When he didn't, she told him he should because he had published a paper on her. She told him that she was a grandmother and happily married to the man she had decided to marry while in that trance in 1930.

Presenting Problem: Indecision

Age Group: Adult

Modality: Individual; outpatient

Problem Duration: (Months)

Treatment Length: One session; two hours

Result: Success. The woman made a decision that she was happy with and it worked out.

Follow-up: 26 years. The woman reported that she was still happy with her decision.

Technique: Hypnosis

Sources: *Collected Papers III*, pp. 207–213; *Phoenix*, pp. 22–24; *Teaching Seminar*, pp. 153–157

Case #211

Case Summary: A college student who had been a frequent hypnotic subject for MHE's experiments and demonstrations sought his help for determining whether or not to marry her fiancé and to figure out how to be happy in that marriage if she went through with it. She gave MHE clear instructions to induce a deep trance and to tell her to plan how she was to think it through and then do so in trance. She did this all silently and with some show of emotion, occasionally talking quietly with herself out of MHE's hearing. He guided her through the process until she appeared to have made some decisions. She told him to awaken her and then to take a slightly negative attitude towards the marriage. If MHE had the negative attitude, she could have a positive one and set out to prove him wrong. He was to take that negative attitude for the next two years and then to drop it. He did so and through letters and news from mutual friends determined that the couple were well adjusted in their marriage.

Presenting Problem: Concern about impending marriage

Age Group: Adult

Modality: Individual; outpatient

Problem Duration: NA

Treatment Length: One session, two hours

Result: Success. The woman thought through the situation, got married and adjusted well.

Follow-up: Five years brought letters and reports of a satisfactory marriage.

Techniques: Hypnosis

Source: *Collected Papers III*, pp. 213–215

Case #212

$\backsim$

Case Summary: A young couple who had already had four children were trying to decide whether he would get a vasectomy or she would get a hysterectomy as a means to prevent more pregnancy. They disagreed on which procedure would be best. MHE had them go into trance and project themselves into the future after such a procedure had been done. Both revealed that if the other had the operation, they would consider that other a "surgical cripple," somehow defective. When they came out of trance with no recollection of these revelations, MHE gently steered them towards the idea, but they only laughed at the absurdity of it and dismissed it. They decided that the man would get a vasectomy. Two years later they returned very angry at MHE, insisting that he should have been more forceful in preventing them from deciding on surgery. He insisted that they had been free citizens who could make their own decisions and he had done all he could at the time.

Presenting Problem: Indecision about operation for birth control

Age Group: Adult

Modality: Couple; outpatient

Problem Duration: NA

Treatment Length: NA

Result: Failure. The couple decided to get a vasectomy, but later regretted the decision.

Follow-up: Two years

Techniques: Hypnosis; future projection

Source: *Life Reframing*, pp. 198–199

Case #213

Case Summary: A woman who had 11 miscarriages was advised to get a hysterectomy. She came to see MHE for hypnosis to help her decide whether or not to get the operation. MHE had her go into trance and project into the future after she had undergone a hysterectomy. She described how depressed she had been since the hysterectomy and thought that if the depression continued for much longer she would commit suicide. MHE brought her out of trance and asked her to remember the important parts of trance. She decided that she had found a new faith in her body, so she was not going to get a hysterectomy. She went on to have five children.

Presenting Problem: Indecision about getting a hysterectomy

Age Group: Adult

Modality: Individual; outpatient

Problem Duration: NA

Treatment Length: NA

Result: Success. The woman decided not to have a hysterectomy and had five successful pregnancies after having had only miscarriages previously.

Follow-up: At least six years.

Techniques: Hypnosis; future projection; posthypnotic suggestion; splitting (remember the important parts of trance)

Source: *Life Reframing*, p. 199

Case #214

7

Marital, Family, and Relationship Problems

FAMILY PROBLEMS

Case Summary: A woman couldn't stand her in-laws visiting three or four times a week. She developed a stomach ulcer. MHE suggested that when the in-laws came to visit, she should become ill: "They certainly can't expect *you* to mop up the floor if you vomit when they come." Each time the in-laws were coming the woman would drink a glass of milk, chat for a while, and then vomit. The in-laws got tired of mopping the floor and eventually stopped coming to visit. The woman's ulcer stopped bothering her. After a few months of not seeing the in-laws, the woman began inviting them *for the afternoon.* When she wanted them to leave she would begin to look ill.

Presenting Problem: Ulcers; problem with in-laws

Age Group: Adult

Modality: Individual; outpatient

Problem Duration: NA

Treatment Length: NA

Result: Success. The woman's ulcer improved and she learned how to control her in-laws' visits.

Follow-up: NA

Techniques: Task assignment (behavioral); utilization (of symptom); symptom prescription

Sources: *Conversations I*, pp. 45–46; *Uncommon Therapy*, p. 153

Case #215

Case Summary: A family came to MHE for therapy. The father found it difficult to agree or disagree with the wife. The wife tended to qualify everything she said in a contradictory way. They had three sons, ages 23, 19, and 17. They had three goals for therapy: first, to get the oldest boy out of the home; second, to get the 19-year-old living on his own; third, to have the 17-year-old move in with the 23-year-old and go to school. Because the mother was the most powerful member of the family and couldn't help voicing opinions, MHE asked her to sit with her mouth shut and her thumbs close together while each family member talked. MHE instructed her to listen carefully so that she could respond to everything that was said when her turn came.

The father was an artist. MHE believed that the man's wife prevented him from painting the things he wanted to paint, causing the man to frequently change mediums. During the approaching summer the father had a teaching job that would require him to live away from home. The father was concerned that if the boys moved out the wife would be very lonely. The mother felt that MHE did not understand her. Each time she made this claim, MHE emphasized the idea that as long as her youngest son was at home, she would have the opportunity to understand that son. When the wife said that MHE did seem to understand her in some regard, MHE mentioned the possibility of the 17-year-old living with his brother. In order to help the mother cope with her sons' moving out and her husband being away, MHE told the mother that she was making the transition from good mother and wife of the past to good grandmother of the future. At the end of three sessions the sons moved out and the husband took the job.

Presenting Problem: Family problems (domination by mother, adult children living at home)

Age Group: Adult/adolescent

Modality: Family; outpatient

Problem Duration: NA

Treatment Length: Three sessions

Result: Success. The sons and husband became more independent and the mother adjusted well to the transition.

Follow-up: NA

Techniques: Linking (mother talk of being understood or misunderstood with talk of the son moving out); redirecting attention (to being a good grandmother from being a good mother)

Sources: *Conversations III*, pp. 23–32; *Uncommon Therapy*, pp. 243–244; pp. 283–284 [This may be two cases condensed into one.]

Case #216

Case Summary: A husband and wife came to MHE with their adolescent. She was their youngest child. Their other children had already left home. They were having a difficult time with the girl. MHE had each tell his/her side of the story while the others kept quiet. After each one had taken a turn, MHE told the girl to take 10 minutes to decide what she would like to say to her parents and in what order she would say it. "At the end of the 10 minutes you'll know what you're going to do and how you're going to do things in the next 10 minutes." After 10 minutes passed she said there was no point in repeating herself because her parents didn't listen. MHE sent the girl out of the office. Then he gave the parents five minutes to decide how they would handle the next five minutes. At the end of five minutes they essentially stated that they'd said a lot of stupid things and had been treating each other with very little respect. MHE decided that they all knew what to do. MHE only saw the family once but later heard that the girl was doing well from another source.

Presenting Problem: Difficulties with adolescent daughter

Age Group: Adult/adolescent

Modality: Family; outpatient

Problem Duration: NA

Treatment Length: One session

Result: Success. The family members realized that they had been treating each other disrespectfully and their relationships approved.

Follow-up: NA

Techniques: Indirect suggestion; task assignment (behavioral); pattern intervention

Source: *Uncommon Therapy*, pp. 273–274

Case #217

Case Summary: A physician asked MHE to see his son. The boy was in high school and had become an ever-increasing management problem. His parents were extremely generous and indulgent with him. He became increasingly demanding and selfish. When the three of them came in, MHE told the boy to sit down and keep his mouth shut. He asked the parents to tell him all the horrible things about their son. When they were done MHE asked the son if their story was accurate. He said, "Hell, no, they left out a lot of stuff because they're too ashamed to tell about it." The boy told MHE more of the horrible things he did. He said that when he did these things his father gave him some money and his mother cried.

MHE told the boy what terms he demanded for the boy's therapy. The boy was to live in a hotel with a fixed budget while his parents went on vacation. The boy would see MHE each day. While the parents were gone the boy read respectable books, got a job, and moved into an apartment with some hard-working friends.

Three days before his parents came home the boy said, "The hell with it." He said he wouldn't see MHE and quit his job. When the parents arrived he greeted them with a four-letter word and became quite stubborn and rebellious. The boy went home with his parents, promising to change. He never changed and eventually he ended up in a psychiatric hospital. From the hospital he called MHE and asked him to take him as a patient. He never showed up for a session. MHE believed the young man would probably end up in prison or a similar institution.

Presenting Problem: Unmanageable adolescent

Age Group: Adult/adolescent

Modality: Family/individual; outpatient

Problem Duration: NA

Treatment Length: (Two weeks)

Result: Failure. The boy's behavior did not improve.

Follow-up: The parents began to be less indulgent with their other children.

Techniques: Task assignment (behavioral); pattern intervention

Source: *Uncommon Therapy*, pp. 274–277

Case #218

ॐ

Case Summary: The parents of a boy named Jimmy complained to MHE about the amount of dawdling the boy did over breakfast and in putting on his socks in the morning. Despite their exhortations to hurry, he typically took two hours to do either task. MHE recommended that the parents spend a week emphasizing that Jimmy was a boy who liked to eat slowly. At the end of that week, on Sunday, the parents were to cook the boy small pancakes one at a time beginning with 15-minute intervals between each, touting it as the perfect solution for someone who liked to eat slowly but preferred his pancakes hot. They were to keep increasing the interval, until the boy was yelling at them to hurry. It took Jimmy less than a week to consistently beat everyone in his family at finishing his breakfast.

Jimmy was invited to a party. On the day of the party, MHE suggested, Jimmy's mother should lay out some socks with holes in them. Jimmy took two hours putting them on. Just before the party, Jimmy's mother insisted that he change into new socks without holes in them. She insisted that Jimmy spend two hours putting them on, as usual. Jimmy pleaded and begged to be allowed to put them on faster, because he did not want to miss the party. She remained firm, telling him that she believed he enjoyed dressing slowly that morning and she still believed it now. Tomorrow, he might tell her something different and she might believe him, she said. The next day, Jimmy told his mother he liked to dress fast, but she insisted he did not have to.

Presenting Problem: Dawdling over breakfast and dressing

Age Group: Child

Modality: Family; outpatient

Problem Duration: NA

Treatment Length: NA

Result: Success. Jimmy started to eat and dress more rapidly.

Follow-up: NA

Techniques: Interpersonal evocation (of wanting to eat and dress faster); symptom prescription

Source: "Double Binds"

Case #219

Case Summary: A father and son came to MHE for therapy. The young man had managed to utterly fail at everything he did, despite his obvious intelligence. MHE complimented him on his ability to always get the lowest possible grade, to be kicked out the naval academy after acing the entrance exam, and on his other feats. MHE told the young man that to do as poorly as he had must have taken great skill and judgment. The boy looked pleased with MHE's assessment of him.

Then MHE told him that he was not going to like the rest of what he was going to hear. It was going to make him very angry, but he would know it was true. MHE began to berate the young man's fiancée as a cheap whore. The man became furious and threatened to strike MHE. "You mean that if I call that tart you call your fiancée a whore, you will really clobber me?" The young man burst into tears and ran out of the office. "Now you've done it," said the father. The father thought the boy would go home and never return for therapy. The boy did go home, but while he was there he broke off his engagement and then returned for therapy.

Presenting Problem: Acting out

Age Group: Adult

Modality: Family; outpatient

Problem Duration: Seven-eight years

Treatment Length: NA

Result: Partial success. The boy recognized that he had a problem and resolved to work on it.

Follow-up: NA

Techniques: Reframing; interpersonal evocation (of anger and shame)

Source: *Conversations III*, pp. 112–116

Case #220

PARENTAL DOMINATION/SEPARATION

Case Summary: A couple in their early twenties who were both attending college came to see MHE because they were distraught over having to have an abortion for the woman. She had gotten pregnant out of wedlock and the couple's parents were pressuring them by saying they would deny further financial support if she did not have an abortion. MHE gathered the impression that they were being bullied by the parents and that they were both rather obsessive-compulsive types. He told them he would help them by telling them the thing they must not think about because if they did it would prevent them from following through with the abortion plan. They were not, under any circumstances, to think of a name for the baby. They went away and returned several days later to tell MHE that they had decided not to get an abortion and had convinced their parents to support them in their decision to get married. After MHE's instruction they had thought of all sorts of names for the baby and each one had made the baby seem more precious to them.

Presenting Problem: Upset over an impending abortion

Age Group: Adult

Modality: Couple; outpatient

Problem Duration: NA

Treatment Length: One session

Result: Success. The couple resolved their upset and decided to have the baby and get married.

Follow-up: The couple both graduated from college with the help and support of both sets of parents. They had several more children.

Techniques: Implication (if they thought of a name for the baby, they wouldn't be able to go through with the abortion); utilization (of their obsessive-compulsive tendencies)

Sources: *Collected Papers IV*, pp. 370–373; *Hypnotherapy*, pp. 360–363

Case #221

Case Summary: A woman who was seeing MHE had become blocked in therapy. She wanted to move out of her parents' house, but couldn't bring herself to make the move. She wanted to go into a library she passed every day but never did. She wanted a better social life but passed up social opportunities. She complained about her job situation but refused to accept a promotion that was available to her. She had the sense that, if she could do even one of these things, she could accomplish all the rest. She demanded that MHE compel her to do these things.

She was a good hypnotic subject, so MHE put her in trance and had her imagine past and then future scenes in imaginary crystal balls. MHE suggested that she see herself in a pleasant scene in the future. She saw herself at a wedding she was to attend three months hence. She was dressed beautifully and danced with several men, one of whom asked her for a date. She was given amnesia for the trance experience. She returned for two more sessions before the wedding occurred and each time she asked MHE to put her in trance and she reviewed the wedding scene again each time. She had amnesia for both experiences. Then she suddenly stopped therapy, upon which she had been very dependent. She returned to see MHE several days after the wedding and described how busy and happy she had been in the months before the wedding. She had done as she had seen in the crystal ball and had been asked for a date by one of her dance partners. She decided that she no longer needed therapy. She eventually married and had three children.

Presenting Problem: Poor social and occupational adjustment; unhappiness

Age Group: Adult

Modality: Individual; outpatient

Problem Duration: NA

Treatment Length: NA

Result: Success. She moved out of her parents' house, got married and made a better adjustment.

Follow-up: At least three years. MHE mentions that she was married and had three children and was seen on an occasional basis through the years.

Techniques: Hypnosis; future projection; amnesia

Source: *Collected Papers IV*, pp. 410–412

Case #222

Case Summary: A physician who was dominated by his mother had failed to benefit from 600 hours of analytic therapy by prominent analysts and was brought to MHE for treatment. He suffered from obsessions, doubts, fears, and compulsions. Even though he was married, his mother still dominated his life. For instance, she had told the newly married couple that they were to honeymoon in their new home, located right next to the doctor's parents' home. Mother selected her son's clothes, cooked his meals for him in his home, and generally told him what to do and what not to do in life. Mother was anti-alcohol and very religious. MHE found out that Mother had accompanied her son to the previous therapy appointments. MHE immediately told the mother that, as a punishment for his recalcitrance, his wife should now accompany him to the office visits. Mother agreed. When the wife came, MHE told her that together they would dethrone the mother from the man's life. The wife agreed. MHE found that the man would not accept suggestions in therapy or in trance, so he told him that the suggestions would not become effective until a later time.

At the specified time, 10 a.m. on a Sunday morning, Mother came as usual to collect her son and daughter-in-law for church. Son was in the kitchen with a half-empty bottle of liquor and was drunk (as MHE had suggested in trance). He told his mother to get her fucking ass to church without him and promptly drank six ounces of liquor straight. He staggered around singing bawdy songs and then passed out. His wife and mother carried him to bed. His mother was so upset and shocked that she went home and missed church for the first time in her life.

When Mother came over to cook breakfast the next day, her son swore at her and told her he was waiting for her so he could have another drink of whiskey. He then pretended to have some liquor (which was actually tea) and staggered off to bed singing about getting drunker by the day. His mother again went home and went to bed upset. The wife cooked her husband all his meals and they and the children all enjoyed it.

The next day the mother burst in and tried to dump out all the liquor in the house and give the couple a lecture, but the man had hidden a flask and drained it before his mother had a chance to stop him. He then shouted obscenities at her and told her to leave his house. Mother stayed away for three months, during which time the man continued to see MHE and to realize how dominated he had been. MHE instructed him to move to a new house when his parents were away on a trip. When the parents came back, he would not tell them where he was living and said that if his mother tried to find out, she would never see her grandchildren again.

After a year, the man restored relations with his parents, but when his mother started to tell him what to put on his plate during Thanksgiving dinner, he took his family and went home. At Christmas dinner, his mother behaved herself for fear that they would leave again. The son tested the mother some time later by offering her a drink of whiskey, which she politely refused, but then sat in silence as the man and his wife each had a drink.

Presenting Problem: Fears; obsessions; compulsions; dominated by mother

Age Group: Adult

Modality: Individual/marital; outpatient

Problem Duration: At least 15 years

Treatment Length: Less than 20 hours

Result: Success. The man broke free of his mother's domination and became free of his fears, obsessions and compulsions. He started to participate in professional activities, eventually rising to prominence in his specialty.

Follow-up: NA

Techniques: Hypnosis; posthypnotic suggestion; task assignment (behavioral)

Source: *Collected Papers IV*, pp. 476–481

Case #223

Case Summary: A young man with asthma lived at home with his mother, who took care of him. MHE judged the mother and the asthma to be unchangeable parts of the man's life. MHE persuaded the young man to take a job at a bank, although the young man had no interest in banking. As time passed, the sessions become less frequent. At each of the sessions MHE asked the young man about a detail of banking which he proceeded to answer with great pleasure. MHE asked him questions about mistakes he had made at work, focusing on how the mistakes were corrected rather than how they were made. The young man came to regard the banking job as a wonderful temporary job to help him make money for college. Gradually he became very enthusiastic about his future. MHE pointed out this change to him. Then MHE asked the young man what he expected about his asthma attacks in the future. "They're damned nuisances," the young man replied.

Presenting Problem: Dependence on mother

Age Group: Adult

Modality: Individual; outpatient

Problem Duration: (Several years)

Treatment Length: (A few months)

Result: Success. The young man became more independent. He started going to school and working at a bank.

Follow-up: NA

Techniques: Reframing; task assignment (behavioral); redirecting attention (on job and on how he corrected mistakes)

Sources: *Conversations I*, pp. 83–83; *Uncommon Therapy*, pp. 66–67

Case #224

Case Summary: Pietro was a 20-year-old man of Italian ancestry who had come to the U.S. with his family when he was four. His father had decided that Pietro would be a famous flute player. He made Pietro practice every day and oriented every aspect of his childhood towards mastering the flute. Pietro came to MHE because his lower lip was extremely swollen and he was unable to practice the flute. His father still determined when he would practice, what exercises he would do, what pieces he would play and how long he would practice each part. One of the father's favorite boasts was that nobody gave him "any lip." He was the absolute master of the family.

When the son came to see MHE he would spend the session raging at MHE. MHE would respond only with casual remarks. Then he hypnotized the man and told him that he needed to unburden himself and free associate. At the end of each session the man would ask when his next appointment would be. MHE would say, "I am recording the hour and day. Be here on time." The man would always return as scheduled. MHE insured this by throwing out remarks like "My birthday is in December," "It's not one o'clock," and "I have five fingers." The man would then show up at one o'clock on December 5th.

The man kept returning for his appointments and berating MHE's ancestors, until one day he declared, "But you're not my father." Three months later his lip was in normal condition. He got a job as first flutist in the Detroit Symphony and then as a flutist in the New York Symphony with private teaching privileges.

Presenting Problem: Swollen lip

Age Group: Adult

Modality: Individual; outpatient

Problem Duration: Three years

Treatment Length: (One year)

Result: Success. The swollen lip became normal and the young man was able to continue his career as flutist.

Follow-up: NA

Techniques: Utilization (of hostility towards father); implication; ambiguity

Sources: *Conversations I,* pp. 91–95; *Hypnotherapy,* pp. 240–246

Case #225

Case Summary: A family came to MHE for therapy. Their only daughter was about to start college. The parents decided that she would live at home and be taken care of. Because they realized that she was likely to fall in love, they were going to build an addition onto the house where she and her husband might live. The daughter was not happy with this plan. MHE spoke to the parents about what might occur after the daughter's marriage: she would become pregnant, deliver a baby, the baby would cry, the baby would learn to walk. MHE told the mother that he suspected her husband would be an overly solicitous grandfather. To the father he said that the wife would probably be an overly solicitous grandmother. The parents both believed their spouse should be kept away from the grandchild. They agreed that when their daughter married she should live away from home. When the daughter had a child, they consulted MHE about how frequently they should visit. He said they should visit no more frequently than one afternoon every six weeks to two months. This arrangement was satisfactory to everyone involved.

Presenting Problem: Family problems (excessive control by parents)

Age Group: Adult

Modality: Family; outpatient

Problem Duration: Several months

Treatment Length: NA

Result: Success. Daughter was able to gain independence and create a satisfactory arrangement with her parents.

Follow-up: NA

Techniques: Age progression; direct suggestion; utilization (of criticalness and controlling)

Sources: *Conversations III*, pp. 42–43; *Uncommon Therapy*, pp. 280–282

Case #226

Case Summary: A college student wrote to MHE. She said that her mother had been dominated by her mother and so had resolved not to dominate her children. As a result she was the girl's best friend, and had been all her life. The girl found that when she went away to college (a Catholic University) she would gain 20 lbs. during the year and then lose 50 when she went home. She wondered why that might be. MHE put the woman in trance. He learned that she had always broken off relationships with boys because they gave her "funny feelings" she couldn't describe. Then he told her that her mother had dominated her in a way that was the opposite of what her grandmother had done. The next time she went home she only lost 18 lbs. MHE told the woman that she was the kind of woman who was the easiest to seduce. He explained to her just how he would do it and she agreed that he was right.

Then he addressed the problem of her weight. He asked her to give him a picture of her in her bikini for Christmas. She brought it to him but was very ashamed because she had been 28 lbs. overweight when the picture was taken. MHE said he didn't want the picture. A year later her weight was normal and she had a steady boyfriend. She decided to quit her job teaching at a Catholic school and to get a job at a public school. MHE also worked with her on test anxiety during one session which Jeffrey Zeig, a student of MHE's, observed. He used hypnosis and told her stories which suggested that, if she were relaxed, she would do better taking the tests.

Presenting Problem: Weight fluctuations; test anxiety

Age Group: Adult

Modality: Individual; outpatient

Problem Duration: NA

Treatment Length: NA

Result: Success. The girl's weight returned to normal.

Follow-up: NA

Techniques: Reframing; task assignment (behavioral); hypnosis; metaphor

Sources: *Experiencing Erickson*, p. 87; *My Voice Will Go With You*, pp. 145–148

Case #227

Case Summary: In 1959, a man sought therapy from MHE because his wife had demanded that he kick his mother out of their home or she would leave him. His mother was very domineering and she had lived with the couple for the five years of their marriage, running the household. The man could not bear to kick his mother out but did not want to lose his wife. MHE had him go into trance and project into the year 1965 and relate to MHE how he had finally gotten his mother to leave and how she had adjusted since that time. He gave a description of how his mother's life and his and his wife's lives had all changed for the better since she had moved out. MHE brought him out of the trance with amnesia for the projection experience and sent him home to discuss the matter with his wife and mother. During those discussions, his mother decided on her own to move out. After that, the man and his wife had three children, although they had previously thought they did not want children.

Presenting Problem: Domineering mother living with married couple; inability to ask mother to move

Age Group: Adult

Modality: Individual; outpatient

Problem Duration: Five years

Treatment Length: NA

Result: Success. The man's mother moved out.

Follow-up: At least four years. The couple had three children after the mother moved out.

Techniques: Hypnosis; future projection; amnesia

Source: *Life Reframing*, pp. 197–198

Case #228

Case Summary: A man named Ralph had attended medical school with MHE. Ralph quit his practice because he was "too neurotic." He came to MHE for help. Ralph gave MHE a long list of his problems: his mother dominated him; he wet his pants; he couldn't stand being waited on by women in restaurants; he couldn't make decisions; and he couldn't play the cello in front of anyone, including his family. MHE saw the man's wife and daughter and they corroborated his story. The daughter particularly complained of the absence of affection and celebration of holidays in their family.

The first thing MHE did was to eliminate the urinating problem. The man had told MHE that as a child he had been made to dig huge bushels of dandelions for very little pay. MHE told the man to put on some old pants and to dig dandelions from 8 a.m. to 6 p.m. without leaving the lawn. During that time he was to drink two gallons of lemonade and to urinate on himself. MHE knew that the man would have to converse with passersby as he sat there in his wet pants. One day of dandelion-digging cured his urination problems.

MHE worked on the man's problems with women and making choices at the same time. He took the man shopping and had a pretty sales girl model underwear for him. He was then forced to make choices about what he would purchase. He made his choices regardless of size. MHE and the man went out to dinner, along with their wives. MHE had coached their waitress to make sure that the man considered all the choices carefully before making a decision.

MHE had Ralph learn to dance and he became very active in square dancing. He even tried calling a few dances. Ralph also was able to give a cello concert for his family.

MHE had Ralph sit out on his lawn with a couple of whiskey bottles, one empty and one half-full. He told his wife to put some rouge on Ralph's nose and cheeks. Ralph was to wear a straw hat and recline with his eyes half-closed and a cigarette dangling out of his mouth. Then his wife should take a picture of him and send it to his mother. After receiving the picture, his mother, who disapproved of drinking and smoking, stopped communicating with him.

The final phase of therapy came at Christmas time. The family had never celebrated Christmas so MHE had Ralph's wife get a tree and presents for everyone. On Christmas Day MHE instructed the family on the proper way to hand out presents: the person giving the present must say "Merry Christmas" and must kiss the receiver of the gift. After a couple tries Ralph mastered this behavior, to his daughter's delight.

A few months later Ralph came to MHE and said that he'd had a pain in his bladder for two months. MHE reprimanded him for not coming in sooner and said that he suspected malignant tumor in the pituitary. MHE's diagnosis was correct and Ralph died two years later.

Presenting Problem: Enuresis; control by mother; fear of females; inability to make decisions

Age Group: Adult

Modality: Individual/family; outpatient

Problem Duration: NA

Treatment Length: NA

Result: Success. Ralph learned to control his bladder and stopped being controlled by his mother. He also learned to interact with females and improved his relationship with his family.

Follow-up: NA

Techniques: Ordeal; task assignment (behavioral and cognitive)

Source: *Teaching Seminar*, pp. 269–281

Case #229

MARITAL PROBLEMS

Case Summary: Henry, a 28-year-old man, was convinced that he did not love his wife and that he had only married her because she resembled his mother, to whom he was strongly attached. In trance he discovered that he also had a strong hatred for his mother, but he wasn't willing to know about this consciously, as it would disrupt his relationships too much. In trance, MHE helped the man forget anything about his wife and mother, except the knowledge that he must have had a mother. Then he had the man see a strange woman sitting in a chair across from him and have the strong sense that the woman's name was Nelly (his mother's name). Henry had frank discussions with Nelly and was able to objectively review her life and her understandings. There followed in subsequent hypnotic sessions similarly frank and objective discussions with two other hallucinated figures, one of Henry and one of his wife, Madge. The real Henry had no recognition of who these people were, due to the induced amnesia. Next, MHE had Henry see those three people in various combinations and in relation to various traumatic experiences from Henry's history. Gradually MHE led Henry into discovering that the people were his mother, his wife, and himself. He realized that his mother was messed up but deserving of a normal amount of respect and affection. He also realized that he loved his wife and that she was different in some ways from his mother. He gradually changed from a critical, compulsive person to a more relaxed, happy man.

Presenting Problem: Thinking he didn't love his wife

Age Group: Adult

Modality: Individual; outpatient

Problem Duration: NA

Treatment Length: More than six months

Result: Success. The man was able to resolve his feelings and relationship with his wife and his mother.

Follow-up: NA

Techniques: Hypnosis; amnesia; positive hallucination

Source: *Collected Papers IV*, pp. 41–47

Case #230

Case Summary: A couple sought therapy from MHE. Each had been previously unhappily married and divorced. They had decided that in their marriage they would share everything. They attended the same movies, even though their tastes were disparate. They always ate the same thing. They went to bed at the same time. When one went to the toilet, the other did the same. MHE recommended that they each attend the type of movie they enjoyed separately and meet together after the movie for dinner. They did not see this as "sharing," so they did not follow his recommendation. They eventually got divorced.

Presenting Problem: Marital problems

Age Group: Adult

Modality: Marital; outpatient

Problem Duration: NA

Treatment Length: (One session)

Result: Failure. The couple disagreed with MHE's advice and eventually got divorced.

Follow-up: NA

Techniques: Task assignment (behavioral)

Source: *Conversations II*, pp. 3–4

Case #231

Case Summary: A couple from out of town came to see MHE for therapy. He was angry because her mother visited excessively. She was mad because he had bought three sports cars in addition to each of their large cars, which had put them greatly into debt. MHE antagonized both of them by accusing the wife of slapping her husband across the face with that "damn mother" of hers, and accusing the husband of slapping his wife across the face with those "damn cars" of his. They stayed for their complete therapy, but went home allied in their anger at him and intent on proving him wrong. The husband sold three cars to pay off some of the debts, and the wife stopped having her mother visit so often. They started getting along very well.

Presenting Problem: Marital problems (angry at each other)

Age Group: Adult

Modality: Marital; outpatient

Problem Duration: NA

Treatment Length: (One or two sessions)

Result: Success. The couple were able to reach a few compromises and they began getting along very well.

Follow-up: The husband sent a letter telling MHE he was right, and the wife sent a similar message through a friend.

Techniques: Reframing; interpersonal evocation (of anger and motivation to prove MHE wrong by changing)

Source: *Conversations II*, pp. 24–25

Case #232

Case Summary: A couple came to MHE for therapy. They came from very different backgrounds. He was from a very proper New England family and she was from a laid-back farm family. The wife's resentment towards the husband manifested itself in their sexual relations. Rather than focusing on their sex life MHE decided to approach the problem from the point of the wife's dissatisfaction with the things her husband did for her. The husband would agree to take the wife out to dinner anywhere she wanted to go, but would end up making all her choices so that she never got what she wanted.

He chose the restaurant, what she would order, and how her food would be cooked. He would bring her flowers on the weekend, but they were never the kind she liked. The wife never objected because she thought he was trying to be sweet.

MHE gave the couple several assignments. First he had the two go out to dinner. The woman would read the directions that MHE had given her. They followed a circuitous path to a restaurant that MHE knew the woman liked. MHE had the woman switch menus with the husband and had her order her own food. The couple had a wonderful time. The next time the two went out they followed a circuitous route of their own invention and then chose the next nice restaurant that the wife saw.

Next, MHE instructed the man to go to a newsstand and get an old newspaper. He was to take the newspaper to a florist and tell him he was playing a joke on someone. The florist was to put an odd collection of flowers in the newspaper. The wife was delighted with them.

For their anniversary MHE told the man to go out and buy everything they would need for a camping trip, including the wife's clothes. He was to pick her up at 4 p.m. and tell her to put on the clothes and get in the car. The camping trip was a great success. On their way back the husband was supposed to get lost. They got lost and ended up spending the night in Yuma and having a great time. The couple soon became avid campers.

Presenting Problem: Marital problems

Age Group: Adult

Modality: Marital; outpatient

Problem Duration: NA

Treatment Length: NA

Result: Success. The couple learned new ways of interacting which led to a more harmonious marriage.

Follow-up: NA

Techniques: Pattern intervention; task assignment (behavioral)

Sources: *Conversations II*, pp. 33–43; *Uncommon Therapy*, pp. 230–233

Case #233

Case Summary: A husband and wife ran a restaurant together. The wife was angry because she wanted the husband to manage the restaurant while she stayed home. Instead she managed the place and he did a lot of the janitorial work. MHE asked the couple which one of them carried the keys. The wife said that they both did but that she always got there first. MHE told the husband that he must get to the restaurant one half-hour before the wife. In that half-hour the man could take responsibility for many things. As the husband assumed a managerial role the wife came into work later and later until she only came in when they were short of help.

Presenting Problem: Marital problems (due to disagreement about professional roles)

Age Group: Adult

Modality: Marital; outpatient

Problem Duration: NA

Treatment Length: NA

Result: Success. The couple changed the way they worked together and their marriage improved.

Follow-up: NA

Techniques: Pattern intervention; task assignment (behavioral)

Sources: *Conversations II*, pp. 44–46; *Uncommon Therapy*, pp. 225–226

Case #234

Case Summary: A husband and wife ran a restaurant together. Every day the wife would come to the restaurant and check up on the husband. This infuriated him. The woman wanted to stop dominating her husband. MHE gave her the task of reporting to her husband. She was to make a list of question comparable to those she asked him. After asking questions about him she was to tell him the answers to the questions about her. The woman got so sick of this that she quit checking up on him.

Presenting Problem: Marital problems

Age Group: Adult

Modality: Marital; outpatient

Problem Duration: NA

Treatment Length: NA

Result: Success. The wife quit checking up on the man's work and their relationship improved.

Follow-up: NA

Techniques: Task assignment (behavioral)

Sources: *Conversations II*, pp. 46–48; *Uncommon Therapy*, p. 224

Case #235

Case Summary: A husband and wife always quarreled about going to the movies. The husband would agree to go to a movie on a certain night and then he would schedule an appointment at that time. MHE suggested that the couple choose a night to go to a movie and let him know. The wife chose the movie and the night. The couple wanted an evening appointment. MHE called the husband and let him know which night was available. It turned out to be the night of the movie but the man thoughtlessly agreed. When the couple came for the appointment the wife was angry. The man said that MHE had played a dirty trick on him. The man asked MHE why he couldn't have given them an appointment on a different night. MHE said, "I could have but I didn't think of it." The man replied, "But you could have thought about it, and I could think about it too."

Presenting Problem: Marital problems

Age Group: Adult

Modality: Marital; outpatient

Problem Duration: NA

Treatment Length: NA

Result: (Success. The man realized that he had been unreasonable and presumably changed his behavior.)

Follow-up: NA

Techniques: Interpersonal evocation; matching

Source: *Conversations II*, pp. 77–78

Case #236

Case Summary: A couple came to MHE because they couldn't resolve an argument over the wife's mother. The two were planning to buy a new house, but they disagreed over whether or not her mother would live with them. The wife wanted the mother and the husband didn't. After hearing a description of the mother's rigidly patterned life, MHE told the couple to postpone their argument until they had purchased the house. The couple went out and purchased a house with an extra bedroom and a den that mother could use. Then they asked the mother if she wanted help packing. The mother said she didn't want to leave where she was and the argument was solved.

Presenting Problem: Marital problems (argument over where mother-in-law should live)

Age Group: Adult

Modality: Marital; outpatient

Problem Duration: A few months

Treatment Length: NA

Result: Success. The mother-in-law made her own decision about where she would live and the argument was solved.

Follow-up: NA

Technique: Utilization (of mother's rigidity); task assignment (behavioral)

Source: *Conversations II*, pp. 78–81

Case #237

Case Summary: A husband refused to compliment his wife. Although she was attractive and charming, he told her that there were many women more beautiful and charming than she. MHE demonstrated how the man might compliment her: he turned to the wife and said, "You know, unquestionably there are many women more beautiful than you, but not for me." The man said he wished he could have thought of it that way. The next day the man was just as "paranoid" against his wife. MHE believed that the wife was playing the role of slowing down the man's hallucinatory and delusional developments.

Presenting Problem: Marital problems (the husband refused to compliment the wife)

Age Group: Adult

Modality: Marital; outpatient

Problem Duration: NA

Treatment Length: NA

Result: Failure. The husband did not change his behavior.

Follow-up: NA

Technique: Direct suggestion

Source: *Conversations II*, pp. 106–109

Case #238

Case Summary: A man with a weak heart dominated his wife by constantly reminding her that he could die of a heart attack at any minute. MHE told the woman to scatter mortuary ads around the house. When the man mentioned his death she would bring up these ads. Sometimes she would add up his insurance policies. Sometimes she would suggest that they take a drive through a certain cemetery. Sometimes she would call up the building contractor in her husband's presence and ask him if he could finish the house before her husband died. These things infuriated him and he quit reminding her of his death. About a year and a half later the man called MHE to ask him how long he should stay in Florida. MHE told him that his children were grown and he had the money so he may as well stay till he stopped enjoying it.

Presenting Problem: Obsession with death; marital problems

Age Group: Adult

Modality: Individual/marital; outpatient

Problem Duration: NA

Treatment Length: NA

Result: Success. The man stopped reminding his wife of the possibility of his death and they began to enjoy themselves.

Follow-up: NA

Techniques: Task assignment (behavioral); ordeal

Sources: *Conversations II*, pp. 139–140; *Uncommon Therapy*, p. 178

Case #239

❧

Case Summary: A husband and wife came to MHE for therapy. Both believed the other to be completely unreasonable. The husband thought the wife couldn't stand to see him have any leisure time because she objected to his working on his car. It turned out that he had been fixing this car up for 12 years and that she'd never gotten a ride in it. MHE asked him if that "wasn't a bit too long to spend on a car?" The man said that it was not. When MHE saw the wife in a later session, she said she had come to realize that the husband was a decent provider although he didn't provide her with much pleasure. She decided to stop fighting him about that car and to start worrying about her own leisure time.

Presenting Problem: Marital problems

Age Group: Adult

Modality: Marital; outpatient

Problem Duration: 12 years

Treatment Length: NA

Result: Partial success. The man continued to spend an excessive amount of time and money fixing up his car, but the wife learned to ignore it.

Follow-up: NA

Techniques: NA

Source: *Conversations II*, pp. 140–142

Case #240

☙

Case Summary: A woman was in psychoanalysis for five years. Her husband brought her to MHE saying that he was sick of paying those bills when she wasn't getting any better. He told MHE that he didn't need any therapy and that he wasn't going to see him again. For the first seven sessions MHE made statements that were at odds with the husband's beliefs and told the woman he was certain the man would agree with these statements. The husband showed up at MHE's office for the next session and told MHE to shut up. The husband said he was going to dictate the therapy his wife should have.

MHE agreed and it turned out that the man suggested just what MHE had in mind. The husband and wife had been married for 17 years. Before their marriage her ambition had been to make a houseful of babies. But the husband had different plans. He told her that he didn't want to father any child that would have as hard a life as he had, so he had a vasectomy. She married him anyway and for 17 years they were unhappy together.

MHE told the couple if they wanted any therapy from him they would have to either separate or get a divorce. The husband said, "This is what we should have been told five years ago." They chose a voluntary separation, which Erickson helped to orchestrate. After six months of separation they were to reevaluate their relationship.

Presenting Problem: (Marital difficulties)

Age Group: Adult

Modality: Individual/marital; outpatient

Problem Duration: 17 years

Treatment Length: NA

Result: Partial success. MHE got the couple to try separating for six months, after which time they would reevaluate their relationship.

Follow-up: NA

Techniques: Interpersonal evocation (of husband coming to see MHE to correct him); task assignment (behavioral)

Sources: *Conversations II*, pp. 148–151; *Uncommon Therapy*, pp. 235–236

Case #241

Case Summary: A woman had been married 14 times. When she came to MHE she told him that there were certain things she didn't want to tell him and she didn't want him to pry. MHE said, "All right, I won't, but if you tell me spontaneously, don't accuse me of prying." At the end of the hour she said that she had no intention of telling him about her first two marriages but she had found that she felt she could tell him anything. Her husband didn't know that she had been married 14 times. They were having difficulties because she forged checks, had affairs, and wrecked his car in a fit of rage. MHE asked her if she was going to tell her husband about the other 13 marriages. She said no. MHE said, "Well that's your answer, stick to it." But she told her husband anyway. The husband asked with how many of her former husbands she had forged checks and committed adultery. She told him. Then he told her that he would stay married to her if she shaped up because he loved her. She shaped up.

Presenting Problem: (13 failed marriages)

Age Group: Adult

Modality: Individual; outpatient

Problem Duration: NA

Treatment Length: NA

Result: Success. The woman confessed to her husband about her previous marriages and stopped forging checks and having affairs.

Follow-up: NA

Techniques: Interpersonal evocation (of rebelliousness when MHE instructed the woman to stick with her decision not to reveal her past to her husband); implication (that the woman would spontaneously tell MHE the things she didn't want him to pry about)

Sources: *Conversations II*, pp. 168–169; *Uncommon Therapy*, p. 234

Case #242

Case Summary: A couple came from another city to see MHE for marital therapy. They had been married over 30 years and had quarreled every day of their married life. MHE suggested that they had had enough of quarreling and asked them if they wouldn't rather start enjoying life. They stopped quarreling.

Presenting Problem: Quarreling; marital problems

Age Group: Adult

Modality: Couple; outpatient

Problem Duration: NA

Treatment Length: NA

Result: Success. The couple stopped quarreling.

Follow-up: NA

Techniques: Redirecting attention; direct suggestion

Source: *My Voice Will Go With You,* p. 55

Case #243

Case Summary: A man and a woman, who were both raised in an extremely conservative Christian sect, got married. They were to have their honeymoon 142 miles away. When they got in the car to drive to the hotel the car heater immediately broke down. When they got to the hotel they were miserable and freezing. It took them until 11 a.m. the next morning to consummate the marriage, although they both were trying to convince themselves to do it throughout the night. They did not enjoy the sex, but the wife became pregnant. After eight months of marriage the two still had not learned how to make love to each other, so they decided the marriage had been a mistake. The man had come to see MHE because they had decided to get an amicable divorce after the baby's birth and he wanted to get divorced better than he had gotten married and wanted help doing it right. MHE told the man that after the wife's six-weeks' checkup he should get a babysitter for their child and take the wife out to a certain hotel for a candlelit dinner to discuss the divorce. He then gave the man step-by-step instructions on how to seduce his wife. The couple stayed married and had two more children.

Presenting Problem: Marital problems; sexual dissatisfaction; desire to get divorced

Age Group: Adult

Modality: Individual; outpatient

Problem Duration: Nine months

Treatment Length: One session

Result: Success. The couple improved their sex life and stayed married.

Follow-up: NA

Techniques: Task assignment (behavioral); direct suggestion

Source: *My Voice Will Go With You*, pp. 129–132

Case #244

Case Summary: A wife called MHE and asked him to make her husband quit smoking. When the husband came in it was clear to MHE that although the man professed to dislike the effects of smoking and how much it cost him, he did not want to quit. MHE sent him home. The wife sent him back and told him to tell MHE that he really did want to quit. Again, after interviewing the man, MHE sent him home because he was convinced that the man would not quit smoking. MHE got the man to let him call up the man's wife while her husband was sitting in MHE's office to hear MHE tell the wife that her husband was a born loser who would not stop smoking.

Next the wife came with the man to a session. MHE explained to the wife that using hypnosis he could give the man motivation to quit, but for the results to last he must want to quit. She told him to go ahead and give him the motivation to quit. MHE suggested that the man put the amount of money it was costing him to buy cigarettes in a jar each time he smoked. For three weeks the man did this and became very excited about using the money he had saved for a vacation. He had never been able to save money before. In the fourth week, he told the wife that he missed coughing, sleeping poorly, and not being able to taste his food and that he had decided to go back to smoking.

Two days later the woman came storming into MHE's office. Tears were streaming down her face. She told MHE that she cried every time she went to the doctor's office. She had also had to quit jobs because she couldn't stop crying. The next day she was taking her children to the doctor's office and she wanted MHE's advice on how to avoid crying. He told her that crying was a very childish thing to do and so she should replace it with another childish thing. She should buy a cucumber pickle and nurse it all the way to the office and all the way home. The next day she came in angry, but not crying, and asked him why he didn't tell her to nurse the pickle while she was there.

Each week the wife came in with a new complaint: the husband would fix things for his mother but not for her; the mother-in-law often dropped by at 4 p.m. and demanded a fancy dinner; the husband and mother would often get a dinner guest drunk enough that he vomited on the dining room carpet, etc. Each time she would bring in a complaint MHE would agree that her husband's behavior was unacceptable. The woman finally filed for divorce.

Presenting Problem: Smoking; uncontrollable crying; marital difficulties

Age Group: Adult

Modality: Individual; outpatient

Problem Duration: NA

Treatment Length: More than four sessions

Result: Partial success. MHE was unable to help the couple with their problems or get the man to stop smoking, but was able to help the woman stop crying when she visited doctors.

Follow-up: NA

Techniques: Hypnosis; utilization (of the man's desire not to spend money on smoking); task assignment (behavioral and symbolic)

Sources: *Phoenix*, pp. 20–21; *Teaching Seminar*, pp. 196–201

Case #245

Case Summary: A couple who had been married for seven years came to MHE for help to resolve a quarrel. Each year they were married they had vacationed in California and Wyoming. The wife wanted a change this year. She wanted to go to North Dakota. The husband objected, saying that California and Wyoming were good enough for him and they should be good enough for her. MHE advised the man to let his wife find out for herself that California and Wyoming were better than North Dakota by letting her take her vacation there while he took his in the usual places. While each was on their separate vacation, the husband called MHE at 2 a.m. to ask him if he had sent them on separate vacations so they could think about getting divorced. MHE told him that he had merely discussed vacations with them. The next night at 1 a.m., the wife called and asked the same question and MHE gave the same reply. When they returned home they divorced. A year later the wife came to see MHE with her new boy-friend and asked his advice about whether the two should get married. After interviewing them, MHE told them that they seemed to be compatible, but that they should be good friends and then discover if that would develop into something more.

Presenting Problem: Marital problem; disagreement

Age Group: Adult

Modality: Marital; outpatient

Problem Duration: NA

Treatment Length: One session

Result: Partial success. The couple resolved their disagreement, but got divorced.

Follow-up: One year

Techniques: Task assignment (behavioral and symbolic); utilization (of the husband's belief that taking a vacation in North Dakota was a bad idea)

Source: *Phoenix*, pp. 39–41

Case #246

Case Summary: A Pennsylvania psychiatrist had been practicing for 30 years and still had not built up a successful practice. He and his wife had each been in analysis for a number of years. They came to MHE for marital therapy. On the first day MHE sent the husband to climb Squaw Peak and he sent the wife to the Botanical Gardens. The husband returned with a glowing report and the wife returned to say how much she hated it. The next day MHE sent the wife to Squaw Peak and the husband to the Botanical Gardens. Once again the husband was thrilled and the wife had nothing positive to say. On the third day MHE let them choose what they would do. The husband returned to the Botanical Gardens and the wife bitterly climbed Squaw Peak again. MHE told them their marital therapy was complete and sent them back to Pennsylvania. They looked at him in disbelief.

When they arrived home, they both went out independently. The wife went and quit psychoanalysis and filed for divorce. The husband also quit analysis and went home and started straightening up his practice. (Later their psychoanalyst and his wife came to see MHE. They also ended up getting a divorce.) The husband called MHE and asked him to talk his wife out of getting a divorce, but MHE told them he had not mentioned divorce during their therapy and would not interfere. They both became much happier.

Presenting Problem: Marital problems

Age Group: Adult

Modality: Marital; outpatient

Problem Duration: Six years

Treatment Length: Three sessions, three days

Result: Success. They were happier after the divorce.

Follow-up: The wife got a job and made a life of her own.

Techniques: Task assignment (behavioral and symbolic)

Sources: *Phoenix*, pp. 93–96; *Teaching Seminar*, pp. 145–148

Case #247

Case Summary: A husband and wife had both been psychoanalyzed: the man by Freud and the woman by one of Freud's disciples. The two of them decided they wanted psychotherapy from MHE. MHE and the husband went to a book sale. As they were walking to the sale, an extremely obese woman came out of a store and began walking about 20 feet ahead of them. "Wouldn't you like to get you hands on that?" the man asked, indicating the woman's rear end. "No, I wouldn't," replied MHE. MHE called the man's wife and told her what her husband had said. "And I have starved myself all these years to keep slim, boyish hips!" said the woman. She resolved to develop a fat behind. A few weeks later the wife asked MHE if he would straighten out her husband in regard to sex. She thought her husband was rather prudish and wished that he would try other positions than the missionary position. MHE did as she asked and their therapy was finished.

Presenting Problem: (Marital difficulties)

Age Group: Adult

Modality: Individual/marital; outpatient

Problem Duration: NA

Treatment Length: NA

Result: Success. The couple's sex life improved.

Follow-up: The husband retired. The woman gained weight and they were both happier.

Technique: Direct suggestion

Source: *Teaching Seminar*, pp. 162–163

Case #248

Case Summary: A nurse told MHE that she had to work hard to support her family and that her husband squandered his paycheck on building a "super car." MHE told the woman that her three-year-old son would be arrested for a crime related to automobiles before he was 15. The woman was so angry that she refused to pay his fee. Eleven years later the woman came to see MHE again. Her son had been arrested for joyriding. MHE's advice to the woman was to insist that the husband drive his super car to the Department of Motor Vehicles (DMV) the next time he had to renew his license. The woman followed MHE's instructions. The people at the DMV refused to let him drive anywhere in his super car and notified the police of its existence. The man had a tow truck take the car to a salvage yard. He came home and apologized to his wife. He told her that he would let her buy a car for him to go to work in and he would give her all his paychecks.

Presenting Problem: Marital problems

Age Group: Adult

Modality: Individual; outpatient

Problem Duration: NA

Treatment Length: NA

Result: Success. The man realized that he had been irresponsible.

Follow-up: NA

Technique: Task assignment (behavioral)

Source: *Teaching Seminar*, pp. 281–284

Case #249

Case Summary: A man and a woman had been married for several years, during which time they had saved their money for a house. The man had dominated the woman during those years. When the time came to buy the house the man insisted that the woman would have no say in it or in how the house was furnished. MHE spoke to the man alone. MHE and the man agreed that the man should be the boss of the family. Then MHE told the man that when a man was really in charge he didn't mind letting his underlings have a say in minor decisions. MHE suggested that the man select 20 floor plans for possible houses and 20 ways to furnish it. Then he would allow the wife to choose from his plans. The husband and wife were both pleased with this arrangement.

Presenting Problem: Marital problem (disagreement about the purchase of a house)

Age Group: Adult

Modality: Individual/marital; outpatient

Problem Duration: NA

Treatment Length: (Two sessions)

Result: Success. The couple was able to reach a compromise about purchasing the house.

Follow-up: NA

Techniques: Utilization (of the man's belief that he should decide major matters and that he was in charge); task assignment (behavioral); reframing

Source: *Uncommon Therapy*, pp. 229–230

Case #250

Case Summary: MHE saw a young couple with marital problems. He told them at the first session that before they returned they were to share a quart of ice cream while sitting on his front steps. When they returned they had not done their task. MHE told them their marital therapy was over and asked them each to write him a letter in a year. A year later he heard from the husband, who told him they had divorced and that he was much happier. When a supervisee asked MHE about his quick dismissal of the couple, he replied that if they did not have the energy to eat some ice cream on his steps he was convinced they would not have the energy to solve their marital problems.

Presenting Problem: Marital problems

Age Group: Adult

Modality: Marital; outpatient

Problem Duration: NA

Treatment Length: Two sessions

Result: Failure. The couple got divorced.

Follow-up: One year later the husband wrote and said he was happier.

Technique: Task assignment (behavioral)

Source: Herbert Lustig, personal communication, 1981.

Case #251

AFFAIRS

Case Summary: A woman MHE treated would get jealous and rage at her husband, who traveled quite a bit for his job. After one of their arguments, she would develop all sorts of physical symptoms until she felt punished enough for her outburst; then the symptoms would subside. After the third interview with MHE, she got jealous of her husband when he wasn't at his hotel to answer her call at the agreed-upon time (she later learned that she had forgotten to take the time zone change into account). She had gone out for an angry walk and had sex with a stranger she met. She was remorseful and certain she was pregnant. She developed a false pregnancy that fooled two gynecologists and then, eight weeks later, realized she had had enough self-punishment and woke up the next day knowing that she wasn't pregnant and ready to give up the somatic self-punishment once and for all. She never again had the symptoms or the jealousy, indicated by a four-year follow-up with the woman and her husband. She was, according to her husband, happy and well-adjusted.

Presenting Problem: Nausea; vomiting; diarrhea; headaches; backaches; jealousy; affair

Age Group: Adult

Modality: Individual; outpatient

Problem Duration: NA

Treatment Length: Six sessions, at least two months

Result: Success. The symptoms abated.

Follow-up: Four years. No recurrence of jealousy.

Techniques: NA

Source: *Collected Papers II*, pp. 209–212

Case #252

Case Summary: One day a mental hospital employee became blind on his way to work. He had left the house in a rage at his wife because she had told a risque story at breakfast. As he rounded a corner he was suddenly unable to see anything but an overwhelming shade of red. After much inquiry from sources other than the patient, MHE discovered the full circumstances that preceded the onset of his blindness. The wife's risque story had been about a red-haired woman. The man's blindness had occurred adjacent to a gas station where a red-haired attendant worked. His wife was having an affair with the attendant. After learning of her affair, her husband had developed an attraction towards a red-haired woman who was one of his co-workers. He and his wife had been fighting a lot and he suspected her of being alcoholic, which she denied.

MHE had the wife come in for a session and she confirmed that she had been drinking and that she had had an affair with the red-haired attendant. The wife declared her intention to break off the affair and asked MHE not to reveal it. MHE put the man in trance and had him regain his sight. He then told the man to study one of MHE's bookplates. Afterwards MHE had the blindness return. When he gave the man a signal the man was able to describe the bookplate, which he found quite mystifying. This increased his confidence in MHE considerably.

The man was eventually able to realize the circumstances that led to his blindness. MHE asked him how he'd like to recover his vision. He said that he'd like to do it gradually, with periods of sight gradually increasing in length. MHE arranged for the man's desires to be met with hypnosis. He and his wife were seen conjointly. Six months later the man reported that he and his wife had reached an amicable divorce agreement.

Presenting Problem: Blindness; (affair)

Age Group: Adult

Modality: Individual/marital; outpatient

Problem Duration: A few hours

Treatment Length: NA

Result: Success. The man regained his sight.

Follow-up: Two years later the man changed jobs.

Technique: Hypnosis

Sources: *Collected Papers IV*, pp. 160–162; *Uncommon Therapy*, pp. 171–173

Case #253

Case Summary: A man brought his wife for therapy with MHE because she had developed an obsession with people's affairs. She avidly read and gossiped about such matters a great deal. Neither husband nor wife had had an affair and they seemed to have a satisfactory sex, home and family life. After several sessions in which the woman felt she was getting nowhere, she asked MHE to hypnotize her. He did and instructed her to begin to speak freely. She declared her inability to do so, but immediately started to do so. This free speaking led her to discuss in great detail the possibility and desirability of her having an affair.

She finally declared that all that she had said so far was only avoiding the real problem. It was that her husband had gotten a vasectomy after they had had all the children they wanted (three). At the time they had agreed on this method, but as the years went on she found that she yearned for making love to someone who was fertile, even though she did not want another child. All the men she had gossiped about and fantasized liaisons with had been fertile, as evidenced by their having fathered children. There was something emotionally unfulfilling about having intercourse with her husband and she thought that she deserved fulfillment as a woman.

MHE told her while she was in trance that what she really wanted was a satisfying emotional experience and that the man she might want to have sex with would only be an instrument for that experience, in that he had only to be a fertile male with whom she did not really want a relationship. He instructed her to have a series of vivid dreams of satisfying sexual experiences she had with her husband right before the conception of each of their children.

She returned and reported that she had been having the dreams and this had only served to increase her desire and impulse to have an affair. In the subsequent trance, MHE instructed her to be able to remember the dreams in her waking state and to have fantasies involving the dream content that would lead to orgasm. She returned and told MHE that it had worked. She had remembered an erotic experience with her husband before they were married and had experienced an intense orgasm while remembering it. The next day she had come across a photograph of her husband that was taken before the birth of their first child and while looking at it had had another orgasm. Looking through some other photographs, she had come across one of a former admirer or hers who was now married with children and instantly had another orgasm while viewing it.

She had satisfying sex with her husband that night and then had a series of dreams about former male acquaintances during which she experienced a number of orgasms. After awakening she deliberately chose to focus on one of the men she had dreamed about and again had an orgasm. When she was picking up her husband at work later that day she had another orgasm when she was greeted by a business associate of the husband, a man who had a large family. That night she and her husband were playing cards with a couple of their friends and she had another orgasm. She reported to MHE that she realized that she could create a satisfying sexual experience anytime she wished and was no longer troubled by her husband's lack of fertility or the impulse to have an affair.

Presenting Problem: Obsessions about affairs

Age Group: Adult

Modality: Individual; outpatient

Problem Duration: Two years

Treatment Length: NA

Result: Success. The woman stopped being obsessed with people's affairs and became more satisfied sexually.

Follow-up: Two years. At that time she was no longer troubled by the obsessions and mostly had erotic dreams about sexual experiences with her husband prior to one of her pregnancies. She was seen during those two years on occasion by MHE to consult about childrearing matters.

Techniques: Hypnosis; splitting (emotional satisfaction from affairs); posthypnotic suggestion; evocation of memories

Source: *Collected Papers IV*, pp. 386–391

Case #254

∽

Case Summary: A woman returned to therapy with MHE after many years. When he had last seen her he had used inhibition technique. The woman said that she had done something that she was both horrified and amused by. She didn't know how much she should tell MHE. MHE suggested that she might tell him a little of the horrifying aspect and a little of the amusing aspect. The woman, who was married, had fallen in love with one of her professors at school. She asked the professor for help in a class taught by another professor and ended up in his office confessing her feelings about him. He said that he would like to kiss her. She said that she couldn't kiss him on the lips, being a married woman, but that he might kiss her between her breasts, since she was wearing a low-cut dress. It didn't go any further. MHE avoided telling her what she should do about the situation. "You know," he said, "It seems to me if you can think the whole thing over, the professor can too." MHE emphasized the fact that the professor had a decision to make, just as she did. At the end of the session she resolved to explore her feelings, particularly her sexual feelings, about the professor.

Presenting Problem: Desire to have an affair

Age Group: Adult

Modality: Individual

Problem Duration: (One-two weeks)

Treatment Length: NA

Result: Success. The woman resolved her problem by deciding to acknowledge her feelings without acting on them.

Follow-up: NA

Technique: Implication (to think it over and make a decision)

Source: *Conversations I*, pp. 193–197

Case #255

Case Summary: A man came to MHE for marital problems. He said again and again how sweet his wife was, yet he was puzzled by her. When he went out of town his wife got lonesome. Then some of his friends would drop in. The man was glad that his wife had someone to keep her company. He mentioned the fact that a friend left a tube of toothpaste on the sink and a discarded razor blade, but he didn't see the significance of it. He talked about how he and his wife quarreled and about how she got pubic lice from her social service work in a poor section of town. Harold kept repeating the same facts. Finally the man said, "You know, if my wife were any other woman, I'd say that she was having affairs." MHE asked the man in what way wife differed from other women. "My God," the man replied, "my wife *is* any other woman." Then he retold his story with recognition of the significant details. He and his wife were able to work out their difficulties and live together happily with MHE's help.

Presenting Problem: Marital problems

Age Group: Adult

Modality: Individual/couple; outpatient

Problem Duration: NA

Treatment Length: NA

Result: Success. The man and his wife resolved their difficulties.

Follow-up: NA

Technique: Implication

Sources: *Conversations II*, pp. 157–164; *Uncommon Therapy*, pp. 247–249

Case #256

꒛

Case Summary: While his wife was out of town, a young husband seduced the maid. The wife was furious when she found out and felt that she could no longer allow the husband in the house. MHE had the three of them come in for a session. MHE let them really let their feelings out to each other. The husband and wife got together and decided to ship the maid to another state where she had relatives. MHE had the wife make the maid pack up the husband's clothes and carry them out to the front yard so that the husband could go off and live by himself. Then, as per MHE's orders, she had the maid bring the clothes back in and repack them and carry them back out. Eventually the wife decided to let her husband come back. She called MHE and asked him to tell her husband to return. MHE told her that any third party could do the job, like the mailman for instance. The wife wrote a letter asking her husband to return. Later the maid reapplied for the job and the couple came banging into MHE's office asking, "What are *we* going to do with this stupid idiot?"

Presenting Problem: Affair; marital problems

Age Group: Adult

Modality: Couple; outpatient

Problem Duration: (A couple of weeks)

Treatment Length: NA

Result: Success. The wife forgave her husband for his infidelity and the couple reconciled.

Follow-up: NA

Technique: Task assignment (symbolic)

Sources: *Conversations II*, pp. 172–173; *Uncommon Therapy*, pp. 175–176

Case #257

꒛

Case Summary: A woman came to MHE for her airplane phobia. MHE asked her to leave the office, to reenter and state her problem. She did so and again told him that she wanted help with her airplane phobia. "Does your husband know about your affair?" he asked her. She asked MHE how he knew and he told her it was the way she sat. She had been seeing her lover for several years. Later she came to see MHE about breaking up with her lover. The lover came to see MHE for his headaches. MHE asked to see the lover's wife. When the wife came in MHE guessed that she, too, had been having an affair. The wife confirmed his guess and told him that it had been her husband's suggestion. He started getting his headaches shortly after the affair began. MHE pointed this out to the man and then asked him what he wanted to do about it. "I'll have my headache," he answered.

Presenting Problem: Headaches; airplane phobia; (affairs); marital problems

Age Group: Adult

Modality: Individual; couple; outpatient

Problem Duration: NA

Treatment Length: NA

Result: Failure. The headaches were not eliminated.

Follow-up: NA

Technique: Hypnosis

Sources: *My Voice Will Go With You*, pp. 188–189; *Phoenix*, pp.115–116

Case #258

Case Summary: A man came to MHE and told him that his (the man's) wife had been having an affair for a week. He had forgiven her and believed that their difficulties could be resolved. MHE excused the man and brought the wife in. She told MHE that her husband did not know everything and that the affair had lasted more than a week. "You mean there have been more men? How many more?" She admitted there had been "at least two." MHE told her "Let's be frank and honest and forthright in our discussion. When the first affair broke off, how did the man tell you that he was tired of you as a piece of ass?" "That's speaking in a very vulgar fashion." "Do you want me to speak in the polite terms that he used and avoid the terms he was thinking?" "He merely said that he guessed he had better return to his wife." She added, "The second man called me a piece of ass after three months." It turned out that her current affair had been going on for 14 days. MHE told her that she must have been awfully tired of the whole thing to let her husband find out so quickly. The woman decided to patch things up with her husband.

Presenting Problem: Extramarital affair

Age Group: Adult

Modality: Individual / marital; outpatient

Problem Duration: NA

Treatment Length: NA

Result: Success. The woman decided to end her affair and work things out with her husband.

Follow-up: NA

Techniques: Implication; shock

Source: *Uncommon Therapy*, pp. 174–176

Case #259

8

Severe Disturbances of Behavior or Cognitions

DESTRUCTIVE/VIOLENT BEHAVIOR

Case Summary: Edward (or Laskarri, in another version) was treated by MHE in the mental hospital. He had been a quiet, isolated man who worked in a factory. One day he had become violently disturbed at work, which led to his commitment to the hospital with a diagnosis of catatonic/hebephrenic schizophrenia. Most of the time he would sit quietly, but three times a day he would become violently disturbed, running frantically around, hiding under beds and shoving beds around. He never gave any explanation for his disturbed behavior or for his disorder in general, even though he was interviewed by several psychiatrists over the course of three years.

MHE decided to use hypnosis with him. One day, when Edward was seated near an immobile, mute patient, MHE sat down and began a trance induction with the mute patient that was really aimed at Edward. Soon Edward was in trance. Catalepsy was induced, during which Edward indicated by head movements that he would like to tell about his difficulties but couldn't find a way.

MHE suggested that Edward begin to have a series of dreams while in

269

trance. Edward dreamed a series of dreams that were to gradually reveal the source of his disturbance, but each with a different content. During the dreams, Edward would shake violently and appear to be suffering a great deal. He would ask MHE to hold his hand before he dreamed and afterwards while he was telling MHE the content of the dream. After several dreams, Edward started to turn his head away from MHE when he approached rather than look attentively at him as he had previously.

For 12 days after that, Edward did not have the usual daily outbursts of violence. On the day that he became violent, he again made eye contact with MHE and again MHE induced trance and hypnotic dreaming. Again, MHE held his hand through the 20-minute disturbing dream. After this dream, Edward did not have another episode of violence for six days. Then he sought MHE out for another hypnotic dreaming session. This was the first time in his three-year hospitalization that he had actively sought treatment. He was hypnotized and asked why he had initiated the session. He reported that he didn't like the hypnotic dreams but that they were better than having the violent episodes on the ward. He had felt another violent episode coming on and wanted to avoid it by having a hypnotic dream.

He proceeded to have another dream with the same emotional content but a different cast of characters and setting. This time he started to experience a little alleviation of the suffering during the dream and a little more recognizable content. In trance, Edward signaled that he would indicate when he needed to have another session by taking MHE's hand as he walked by him.

After an 11-day interval with no disturbed behavior, Edward grabbed MHE's hand and spontaneously went into trance. MHE instructed him to have another dream with less disturbance of emotion and clearer, more recognizable content. The dreams started to have clear and repetitious characters—a man, a big woman, and a smaller woman—and they were always abusing Edward physically in some way.

Finally, Edward indicated that he was ready to have a dream that would clearly reveal the source of the problem. He dreamed a dream that revealed that his parents and older sister had systematically verbally and physically abused him to take out their frustration and anger at having lost the status they had enjoyed in their country of origin when they came to America and were treated as "dumb immigrants." Since Edward was born in America and could speak English, they heaped their scorn and abuse on him. Once Edward realized this, he shortened his name and got away from his family. He got a good job and raised a family. His father died from abusing alcohol, his mother died of cancer and his sister committed suicide. [In another version, he had an older brother who had protected him. That older brother was another character in the dreams.]

Presenting Problem: Violent behavior, mutism

Age Group: Adult

Modality: Individual; inpatient

Problem Duration: Three years

Treatment Length: Three months

Result: The man stopped having disturbed, violent outbursts and got out of the hospital.

Follow-up: It is unclear how MHE obtained follow-up information. He merely notes in the write up that "the years have passed." Edward got a better job than he had had when he entered the hospital. He married and raised a family.

Techniques: Hypnosis; hypnotically-induced dreams

Source: *Collected Papers IV*, pp. 58–66 and pp. 331–334

Case #260

Case Summary: A 22-year-old man, newly married, asked MHE's help to cease his reckless driving. He was somewhat ambivalent about the request, however. He had been a stunt driver and was confident that he could control a car under any condition. He was a bit worried about the safety of his wife though and thought he needed to give up his dangerous driving habits. He would usually drive 90 m.p.h. on straight stretches and 70 to 90 on mountain roads. He declared that hypnosis probably wouldn't help him and that he would have to stop in his own way. MHE seized upon this statement and repeated it again and again until it became the trance induction and treatment. MHE offered the man no other suggestions and roused him from the trance by saying that nothing that the conscious mind would find important was said in trance.

The man expressed his regrets that he wasn't hypnotizable and reiterated his belief that he would just have to find his own way to stop the reckless driving. Two weeks later he stopped in to report that he was still driving dangerously and was still having his wife accompany him and that he guessed he'd just have to find his own way to stop. Two weeks after that he came in happy to report that he had handled the problem in his own way. He had driven alone on a mountain road one day and decided to have one last fling with dangerous driving and had lost control of the car, which plunged off the cliff. He had just barely managed to jump out of the car in time to save himself. He had since gotten a safer car and was driving safely.

Presenting Problem: Reckless driving

Age Group: Adult

Modality: Individual; outpatient

Problem Duration: NA

Treatment Length: One session

Result: Success. The man stopped driving dangerously.

Follow-up: NA

Techniques: Hypnosis; utilization (of the man's belief that he had to stop in his own way)

Source: *Collected Papers IV*, pp. 233–234

Case #261

❧

Case Summary: A very bright eight-year-old [seven-year-old in another version] boy had become a troublemaker after his mother, a single parent, started dating men. He began destroying things and rebelling in school and in the neighborhood. His mother brought him to see MHE. She had tried normal discipline, but the boy was too much for her, even with the help of relatives and the school. The boy told MHE that nobody could stop him from being the toughest hoodlum in Arizona. MHE asked the boy if he was afraid of him (MHE) giving the mother some advice. He said he wasn't. The boy scornfully asked MHE if he was going to recommend the mother spank him, but MHE replied that the only thing that would be done was to give the boy an opportunity to change his own behavior.

MHE gave the mother a plan while the boy was out of the office. Mother was to arrange for the other children to be taken care of by her parents for the day. She was to prepare some food, some drink, a good book and a telephone at a convenient spot in the living room. She was to have a showdown with the boy the next day. MHE suggested that the boy "really take his mother to the cleaners" the next day.

The next morning the mother awakened the boy and suggested that they have a good breakfast before starting the day. The boy threw his eggs on the floor and demanded bacon. She prepared bacon. He threw some more stuff on the floor. In response to this, Mother quietly went to the bathroom. When she came back she sat on her son. The boy cried, struggled and threatened her. She held firm and told him that as she did not know how to help him control his behavior, she would just sit there until she thought of a way. Since she was sure she would not be able to come up with a plan, she would have to sit there for some time. He would probably be the one who would have to come up with a plan, she told him, since she had run out of ideas.

She had thought that she would be too big to sit on him, but MHE had reassured her and told her that she would have a hard time even staying on him. She found this true. The boy would go through fits of struggling, threatening her and yelling obscenities, then would collapse sobbing in exhaustion. She sat on him most of the day. After many promises to be good, which she rejected as insincere, he finally convinced her that he had a plan about how to control his behavior. She let him up. He asked for supper, but she told him that since he had missed breakfast, he would have to wait for breakfast the next day, since he couldn't start his meals with supper. He quietly acquiesced and sobbed himself to sleep in his room.

The next day, he was given oatmeal for breakfast, one of his least favorite foods. He started to protest, but then ate it. His mother told him that she had made extra helpings, so if he didn't finish it at breakfast, he would have to have it for lunch and supper. He tried but wasn't able to finish it all for breakfast and had to eat the rest of it cold at lunch. That day he went to each of the neighbors whose property he had destroyed, apologized, and promised to make amends. He returned to school and apologized to his teachers. Things settled down at home.

After several months, after an argument with one of his sisters, the boy suddenly declared that he was tired of towing the line and that he would stomp anybody who got in his way, including MHE. When Mother's usual discipline methods failed to stop this, she brought him to see MHE and said that the boy had threatened to stomp MHE's office. MHE sent the mother away and challenged the boy to stomp as hard as he could. The boy said he could stomp 1000 times if he wanted, but MHE was skeptical. He said that such a small boy would almost certainly not be able to stomp even 50 times without getting tired and wanting to sit down.

The boy started stomping and MHE praised his stomping ability, but again doubted that the boy could keep it up. The boy did slow down at about 30 and finally declared his intention to stay standing up. MHE again expressed doubt that the boy could remain standing without fidgeting for the whole session. MHE went about his business, making case notes. The boy started to lean on the chair when he thought MHE wasn't looking and to sit down when MHE went out of the room, always standing up when MHE came back into the room.

When mother returned two hours later, MHE told her that what had occurred in the office was a secret between the boy and himself. On the way home, the boy told his mother that MHE was a nice doctor and there was no further trouble. When the mother decided to get married some time later, the boy wouldn't fully accept the stepfather until he found out that MHE approved of the man.

Presenting Problem: Rebelling, threatening and destroying property

Age Group: Child

Modality: Family/individual; outpatient

Problem Duration: NA

Treatment Length: (2 sessions)

Result: Success. The boy stopped destroying things and defying his mother and his teachers.

Follow-up: Two years. When the boy's mother decided to get married, he refused to accept the stepfather completely until he found out that MHE approved of the man.

Techniques: Task assignment (behavioral); utilization (of mother's hostility toward the boy and the boy's rebelliousness)

Sources: *Collected Papers IV*, pp. 507–515; *Conversations III*, pp. 135–138; *Uncommon Therapy*, pp. 213–221

Case #262

Case Summary: Ruth was a very disturbed 12-year-old in the state hospital. She would plead with the nurses to buy her some candy. When the nurse gave it to her she would thank the nurse ever so politely and kick the nurse in the shins or she would hug the nurse in gratitude and rip the nurse's shirt. Ruth was very destructive. In the previous year she had done $5,000 worth of damage to the hospital. The superintendent was forced to put Ruth into a seclusion room where she promptly began destroying the bed and tearing the plaster off the walls. When the superintendent called in MHE she had already done $400 worth of damage. MHE asked him if he would be willing to accept $400 to $500 more damage in place of a higher bill. The superintendent agreed.

MHE entered Ruth's room and told her she'd been doing a very inefficient job of tearing the plaster off her walls. He showed her how she could make a hammer to destroy the wall from strips of her gown and the laths from the wall. Ruth was shocked. Then MHE told her to sit down and help him pull the radiator out of the floor. When the job was done Ruth burst into tears and said, "You're a doctor, you shouldn't do things like that." From then on whenever Ruth got destructive the nurses had only to threaten to call Dr. Erickson. Ruth didn't want to see him when she was disturbed but she asked for him when she was feeling good.

Presenting Problem: Destructive behavior

Age Group: Child

Modality: Individual; inpatient

Problem Duration: NA

Treatment Length: One visit

Result: Success. Ruth stopped damaging the ward.

Follow-up: NA

Techniques: Matching (violence); symptom prescription; shock

Sources: *Conversations III*, pp. 80–82; *My Voice Will Go With You*, pp. 229–231

Case #263

Case Summary: A very vicious little boy made his stepmother dance on the kitchen floor for an hour by threatening to beat the baby with a bicycle chain. The father brought the boy in to see MHE. MHE saw him for a while until he finally said that they didn't like each other and that he was going to ask the father to take his son to another psychiatrist.

Presenting Problem: Cruelty; threatening

Age Group: Child

Modality: Individual; outpatient

Problem Duration: NA

Treatment Length: (A few sessions)

Result: Refusal. MHE refused to treat the child.

Follow-up: NA

Techniques: NA

Sources: *Conversations III*, pp. 133–134; *Uncommon Therapy*, p. 201

Case #264

Case Summary: A man came to MHE for help controlling his explosive and violent temper. The man lived on a farm and MHE asked him how he heated the house. The family had a wood burning stove which was fueled by the wood the man chopped himself. MHE asked the man what kind of wood he chopped. He said that he cut oak and ash but not elm because it was too hard to split. MHE told the man that he had to "split the hell out of" a block of elm whenever he got angry.

Presenting Problem: Explosions of temper

Age Group: Adult

Modality: Individual; outpatient

Problem Duration: NA

Treatment Length: NA

Result: (Success. The man learned how to avoid taking his anger out on his family.)

Follow-up: NA

Techniques: Task assignment (behavioral)

Source: *Teaching Seminar*, pp. 195–196

Case #265

Case Summary: Big Louise was 6′6″. She was a bouncer in the speakeasies of Providence, Rhode Island in the 1930s. She had a hobby of beating up policemen and sending them to the hospital. Finally the Chief of Police had her committed to an insane asylum as being dangerous to others. Big Louise was not happy about being in the hospital so she did $500 worth of damage to the ward each month. MHE made friends with Big Louise. One day she had the nurses bring him to talk to her. When MHE came in she was pacing. He asked her to sit down and talk to him about New England winters. Ten minutes later MHE signaled the nurse. As per MHE's instructions, 14 student nurses rushed in and started destroying the ward. Big Louise pleaded with them to stop but they ignored her. That was the last time Louise did any damage.

Presenting Problem: Violent behavior

Age Group: Adult

Modality: Individual; inpatient

Problem Duration: NA

Treatment Length: NA

Result: Success. She stopped damaging the ward.

Follow-up: Louise got a job in the hospital laundry, got a discharge, and married another hospital employee.

Technique: Symptom displacement

Source: *Teaching Seminar*, pp. 224–226

Case #266

Case Summary: A husband and wife came from California to see MHE. The man said he wanted MHE to talk some sense into his bride. The man explained that his first child had to be a boy. If not, he would shoot his wife and the baby. The man was a lawyer with a good practice. MHE discussed the medical impossibility of determining the sex of a child. He then suggested that the couple should file for a divorce. The man should take a trip somewhere to visit some friends. While he was gone the wife should pack up and move to another town, keeping her address a secret. The next day the couple agreed to carry out his suggestion. After the divorce was granted the man thanked MHE for his intelligent advice. He said that he would think the matter over again before he married. MHE suggested that in the future he discuss the matter with a potential bride before marrying her.

Presenting Problem: Husband threatened to kill the wife if she didn't give him a son.

Age Group: Adult

Modality: Marital; outpatient

Problem Duration: NA

Treatment Length: Two sessions

Result: Success. The husband did not kill the wife and the couple divorced. The man agreed to reevaluate his position before marrying again.

Follow-up: The wife kept her address a secret.

Techniques: Direct suggestion; task assignment (behavioral)

Source: *Uncommon Therapy*, pp. 176–177

Case #267

DELUSIONS/HALLUCINATIONS/PSYCHOSES

Case Summary: A 24-year-old woman was diagnosed as paranoid schizophrenic after she had auditory and visual hallucinations and became antagonistic towards her parents and her siblings. She had been hospitalized and various psychoanalytically-oriented psychiatrists had attempted to treat her, to no avail. She repeatedly mocked their attempts and put them on the defensive. They finally gave up their efforts, declared her untreatable, and recommended electroshock treatments. The woman and/or her family had been unwilling to have electroshock used and so she was taken out of the hospital and brought to MHE for treatment. She took a mocking stance towards MHE and told him her family wanted him to hypnotize her into sanity. She would be interested, she told him, in seeing what kind of ass he was going to make of himself.

MHE told her that he hoped not to make an ass of himself, despite his potential for doing so, but that he only intended to bore her for the two-hour session. She admired his honesty, she told him, because most psychiatrists fancied themselves interesting. MHE proceeded to read her an article about working with resistant patients which included a long induction script. He recommended that she listen with resentment at the boredom she was to experience and to make sure she didn't go to sleep. She sat with a scornful expression on her face until she realized that her right hand was lifting up in response to the suggestions being read in the script. She then cooperated in treatment and was able to reenter college and get along better with her family. She continued in therapy with MHE, even though her psychotic symptoms were gone.

Presenting Problem: Hallucinations; paranoid schizophrenia; hostility towards family

Age Group: Adult

Modality: Individual; outpatient

Problem Duration: At least two years

Treatment Length: More than 10 sessions

Result: Success. The woman's family said she was the best they had ever seen her in her life. She said she needed more understanding of herself, but understood her hallucinated persecutory perceptions were in the past.

Follow-up: MHE continued to see her in therapy with no recurrence of the symptoms. She was making an excellent adjustment, enrolled in college and seeing MHE weekly.

Techniques: Hypnosis; utilization (of her hostility)

Source: *Collected Papers I*, pp. 318–320

Case #268

Case Summary: A woman who was very close to her roommate became distressed after her roommate became catatonic and had to be hospitalized. She was afraid she would become catatonic herself and there was some evidence that it was happening. After consulting four psychiatrists, two of whom said they were too busy and two of whom said they did not have the training to deal with her situation, she entered treatment with MHE.

Things were going slowly until one day she entered MHE's office wearing a new outfit and declared that she was either getting better or going crazy, she did not know which. In hypnosis, she still didn't know whether the new clothes were a sign of improvement or of an imminent breakdown. Then she remembered a dream which disturbed her and declared that she no longer wanted to remember anything and was going to leave therapy and go visit her friend in the psychiatric hospital. Once there, she was going to do something bad.

Although he spent four hours trying, MHE could not dissuade her from this course. Finally, in desperation, he requested that she go out of his office and return to give him once again that good feeling he first had when he saw her enter his office that day with a new outfit on. She did and promptly developed an amnesia for all that had occurred that session, giving MHE the chance to arrange for a different course of events that would not conclude so hopelessly. He was successful and therapy continued until her adjustment was good.

[In another version, MHE used her as a demonstration subject for a group of medical students and had her see her former roommate across the room. She therefore made the distinction between her and the woman and found her own identity. She was so proud of having been a part of teaching the students that she hadn't noticed she had accomplished this.]

Presenting Problem: Fear of catatonia/psychosis

Age Group: Adult

Modality: Individual; outpatient

Problem Duration: NA

Treatment Length: NA

Result: Success. The woman lost her fear of going insane.

Follow-up: Over eight years.

Techniques: Hypnosis; structured amnesia; [positive hallucination; dissociation]

Sources: *Collected Papers II*, pp. 282–285; *Mind-Body Communication* p. 58

Case #269

Case Summary: A man in his mid-twenties had obsessions about being homosexual, was attracted to a man he worked with in a "horrible, sentimental way," was fearful and shy, was agoraphobic and claustrophobic, had insomnia and saw women in a visually distorted manner in which they all looked like rotting corpses. MHE was not making much progress with him and wanted to use hypnosis. The man was wary of hypnosis, but agreed reluctantly when MHE taught him time distortion and told him he would only have to do an experiment of 10 to 20 seconds in hypnosis. MHE had him review every life experience related to his problems in a time distorted 20 seconds.

After successfully reviewing many life experiences during the allotted time, the man got insight into the cause of his problems and got relief from them. The problems stemmed from his anger and feelings of betrayal when his mother died when he was 10, not keeping her promise to make him a birthday cake after imploring him to trust her. It was triggered in his adult life by hearing the news that his father had terminal cancer and that his father and stepmother were about to celebrate their "10th birthday" of being married.

Presenting Problem: Obsessions; phobias (claustrophobia and agoraphobia); insomnia; hallucinations

Age Group: Adult

Modality: Individual; outpatient

Problem Duration: More than six months

Treatment Length: A number of weeks

Result: Success. The man got relief from his phobias and obsessions.

Follow-up: NA

Techniques: Hypnosis; time distortion; direct suggestion

Source: *Collected Papers II*, pp. 286–289

Case #270

꿈

Case Summary: A woman hallucinated six nude young men floating above her at about ceiling height everywhere she went. They talked to her about art, literature, music and sex. She came to MHE because she wondered how she could function with these men following her everywhere. She told MHE that she had gotten two divorces because her husbands had become upset when she had revealed to them that she spent hours floating in the clouds and living in a glass castle at the bottom of the ocean. She had lately been sitting in her apartment for a week at a time taking her trips.

When she sat down in the office she asked MHE why he kept a large bear trap set next to his desk. He told her that he couldn't explain the matter in one session. Next she looked into an alcove and asked whether it wasn't rather unprofessional to keep six nude dancing girls in his office. MHE said that if she could have her nude young men, he could see no reason for him not to have his dancing girls. The woman didn't like the way her young men were looking at the girls. MHE assured her that the girls were only interested in him and that the men were only interested in her. Once when walking to answer the phone, MHE almost walked into the bear trap but she restrained him. After that he always walked around the trap, which he told her he would eventually have removed.

Gradually MHE raised the question of when the young men should be present. He said that sometimes he kept his dancing girls out of sight if he thought other people wouldn't appreciate them. Eventually she left her young men in MHE's closet where she could come to visit them when she needed to. She was able to get jobs as a high school teacher, a counselor and then as a secretary to the president of a large corporation. She suggested that since MHE had come up with the idea of keeping her nude men in the closet, he might be able to come up with an idea of where to put her psychotic episodes. MHE suggested she put them in manila envelopes. She thought this was a good idea and periodically she would bring or send an envelope to MHE which contained her psychotic episodes. He was to put them in his files. She came to examine them years later and told MHE that she was now sure she could trust him, because he had kept her psychotic episode envelopes as he had promised.

Presenting Problem: Hallucinations; catatonia

Age Group: Adult

Modality: Individual; outpatient

Problem Duration: NA

Treatment Length: NA

Result: Partial success. The woman was able to remained employed and to keep her hallucinations and catatonic episodes within reasonable limits.

She was also able to retain a civil service job for many years. She was self-supporting.

Follow-up: She was married eight times and for a time became dependent on alcohol, but went to Alcoholics Anonymous and was able to remain sober. She was never able to establish a savings account.

Techniques: Utilization (of symptom); anchoring the symptom (the nude young men in the closet; the psychotic episodes in the manila envelopes)

Sources: *Collected Papers IV*, pp. 70–74; *Conversations I*, pp. 232–235; *Healing in Hypnosis*, p. 116

Case #271

Case Summary: MHE saw a professional woman who had the sense that there were monsters floating behind her and peopling her bedroom. She wasn't certain whether they were dreams or real. MHE thought she was prepsychotic, not psychotic, because she had enough insight to doubt the hallucinations. He had her go into trance and visualize a series of 14 crystal balls in which she would see scenes from her past in the first 12, the present in the 13th and the future in the 14th. He kept telling her to see the scene in the crystal ball and not to look at the 14th one yet. In the first few, she saw pleasant scenes of her childhood, but as they got closer to the present, they started to get more menacing and disturbing. He then had her create a new ending and see it in the 14th crystal ball. She saw a scene of a happy version of her going swimming two months in the future (she had previously had a fear of swimming). She actually went swimming two months later, faced some difficult feelings and ultimately became happier and better adjusted, heading a professional department and happily married.

Presenting Problem: Hallucinations

Age Group: Adult

Modality: Individual; outpatient

Problem Duration: NA

Treatment Length: NA

Result: Success. The woman stopped having disturbing visions and become more professionally and personally adjusted.

Follow-up: It's not clear how the follow-up information was obtained.

Techniques: Hypnosis, positive hallucination, age progression, presupposition ("Don't look at the 14th crystal yet.")

Source: *Collected Papers IV*, pp. 85–87

Case #272

Case Summary: A woman's husband told MHE that the woman was catatonic. When she arrived in his office, knowing that he was a hypnotist, she immediately went into a trance and started asking him about the roses that were floating in the air. MHE had her place the roses in an imaginary vase, then to see them change colors, then to change into a rosebush, then into some roses that MHE had never seen. This last suggestion induced an age regression and she saw herself at a younger age watching her father cut roses. Over the course of treatment, the woman would describe her younger self in relation to the roses. Gradually, the girl in the visions started to grow up, going from early childhood through college years. It turned out that her husband was a petty criminal, a voyeur, and an exhibitionist who was finally sent to prison. She recovered from her psychosis and was able to hold a responsible job position.

Presenting Problem: Catatonia; hallucinations

Age Group: Adult

Modality: Individual; outpatient

Problem Duration: NA

Treatment Length: NA

Result: Success. The woman was no longer psychotic and was able to hold a job.

Follow-up: NA

Techniques: Hypnosis; utilization (of the hallucinated roses); age regression

Source: *Collected Papers IV*, p. 121

Case #273

Case Summary: A patient in Worcester State (Mental) Hospital spent his time anxiously winding string around the bars of his window to protect him from enemies. MHE started helping him wrap string and pointed out to the man that there were cracks in the floor and the door that should be stuffed with paper to keep his enemies out. Then MHE pointed out that the man's room was only one of many in the building and that to be really safe he needed the help of the hospital attendants. Then MHE spread the guardian factor to the hospital staff, the Board of Mental Health in Massachusetts, the governor, and the state police. Then it was expanded to adjoining states, then to the United States. As a result, the man was able to comfortably wander around the grounds and stopped his anxious winding of string. He worked in the hospital shops and was much less of a problem.

Presenting Problem: Anxious behavior; paranoia

Age Group: Adult

Modality: Individual; inpatient

Problem Duration: NA

Treatment Length: NA

Result: Partial success. The man stopped his anxious behavior and was much less trouble in the hospital.

Follow-up: NA

Techniques: Utilization (of paranoia); pattern intervention; joining

Sources: *Collected Papers IV*, pp. 335–336; *Experiencing Erickson*, pp. 91–92

Case #274

Case Summary: On January 1st a man came to MHE because he believed that he would die of heart failure that night. MHE said, "All right, call me up tomorrow morning and tell me you are dead." That night at 11 o'clock the man called to say he was dying. MHE told him to call in the morning. The next day the man once again expected to die that night; he called MHE and was told to call back in the morning. This ritual went on every day for the next few months. In February MHE began reciting for the man all the days that he'd been wrong about dying. This infuriated the man. The man continued to call MHE throughout the spring, with MHE repeatedly reminding the man of all the times he'd been wrong. Finally, in June the man said, "I'm going to change that record. I don't think I'm going to die tonight, but I don't know about tomorrow night." MHE said, "Call me next week." The man called the next week and agreed that the issue had been settled.

Presenting Problem: Delusion

Age Group: Adult

Modality: Individual; outpatient

Problem Duration: NA

Treatment Length: (Five months)

Result: Success. The man stopped believing that he would die.

Follow-up: The man returned to college.

Technique: Implication (that the man would be alive in the future)

Source: *Conversations I*, pp. 81–82

Case #275

Case Summary: Herbert stood in a corner in his nightshirt. He'd been in the hospital for six months and had stood in the corner night and day. Herbert had to be tube fed. He believed that he had no throat, no stomach, and no bowels. He believed that the doctors only pretended to tube feed him. MHE assured him that he would convince him that he had a colon, a throat, a stomach and that he was being fed. Herbert was skeptical. When the time came, MHE tube fed Herbert a concoction of raw cod-liver oil, vinegar, baking soda, eggnog and milk. The food made Herbert belch with a taste like rotten fish. After several such meals he admitted that he was being fed and that he had a stomach. He asked that he not be fed any more rotten fish.

Then he reminded MHE that he still did not believe he had a colon. MHE had him restrained in bed and given a cathartic which was scheduled to take effect at 6 a.m. At 6 a.m. the man started yelling to be taken to the bathroom. MHE replied that it was impossible since he had no colon. Herbert finally crudely told MHE what would happen if he didn't believe he had a colon.

Next the man said that he couldn't possibly eat solid food or put a glass to his lips. MHE told him that in the morning he would pound on the dining room door and demand to be let in. He would then enter and drink a glass of milk. Herbert did not believe him. MHE's prophecy came to be because he had put a generous dose of salt in Herbert's tube feeding that night.

To teach Herbert to eat food, MHE sent him outdoors in mid-winter. When he came in he had him stand in the corner of the kitchen amongst all the good smells and watch the cook eat, until Herbert demanded to join in.

Herbert had a history of gambling and was an expert at cards. He refused to participate in ward activities. MHE forced him to watch a group of extremely deteriorated patients play a nonsense game of cards. This frustrated Herbert so much that he agreed to teach one of them a real game. In time Herbert was discharged and hired by the hospital.

Presenting Problem: Delusions (belief that he had no digestive system); refusal to eat

Age Group: Adult

Modality: Individual; inpatient

Problem Duration: (At least six months)

Treatment Length: NA

Result: Success. Herbert gave up his delusions about his digestive system and began eating again.

Follow-up: Herbert was discharged from the hospital and employed.

Techniques: Evocation (of motivation and body experience); task assignment (behavioral)

Sources: *Conversations I*, pp. 226–228; *Uncommon Therapy*, pp. 287–290; *My Voice Will Go With You*, pp. 202–209

Case #276

Case Summary: John and Alfredo were both hospitalized independently. Each believed that he was Jesus Christ. MHE put the two men in a room

together. Each would accuse the other of being crazy. One day John realized that he and Alfredo were saying the same things and that perhaps both of them were crazy. MHE agreed with him and said that the ward nurses held the same view. MHE also pointed out that the way the man had been screaming that he was Jesus Christ was not very Christ-like. John asked MHE to take him to the library so he could test his theory. They picked out a book and John looked through it. "There's a capital t and an h, there's an o, and there's an r, and there's an n" and so on (the man's last name was Thornton) until he found all the letters of his name and deduced that the book must be about him. MHE then found all the letters of his own name and made the same claim. John said, "Somebody's crazy. It isn't you. Let me think it over awhile." John discarded his delusions and eventually got discharged and got a job. Four years later he was still gainfully employed.

Presenting Problem: Delusions (belief that he was Jesus Christ)

Age Group: Adult

Modality: Individual; inpatient

Problem Duration: NA

Treatment Length: NA

Result: Success. John discarded his delusions and got a job.

Follow-up: John was still employed four years later.

Techniques: Utilization (of delusional beliefs); matching (finding the letters to both of their names in a book); task assignment (behavioral and perceptual)

Sources: *Conversations I*, pp. 229–230; *My Voice Will Go With You*, p. 201

Case #277

Case Summary: MHE started treating John, a schizophrenic, in the early 1960s. MHE quickly decided that John's family wasn't helping him, so he got them to establish a trust fund for him, which allowed him to be independent from them. At first John drove to the sessions, but when his symptoms became so severe that he couldn't drive, MHE and Mrs. Erickson found him an apartment within walking distance of MHE's office. MHE had his daughter Kristi accompany John to the dog pound to get a dog. When it soon became clear that John's apartment was too small for keeping a dog, MHE offered to give John's dog, Barney, a home. It was to be clear that the dog was John's, however, and he was to come to MHE's house twice a day to feed and care for Barney.

After a while, MHE stopped having John have therapy sessions, and used his visits as informal treatment. MHE terrorized Barney by swatting at him with a fly swatter and blowing a loud horn when Barney approached him, so Barney wouldn't become attached to MHE. MHE then wrote John a whole series of letters allegedly from Barney describing events in the Erickson household and anecdotes about life in general. This was followed by a series of limericks, again allegedly written by Barney, for John about Barney's relationship to John, life in general and more about the Erickson family.

When MHE died in 1980, Barney died too, both of them having been ill for some time. Mrs. Erickson took John to the pound, where they each picked out a new puppy of the same breed that Barney had been. John continues to visit the Erickson house each night to watch television with Mrs. Erickson and he looks after the house and the pets while Mrs. Erickson is traveling.

Presenting Problem: Schizophrenia

Age Group: Adult

Modality: Individual; outpatient (from sessions to visits)

Problem Duration: At least 15 years

Treatment Length: Almost 20 years

Result: Partial success. John's life became more stable although he was still schizophrenic.

Follow-up: After MHE's death, John continued to be stable for at least five years.

Techniques: Indirect communication; task assignment (behavioral)

Source: *Experiencing Erickson*, pp. 20–27

Case #278

Case Summary: A psychotic man sought hypnosis from MHE to help him accomplish some bizarre schemes he had for changing the world. MHE told the man that he could not hypnotize him because he had such quick eye movements.

Presenting Problem: Desire for hypnosis to realize plans; (psychosis); (delusions)

Age Group: Adult

Modality: Individual; outpatient

Problem Duration: NA

Treatment Length: One session

Result: Dismissal. MHE dismissed him from treatment and refused to hypnotize him.

Follow-up: Jeffrey Zeig, a student of MHE's, saw him some years later for the same problem.

Techniques: NA

Source: *Experiencing Erickson*, p. 78

Case #279

Case Summary: A patient in a psychiatric hospital spent all of his time standing around. He never spoke to anyone. One day MHE approached him with a manual floor polisher. He put the man's fingers around the handle and said, "Move that floor polisher." At first the man only moved the polisher an inch back and forth. Each day MHE instructed the man to polish a greater area of the floor until he was polishing the entire ward. Soon the man began to complain that MHE was abusing him by making him polish floors all day. MHE suggested that he might try making beds. The man tried making beds. Gradually the man began to talk about his delusions. The man remained psychotic, but within a year's time he was able to function in the outside world.

Presenting Problem: Inactivity; lack of communication; psychosis; delusions

Age Group: Adult

Modality: Individual; inpatient

Problem Duration: NA

Treatment Length: NA

Result: Partial success. The man was able to function in the outside world.

Follow-up: NA

Techniques: Task assignment (behavioral); direct suggestion

Source: *My Voice Will Go With You*, pp. 199–200

Case #280

ॐ

Case Summary: A patient in the mental hospital went around telling people he was Jesus. MHE told him that since he was on earth to serve mankind, there was a task he could do to serve people. Since it was desirable for the doctors to play tennis during their recreation hours because they were using the muscles God gave them, could the man possibly help by smoothing the dirt on the tennis court? God surely did not intend for all those lumps to be in the tennis court, MHE told him. The man agreed and became an excellent tennis court keeper. After some time, MHE mentioned that he understood that the man was a carpenter (Jesus had been a carpenter). The man could only agree that he was. MHE told him that to serve mankind, the psychology laboratory could use his carpentry skill to have some bookshelves built. The man became the psychology laboratory handyman.

Presenting Problem: Delusion

Age Group: Adult

Modality: Individual; inpatient

Problem Duration: NA

Treatment Length: NA

Result: Partial success. The man still had delusions, but became engaged in productive activities.

Follow-up: NA

Techniques: Task assignment (behavioral); reframing; utilization (of the man's belief that he was Jesus Christ)

Sources: *Phoenix*, p. 43; *Uncommon Therapy*, p. 28

Case #281

❧

Case Summary: A young man from Los Angeles called MHE for therapy. He was afraid that he would go into orbit and this delusion intruded upon him constantly. The man had gotten a job in an underground mine to escape going into orbit, but it had not helped. Other psychiatrists had wanted to give him electroshock treatments. MHE had him come to Phoenix and get a job in a warehouse. First MHE tried to distract him with a new obsession by having him count his steps as he walked along the street while he was memorizing street names. When that did not work, MHE told him that it apparently was his fate to go into orbit, so he should get a canteen of water and some salt pills and hike around on the top of some local mountains. He was to report at 10:30 p.m. after being up there all day if he did not go into orbit. After some time doing this, the man started to doubt that he would go into orbit. Then his sister from California asked MHE if her brother could come to California to do some odd jobs for her. MHE told him he could go because she lived near mountains and he would always be able to hike up to the mountains with his canteen if he felt as if he were going to go into orbit. Several months later, he came back to visit MHE and told him he realized that the fear of going into orbit was a crazy delusional idea and thanked MHE for saving him from the state mental hospital. The man got a new job in Phoenix and then moved to Wisconsin with MHE's approval. He got married to a woman with a child and was happy being a husband and a father. MHE never charged him for his treatment.

Presenting Problem: Delusion

Age Group: Adult

Modality: Individual; outpatient

Problem Duration: NA

Treatment Length: NA

Result: Success. The man stopped having the delusion, got married and got a steady job.

Follow-up: A couple of years.

Techniques: Task assignment (behavioral and cognitive); utilization (of the man's belief he would go into orbit); redirecting attention

Source: *Phoenix*, pp. 44–46

Case #282

9

Miscellaneous Problems

SELF-IMAGE/BODY-IMAGE PROBLEMS

Case Summary: A patient of MHE's, the mother of a 14-year-old girl, told MHE that her daughter thought her feet were too large. Consequently, she had become extremely withdrawn, refusing to go out of the house and refusing to talk to anyone. MHE told the mother that he would make a phony house call and that she (the mother) should go along with whatever MHE did. MHE then examined the mother's chest, after arranging for the daughter to be there as a chaperone. After examining the mother, MHE "accidentally" stepped back onto the daughter's bare toes. When she cried out in pain, he turned to her and said angrily, "If you would grow those things large enough for a man to see, you wouldn't get them stepped on." Shocked at first, the girl quickly recovered and seemed pleased. Before MHE left the house, the girl had asked her mother if she could go out to a show. There was no further trouble about the feet.

Presenting Problem: Body-image; thinking feet are too big

Age Group: Adolescent

Modality: Family; outpatient (home visit)

Problem Duration: Two weeks

Treatment Length: One visit

Result: Success. The girl stopped thinking that her feet were too large and made a better social adjustment.

Follow-up: NA

Techniques: Implication; interpersonal evocation

Sources: *Collected Papers II*, pp. 315–316; *Conversations III*, pp. 12–14; *Uncommon Therapy*, pp. 197–198

Case #283

Case Summary: Harvey was 29-year-old man brought to a seminar as a challenge for MHE by psychoanalytically-oriented therapists who didn't think much of hypnotherapy. He was very unassertive and had all sorts of aches and pains. He had been in treatment with a psychiatrist for several years. He was bullied by people at work and never stood up for himself. He held a job far below his capabilities. He was not able to write legibly or tie his shoes or tie neatly. He was always making social mistakes that kept him from developing romantic relationships. He always assumed he would fail.

MHE put him into trance using authoritarian techniques since Harvey always tried to please authorities. He had Harvey learn to positively and negatively hallucinate. MHE then had him write the phrase, "It's a beautiful day in June," and he wrote it almost illegibly. MHE had a seminar attendee write a sample of the same phrase in good handwriting and MHE praised it excessively. Harvey was ashamed of his writing. MHE asked him if he would like to be able to write like the other man had and Harvey said he'd give anything to be able to.

Next MHE had Harvey forget he was Harvey and hallucinate scenes from his past in imaginary crystal balls, not recognizing that they were images of himself. [In another version MHE had Harvey assume the identity of one of the medical students in the seminar in order to get an impersonal view-point.] Harvey saw some traumatic scenes, including one in which he got punished for writing with his left hand. MHE had him awaken and write the phrase with his *right* hand (that is, the correct one, the left) without being aware that he had written it. He wrote it very well. When others in the room tried to convince him he had written it, MHE instructed, he was to call them damn liars. He did.

Then MHE had him watch the paper and find out who wrote the phrase next. When Harvey noticed himself writing it automatically, he became convinced that it was his handwriting after all. He went around the room and made everyone present praise his writing. He tied his shoes and tie neatly before leaving. He went back to work and started asserting himself. He recopied all his illegible records and got a raise and promotion. He also started dating and got married.

[In another version, Harvey was given a series of sheets of paper on which he legibly wrote a series of messages to himself to read sequentially after he came out of trance. The messages would convince him that he had written the pages and that he could write legibly.]

Presenting Problem: Poor handwriting; inability to tie shoes and tie neatly; unassertiveness; somatic complaints; poor self-image; poor relationships

Age Group: Adult

Modality: Individual; outpatient (demonstration)

Problem Duration: NA

Treatment Length: NA

Result: Success. Harvey started asserting himself on the job and with his psychiatrist and started dating women.

Follow-up: 40 years. The therapy took place in 1937 and MHE reported in 1977 that Harvey was still getting along well.

Techniques: Hypnosis; positive hallucination; automatic handwriting; dissociation (from own identity)

Sources: *Collected Papers IV*, pp. 81–85, and pp. 491–498; *Experiencing Erickson*, pp. 10–12

Case #284

Case Summary: A woman who had been divorced three times sought hypnosis from MHE for persistent feelings of coldness in her buttocks. These had developed after a disastrous first marriage, when she discovered that her

husband was an alcoholic and he roughly tried to consummate the marriage on the wedding night while intoxicated. When she failed to respond to his rough approach, he told her she had a "frigid ass" and that he was going to find a prostitute who would respond to his needs. Subsequent attempts to have intercourse were also unsuccessful and her husband always attributed this to her cold ass, which she feared was true. She tried to make the marriage work for a year, but it ultimately failed.

Some time after her first divorce, she married an effeminate man who was attached to his mother and male friends and who found her body repulsive. Their sexual encounters and her lack of response to him only further convinced her of the truth of her first husband's diagnosis—that she had a frigid ass.

She had resolved to give up the idea of marriage, but had met an older gentleman who seemed to be quite sensitive and who seemed to care for her. On the wedding night, it became apparent that he had married her to swindle her out of her money. When he realized that she was onto his scheme, he violently raped her and gave her the same label her first husband had given her.

She had recently met another man with whom she was contemplating marriage and who seemed more suitable, but she wanted to insure the same problem did not recur. She asked MHE not to do psychotherapy, but to use hypnosis to take away the cold feeling in her rear. He trained her thoroughly in hypnosis. Next MHE told her to make a systematic inquiry into how much hot water she could stand in in the bathtub until it raised goosebumps only on her legs. She accomplished this. Then in trance, MHE suggested that since she now knew that heat could produce the symptoms of cold, that could be true of her thighs and buttocks as well. He went on to describe the thrills and chills and tingles that run down a little girl's spine when she gets a doll she didn't expect, the tingling delights of sledding on a cold day, the joys of a cold dish of ice cream on a hot summer's day and other situations in which cold was linked to pleasure. MHE told her she should develop a secret, private knowledge that her body could experience heat from a subjective cold response and to keep this knowledge from her conscious mind. She told MHE soon after that that she had decided that she rather liked being a "frigid-ass." She married and started a family.

Presenting Problem: Cold buttocks

Age Group: Adult

Modality: Individual; outpatient

Problem Duration: NA

Treatment Length: NA

Result: Success. The woman was no longer troubled by cold buttocks.

Follow-up: MHE mentions that years have passed and the woman was enjoying her fourth marriage and had a child.

Techniques: Hypnosis; task assignment (behavioral and perceptual); reframing (cold feelings can be the result of heat)

Source: *Collected Papers IV*, pp. 218–222

Case #285

Case Summary: A 30-year-old divorced man lived alone and had a wretched life. He had no friends, had a bad job, lived in a shoddy boarding house and visited his doctor two to four times per week complaining about imaginary aches and pains. He was finally referred to MHE for hypnotherapy. MHE spent a month of weekly three- to four-hour sessions training the man in various hypnotic skills. Then MHE had him hallucinate a series of scenes from his life in imaginary crystal balls. As the man reviewed them, he concluded that anyone who had that kind of history had not much of a chance. He left that session quite depressed. The next session he outlined his small goals of attaining adequate health and a slightly better adjustment socially. He left that session depressed as well.

At the next session he was told that at some time in the future MHE would have him return and review the progress he had made in therapy that had enabled him to develop a normal life. Then he was hypnotized and was induced to see scenes of himself in the future in the hallucinated crystal balls. He was to see scenes of the successes he experienced as a result of successful therapy. He described a number of scenes in which he saw himself acting more assertively, asking for and obtaining a raise on his job, giving speeches, going out with several attractive women and generally being happy and confident. MHE induced an amnesia for the trance experience. At the next session he oriented the man to the future and had him feel as if he were returning for a follow-up interview with MHE. He described the changes he had made since ending therapy. He was given amnesia for that experience as well. He was given another appointment for two months in the future. When he returned he had made the changes that he had only hallucinated before.

He had a raise, a new girlfriend, a better position at work, and he had moved to nicer quarters. He had given several speeches and had stopped having all his aches and pains. Two years later he was still doing well and was making plans to marry his girlfriend.

Presenting Problem: Hypochondria

Age Group: Adult

Modality: Individual; outpatient

Problem Duration: Three years

Treatment Length: Seven sessions

Result: Success. The man stopped complaining of aches and pains and made many other positive changes in his personal, social and occupational situations.

Follow-up: Two years

Techniques: Hypnosis; amnesia; positive hallucination; age projection

Source: *Collected Papers IV*, pp. 397–404

Case #286

Case Summary: A sophomore in college had been in an automobile accident in her early teens that had left her with a small scar on the right side of her mouth. She had developed a habit of hiding the scar from anyone's sight. She would continually cover the right side of her face. Although right-handed, she had learned to eat with her left hand so she could keep her face hidden with her right hand. She could not drive a car because that would leave her face uncovered. She would only go out on dates at night and then only walk on the right side of the boy she was dating. She would not even smoke cigarettes while she was walking with her dates because she was afraid that her date would see her scar in the glow of the cigarette. (She did, however, enjoy kissing boys, as long as it was dark.) Her parents and several plastic surgeons had assured her the scar was so small that most people wouldn't notice and that plastic surgery wasn't needed.

She sought MHE's help in adjusting to her handicap. Even while seeing him, she kept her face covered with her hand. MHE had her make a self-portrait of her face and draw the scar as accurately as possible. She did the portrait and seemed confused after she did. MHE next hypnotized her and told her that she should investigate and learn everything she could about beauty patches that women used. Then she was to make a number of sketches showing various beauty patches and their locations on women's faces. She was to forget that these were trance suggestions and was to wonder why she was doing it.

When she brought the sketches back two weeks later, MHE slipped her self-portrait in among them and, after looking at them, laid them on a table and asked her to comment on each of them. She failed to recognize her self-portrait initially and was quite fascinated at the beauty patch that was a six-pointed star, because she only remembered drawing five-pointed stars as beauty marks. Once she realized that the six-pointed star was really her scar, she faltered in her speech and appeared shocked and confused.

MHE told her that her own self-portrait and her description of it indicated that it was like a beauty mark. He told her that she should go on dates and kiss boys underneath the porch light from now on and wonder which side of her mouth they were going to kiss her on, the right or the left.

[In one version MHE has her carry two heavy handbags on her date so she will keep her hands down.] MHE suspected that the dates would kiss the side with the beauty mark, the right side. She subsequently reported that her dates usually kissed her on her right side. MHE thought that this was because she was curious and when she was curious she always tipped her head to the left so that the date had to kiss her on the right. She lost her compulsion to hide her scar and made a good adjustment.

Presenting Problem: Shame about scar; hiding a scar on her face with her hand; behavioral restrictions associated with having to hide the scar constantly

Age Group: Adult

Modality: Individual; outpatient

Problem Duration: About seven years

Treatment Length: At least three sessions

Result: Success. The woman lost her compulsion to hide her scar and her shame about it.

Follow-up: Six years. She was subsequently married and had four children.

Techniques: Hypnosis; task assignment (behavioral); reframing (scar into beauty mark)

Sources: *Collected Papers IV*, pp. 465–469; *My Voice Will Go With You*, pp. 64–66

Case #287

Case Summary: A woman was brought to MHE by her husband because she had tantrums of anger at her husband and bouts of crying, although they seemed to have a good relationship. She had never offered any explanation for these outbursts to her husband. She told MHE that she had been raised by a mother who told her every day of her childhood that, since she was unattractive, she had better develop a good personality or she would never marry. She did develop a good personality and attracted many dates, but she kept rejecting them after they would "lie" to her. They would tell her she was attractive and this would disgust her.

She had finally settled on her husband as a mate because he had told her that he found her personality fascinating. As the years passed, he started telling her that she was pretty, especially after the birth of their child. She remembered, however, what her mother had said about her unattractiveness and also that her mother had told her that, after the birth of children, what little beauty a woman had was gone. She had noticed that her nipples had become deeply pigmented after the birth of her son, which confirmed her mother's prediction, as it was clearly unattractive. So when her husband would compliment her on her looks, she would find herself getting angry to the point of rage at his "lying."

She would not be swayed by MHE's or her husband's assurances that she was attractive—she knew otherwise. MHE learned that she thought that her son was the image of her husband, except that her husband had a mustache. He also learned that she often read fairy tales to her son. MHE gave her suggestions to tell fairy tales in trance and to discuss her husband's mustache. She did so. One of the fairy tales she told was "The Ugly Duckling."

MHE then told her that she should go home and, as a joke, paint a mustache with an eyebrow pencil on her son. When she returned, she told MHE that the mustache was grotesque on her son because it didn't fit him as it did her husband. MHE told her that there was a deeper meaning in that, but she wouldn't discover it right away. He then told her while she was in trance that a certain fairy tale would keep coming to her mind and that that would somehow fit with the mustache on her son's face. He also suggested that she would do something immediately before the next session to indicate that her unconscious was complying with the suggestions.

She came late to the next session because she had been delayed at the beauty parlor, having just had a complete makeover. She had been obsessed with "The Ugly Duckling" story since the last session and now realized that what was appropriate for a child was not appropriate for an adult. She had come to realize that her husband genuinely thought she was attractive and had enjoyed her darkly pigmented nipples. MHE told her that when her husband came home from work that night, she was to ask him if he wanted to take a pretty girl out to dinner that night. The husband was so astonished by this behavior that he agreed and forgot a business appointment that evening.

She came in for another appointment three months later and asked if she should reveal to her husband the silly ideas she had from childhood about being unattractive. As it appeared that the husband had lost all curiosity about the problem now that it was resolved, MHE recommended against telling him.

Presenting Problem: Unexplained anger and crying; negative self-image

Age Group: Adult

Modality: Individual; outpatient

Problem Duration: NA

Treatment Length: Five sessions

Result: Success. The anger and crying episodes stopped and the woman adjusted her self-image to a more positive one.

Follow-up: One year. The couple referred another couple in the hope that MHE could help that couple as much as he had helped them. They seemed to be happily adjusted.

Techniques: Hypnosis; posthypnotic suggestion; task assignment (behavioral)

Source: *Collected Papers IV*, pp. 470–475

Case #288

❧

Case Summary: A 35-year-old woman named Grace came to MHE because she wanted a husband and children. Her personality and appearance were such that men did not find her attractive. She was somewhat overweight, very dirty and unkempt, and her clothes were loud and ill-fitting. She was very cold and impersonal with those she was not close to but she could be very charming and interesting company when she chose to be.

Grace was coaxed by a friend, Agnes, to seek therapy from MHE because she was suicidally depressed. She was reluctant to seek therapy because she had little money. MHE told her that her therapy would be free as a favor to Agnes, who was also a friend of his. She told MHE that her present life was unbearable and he must help her. MHE told her to go home and decide if she was ready to accept any therapy he would give her, no matter how severe. He told her that her payment for therapy would be complete obedience to his instructions. The only choice she would have is that she could tell the instructions to Agnes, and if she approved, the patient would have to do the task.

She returned in three days and promised to comply with anything short of murder. MHE began by asking how much money she had. She said that she had $1,000 to spend. MHE told her to expect to spend $700 of it on herself. Then he began systematically and impersonally listing all of the faults of her appearance, giving her concrete evidence by having her use a mirror. He told Grace she could correct all these things herself and that they were the product of willful self-neglect. He then handed her a washcloth and instructed her to wash one-half of her neck, so that she could see the contrast.

At the next interview she returned, clean and well-groomed, although she still wore the same sloppy, clashing clothes. MHE discussed the changes she had made in an impersonal manner. MHE then told her, "Once you are stripped of your repressions, your own awareness of what had been so horribly repressed would be continuously present in your consciousness and would compel you to behave normally and rightfully with a pleasing and satisfying self-awareness." He revealed the repressed thought at the end of the session, "You have a pretty patch of fur between your legs." He instructed her to go home and, after her shower, explore that pretty patch of fur. Next he had her look at the two badges of womanhood that were on her chest. She should explore them visually and tactually.

At the next session MHE gave her elaborate instructions on how to prepare for the company dance, including which beauty specialists to see and how to go about making her own gown. She was to return when she was dressed for the dance. In a few weeks she returned on her way to the dance, dressed to a "T" and looking animated and vivacious.

Presenting Problem: Inability to get a mate

Age Group: Adult

Modality: Individual; outpatient

Problem Duration: NA

Treatment Length: Four sessions

Result: Success. The woman started dressing better and taking better care of her appearance. She was married within a year following therapy.

Follow-up: At least five years. The woman was married to a college professor/doctor and had four children.

Techniques: Task assignment (behavioral); hypnosis

Sources: *Collected Papers IV*, pp. 482–490; *Conversations I*, pp. 159–165; *Uncommon Therapy*, pp. 91–94

Case #289

Case Summary: A high school girl came to MHE for hypnotic therapy after hearing him speak at her school on hypnosis. She had become withdrawn and started failing in her schoolwork after moving and entering a new high school. She thought because she only had one double-sized incisor that she was unattractive and "a freak." She had sought treatment without her parents' knowledge because they wouldn't understand her concerns. She thought that MHE could probably hypnotize her with a glance and that she probably would not even know she was in trance, which probably explained why she could talk so freely to him.

She usually hid her mouth in any way she could, by refusing to eat in the school cafeteria, by keeping her upper lip closed over her upper teeth, by refusing to smile or laugh, etc. MHE noticed that she used a great deal of the slang talk of teenagers of that time period and decided to use this ability. He encouraged her to show off her slang in the sessions. He also learned that she was quite gifted at imitating accents from around the world and encouraged her to demonstrate that ability during sessions.

She greatly enjoyed these activities and MHE gradually started to steer the discussion towards slang and pun expressions for or involving teeth. He sent her out to research and return with as many slang expressions involving teeth as she could find. She came back and reported them to MHE in various accents and finally realized what he was having her do and how enjoyable the subject of teeth had become. He then reminded her of the popular phrase, "That's my Pop," and told her to go home and recite the phrase, "That's my maw," in front of a mirror. If she did not get it, she was to consult a dictionary. ("Maw" is another word for mouth and for mother.) She came back smiling and repeating the phrase at the next session. After that she made a good adjustment in high school.

Presenting Problem: Shame about teeth; avoidance of people and situations; failing in schoolwork

Age Group: Adolescent

Modality: Individual; outpatient

Problem Duration: NA

Treatment Length: Six sessions

Result: Success. The girl stopped being so withdrawn and ashamed of her teeth. She also did better academically.

Follow-up: MHE heard from teachers that she was popular and well-adjusted.

Techniques: Utilization (of slang and ability to imitate accents); task assignment (behavioral and cognitive)

Source: *Collected Papers IV*, pp. 500–502

Case #290

Case Summary: A 21-year-old woman sought therapy from MHE because she felt so hopeless about her life that she had decided to kill herself in three months. She paid MHE in advance for the sessions and then told him about her situation. She was an unwanted child and her parents had died in a car accident soon after she graduated from high school. She had drifted from job to job and place to place, never satisfied with herself and her situation. She thought herself very unattractive, mostly because she had an 1/8″ gap between her two front teeth. She kept it and her face hidden much of the time. She would have liked to get married and have children, but she knew it was impossible for someone who was as unattractive as she was.

MHE thought she was pretty, but noticed that she dressed and looked as unattractive as possible. She cut her own hair and it was uneven. She wore unflattering clothes that had rips in them and were of unmatched colors.

During the next four sessions, she insisted that MHE talk and earn his fee, but he managed to learn from her that she was attracted to a young man at work and he seemed to be attracted to her, although she could not recognize his attraction. She would endeavor to be at the water fountain when he was there and he did the same.

The next four sessions, MHE had her in light trance and suggested that she get new clothes and a new hairstyle, convincing her that she might as well have one last fling before she died. Next he had her practice squirting water through the gap in her teeth while naked in the shower until she could squirt with accuracy. She regarded this assignment as frivolous, but dutifully complied.

During the next few sessions, MHE built up the idea of using her new-found squirting skill to play a practical joke on the young man at work. At first she was unwilling to do it, but gradually she was persuaded. MHE suggested that she dress in her nicest new clothes, fix her hair and meet the young man at the drinking fountain. When he appeared, she should get a mouth full of water and squirt it at him through the gap in her teeth. Then she should take one step towards him, turn around, and "run like hell."

She did and the young man ran after her, caught her and kissed her in retaliation. The next day, he met her at the fountain with a water pistol and squirted her. She replied with a squirt of water through her teeth at him, which resulted in another kiss. Soon they were dating.

She missed several appointments and returned to tell MHE what had transpired. She then asked MHE to give her a cold, factual appraisal of herself, since she had been doing quite a bit of thinking on the subject. He told her that she had appeared as a person who didn't take good care of herself or care for herself, much in contrast with the person he saw in front of him now. She had perceived the gap in her teeth as a liability then. Furthermore, she had cooperated in her therapy and by her own efforts had changed her life. She now had evidence from a masculine point of view that she was attractive.

Several months later MHE received an announcement in the mail of her engagement to the young man and six months later an announcement of their marriage. Fifteen months later, MHE received a snapshot of the couple's home, an announcement of the birth of their first child, and news of her husband's promotion.

Presenting Problem: Suicidal intentions; negative self-image; shame about teeth; poor dress and appearance; avoidance of people

Age Group: Adult

Modality: Individual; outpatient

Problem Duration: NA

Treatment Length: 13 sessions, three months

Result: Success. The woman started dressing better, dating and got married. She gave up the idea of suicide.

Follow-up: The woman referred several people to MHE through the years and they always spoke highly of her.

Techniques: Task assignment (behavioral); hypnosis; utilization (of the gap in her teeth)

Sources: *Collected Papers IV*, pp. 502–505; *Phoenix*, pp. 131–132; *Uncommon Therapy*, pp. 71–73

Case #291

Case Summary: The wife of an intern on the staff of the hospital in which MHE worked sought therapy from him when she became pregnant. She was afraid that due to her poor childhood experiences she was unequipped to raise a child. She was unwanted by her mother, who gave over her care to an aunt in exchange for room and board. The aunt was rather cold and distant and much of the girl's life was spent playing alone. Her father was affectionate when around, but spent most of his time traveling on business.

MHE told her to come to the next session and tell him all her fears and anxieties in great detail. She came to the next session very emotional and fearing a breakdown. MHE reassured her and induced a trance. While she was in trance, he started evoking recent memories and introducing false memories of himself in those situations. Then he would induce amnesia for the hypnotic nature of those memories. This was to prepare her to age regress to childhood and have MHE be "The February Man" (see also Case #162), a kindly friend of her father's who visited her yearly during childhood and became a positive adult role model. In various sessions, he appeared again and again in her memories and became a trusted confidant and friend. He induced amnesia for all these hypnotic experiences.

There was a crisis during treatment when her mother wrote her and told her that she did not want to be called "grandmother," in essence rejecting the baby before it was born. MHE regressed the woman to a time before the writing of the letter and prepared her for it, so it was no longer a crisis.

Near the end of treatment, MHE arranged to have her forget that she had ever seen him for therapy but to seek his help to learn hypnotic analgesia for childbirth. She came for hypnotic childbirth training and used it successfully. She returned for a "booster shot" of hypnosis for the birth of her second child two years later and was found to be well-adjusted.

Presenting Problem: Fear of inadequate parenting abilities

Age Group: Adult

Modality: Individual; outpatient

Problem Duration: NA

Treatment Length: Six months

Result: Success. The woman made an adequate adjustment to parenting and had three children.

Follow-up: At least three years

Techniques: Hypnosis; age regression; amnesia; analgesia

Sources: *Collected Papers IV*, pp. 525–542; *Hypnotherapy*, pp. 460–477; *Uncommon Therapy*, pp. 179–182

Case #292

Case Summary: A woman with very poorly combed hair came to MHE because she was having trouble with her job. Her boss repeatedly told her to comb her hair, although she claimed to be doing "her level best." MHE asked her how afraid she was of looking her best. He told her that she could find out by going home and washing her hair. "You are going to find out a number of things about yourself." When the woman returned, she reported that she was now combing her hair very nicely. She also told MHE that after her shower she studied her body, front and back, in the mirror and found that she felt good about it. The woman's relationship with her boss improved.

Presenting Problem: Job difficulties; (negative self-image)

Age Group: Adult

Modality: Individual; outpatient

Problem Duration: NA

Treatment Length: (Four sessions)

Result: Success. The woman's job situation improved and her self-image improved.

Follow-up: NA

Techniques: Ambiguity ("a number of things"); task assignment (behavioral)

Sources: *Conversations I*, pp. 27–28; *Uncommon Therapy*, p. 105

Case #293

Case Summary: A 50-year-old woman came to MHE for therapy. She had an extremely low opinion of her life. She said that she was an alcoholic, a parasite, and that she hated her family, whom she lived with on a wealthy ranch. The woman had undertaken many successful business ventures during her life, all of which she had eventually destroyed. She was extremely critical of everyone around her. She criticized her mother for growing grasses in the backyard. She thought all married men were no good. She told MHE that he was a fool to work with her because she'd been rejected by other prominent psychiatrists.

MHE began by asking her what one of her accomplishments was. She replied that she started a ceramics business. The woman returned for sessions off and on. She was very self-pitying and made little improvement. During one session MHE discussed the grasses that her mother planted. He intentionally stumbled over the name of a certain grass and pretended to be unable to spell it. As he had hoped, this encouraged the patient to remark on his stupidity. The woman finally decided that she would continue coming to MHE once a month for advice. At one session the woman asked why MHE kept her as a patient. He told her that it certainly wasn't her sex appeal, since he was not at all attracted to her, so he must have seen something in the way of brains and personality and ability. She asked the same question several times later. Each time he would say brains, personality or ability, but he never would commit to just one of the qualities.

Presenting Problem: Critical of others; unhappy; business problems; negative self-image

Age Group: Adult

Modality: Individual; outpatient

Problem Duration: NA

Treatment Length: NA

Result: Failure. The woman never made any significant progress.

Follow-up: NA

Techniques: Reframing; utilization (of behavior and of beliefs)

Source: *Conversations I*, pp. 184–190

Case #294

Case Summary: A woman wrote to MHE several times asking if he would take her as a patient. He was surprised to see that she was writing from Phoenix, where they both lived, instead of calling him on the phone, but each time he wrote back saying that he would accept her in therapy. It took her three months to finally work up the courage to come to see MHE for a session; then she asked to be given a session after dark, so no one would see her.

When she finally came in she indicated, in a rather indirect manner, that she had a problem with passing flatus. She was attending college and had passed gas rather loudly while writing on the blackboard at the front of the class. She was so ashamed that she ran out of the classroom and stayed in her house for several months, avoiding people. MHE gave her a lengthy oration about athletes, muscle contraction, and the proper functioning of the bowels. He also explained that there is a proper place for certain activities—we don't brush our teeth at the dinner table—and that one must respect the needs of every part of the body. Sometimes, he explained, the needs of the body supersede the proper place and time for things, as when one is driving and gets sand in one's eyes.

He found out that she was a converted Catholic and MHE knew that they were especially devout. So at the second session, he accused her of being impious and making a mockery of God and told her that she should be ashamed of herself. She protested but he said he could prove it. He showed her his anatomy book and told her that no human engineer could make a valve that opened downward and let air out but contained liquid, solid and air. He told her that she should demonstrate her respect for God's handiwork by cooking a pot of beans, dancing nude in her house and learning why the people in the Navy called beans "whistleberries." He told her to practice "making little ones, making big ones, loud ones, soft ones." She did.

She later got married and returned to college. [In another version, MHE says that her sexual relations with her husband had been poor because she feared passing flatus, so it seems that she was already married in that version.] After therapy she had a baby and when MHE visited her in her home she breast-fed the baby in front of him with no shame.

Presenting Problem: Embarrassment (about flatulating); avoidance of people

Age Group: Adult

Modality: Individual; outpatient

Problem Duration: Three-six months

Treatment Length: NA

Result: Success. The woman returned to college and stopped hiding from people.

Follow-up: At least one year.

Techniques: Reframing; task assignment (behavioral); utilization (of shame and religious beliefs); analogy

Sources: *Conversations I*, pp. 213–216; *My Voice Will Go With You*, pp. 151–152; *Phoenix*, pp. 76–78; *Uncommon Therapy*, pp. 167–169

Case #295

Case Summary: A psychiatrist from another state, who had been a student of MHE's, referred a woman with whom he had been working unsuccessfully for three years. She was 50 years old, recently widowed, and had an adequate income. When she came to see MHE, he noticed that she wore a very tight blouse and had no breasts. He told her that he was a man and had a right to see bumps on her chest. Therefore, the next time she came to see him, she should have a pair of "falsies" on. He didn't care if they were small, medium, or large. She returned for the next session wearing medium-sized falsies. They had a discussion of her general situation. After that she returned home happy.

Presenting Problem: (Unhappiness)

Age Group: Adult

Modality: Individual; outpatient

Problem Duration: At least three years

Treatment Length: NA

Result: Success. The woman was no longer unhappy.

Follow-up: The psychiatrist who had referred the woman met MHE a month later and told him that when she returned to her home she was a different woman and was happy. Since she was in Phoenix such a short time, the psychiatrist was amazed at the difference, but the woman would not tell him what MHE had done with her.

Techniques: Task assignment (behavioral)

Source: *Experiencing Erickson*, pp. 141–142

Case #296

Case Summary: A man saw himself as very inferior because he was slightly less than six feet tall, which was the height of real men, in his view. He also weighed slightly less than a real man should weigh. He lived with his parents and sold 10th-rate used cars. He saw himself as a poor, miserable, s.o.b. shrimp. MHE got him to move out of his parents' home and change his self-image. The man became the manager of a new car dealership.

Presenting Problem: Poor self-image; dependency on parents

Age Group: Adult

Modality: Individual; outpatient

Problem Duration: NA

Treatment Length: NA

Result: Success. The man started to see himself in a better light and got a new job.

Follow-up: NA

Technique: Task assignment (behavioral)

Source: *Mind-Body Communication*, pp. 86–87

Case #297

Case Summary: A woman in her thirties reported being sexually molested regularly by her father from age six to 17, when she left home. She worked her way through high school, college and graduate school, all the while feeling inferior, ashamed, and indecent, hoping that the education she got would help her to feel better about herself. When the education didn't seem to make any difference in her feelings of self-worth, she just gave up and became a prostitute, living with one man after another. Sex was a horrible experience for her, as a man's erect penis terrified her and, when confronted with one, she became helpless, weak, and passive. MHE told her that she was stupid to be afraid of a bold, erect, hard penis, because she had a vagina and a vagina can take the biggest, boldest, most assertive penis and turn it into a dangling, helpless object. She could take a vicious pleasure in reducing it to a helpless, dangling object. She found that she did take pleasure in that and found that, as she did so, her feelings of self-worth increased.

Presenting Problem: Self-esteem; sexual problem (fear of erect penises)

Age Group: Adult

Modality: Individual; outpatient

Problem Duration: Since childhood

Treatment Length: NA

Result: Success. The woman lost her fear of penises and her self-esteem improved.

Follow-up: NA

Techniques: Reframing; linking (having a vagina with power)

Source: *My Voice Will Go With You*, pp. 36–37

Case #298

Case Summary: An eight-year-old girl had turned bitter and hateful. Her mother had been to see MHE for some pain control. MHE found out that the girl was bitter because she had a lot of freckles and the children at school teased her about them. She hated her freckles and she hated everyone. When her mother brought her to see MHE, she wouldn't come out of the car because she said she hated MHE. MHE had her mother drag her into the office and leave. MHE immediately accused the girl of being a thief and a liar. She defended herself but he said he had proof of his allegations. He had found out from her mother that she loved to eat anything made with cinnamon. He told her that she had been climbing up to steal some cinnamon cookies out of the cookie jar and the jar had spilled all over her face. The proof was on her face, he said, and called her "Cinnamon Face." She burst out laughing with relief after hearing his proof and they had a nice chat. They carried on a correspondence after that and the girl stopped being so bitter and hateful. She sent him a letter with a drawing of a girl with freckled face that was smiling and signed it "Cinnimon Face" [sic].

Presenting Problem: Being hateful

Age Group: Child

Modality: Individual; outpatient (and by mail)

Problem Duration: NA

Treatment Length: NA

Result: Success. The girl stopped being hateful.

Follow-up: MHE kept up a correspondence with her.

Techniques: Shock; reframing

Sources: *My Voice Will Go With You*, pp. 152–154; *Phoenix*, pp. 79–80

Case #299

Case Summary: A man named Harold came to MHE for therapy. Harold was in a pathetic state. He was filthy, unshaven, his hair and clothes were ragged, and his workman's boots were held together with twine. He lived in a shack and ate discarded vegetables and cheap meat. Harold believed that he was a no-good moron. He was also terrified of women and considered himself homosexual. In his opinion all he had going for him was his ability to work hard. He used manual labor to distract himself from feelings of misery and the desire to commit suicide. MHE told the man, "Listen you, listen to me. You're nothing but a miserable moron. You know how to work, you want help. You don't know nothing about doctoring. I do. You sit down in that there chair and you let me go to work."

Throughout therapy MHE used trance states of varying intensity to avoid Harold's resistance. MHE used several techniques to raise Harold's self-esteem. When Harold told MHE that the Bible was the most important thing in the world, MHE remarked on the passage in the Bible which discusses the importance of manual laborers. MHE told Harold that his body was nothing but a machine and that it was his job to care for that machine properly as he would care for farm machinery. MHE talked to Harold about the intellect and judgment required for efficient manual labor. He also told Harold about idiot savants. MHE told him he was "neither an idiot nor a savant, just somewhere in between."

These sessions led Harold to seek better living conditions, to care for himself, and to seek a better paying job. MHE wanted Harold to continue his education although Harold was confident he was too stupid. MHE had Harold take an algebra course, knowing full well that he would fail. When Harold reported his failure, MHE told him that his (Harold's) error had been enrolling to discover "if he would pass" the course rather than "that he could not."

Next MHE began encouraging Harold to socialize. He introduced him to Joe but forbid him to discuss the friendship with him. Although Joe was confined to a wheelchair, he was independent and supported himself. Joe had a large supply of knowledge and was very enterprising. He served as an inspiration for Harold. MHE told Harold to go to the library, where he gradually began to expand his knowledge. Harold was emotionally distressed by the subjects of cooking and writing. MHE discussed both subjects as great accomplishments, but also as something that the feeble-minded, even women, could do. Harold was encouraged to study the subjects and to master shorthand and typing. This led to his employment as an amanuensis for an eccentric intellectual who taught him a great deal. MHE also encouraged Harold to study music. MHE wanted him to learn to play the guitar eventually but he had him start with piano lessons. His teacher was an elderly woman.

After Harold got a managerial position in an office MHE hypnotized him and gave him the suggestion that at the next interview he would pose a question which was a tentative suggestion. Harold returned and said he'd like to go to college even though he knew he'd flunk out. He enrolled in college the next semester and was astonished to find that he received good grades at mid-semester. MHE told him not to put too much weight on these grades because the teachers had not had enough time to assess him. At the end of the semester he got all A's.

Next MHE began focusing on Harold's fear of women. Harold had never had anything to do with women and insisted that he didn't want to have any part of them. Early in the therapy MHE had assigned Harold to make friends with a total stranger. He arranged it so that Harold would meet a couple who MHE knew would be friendly. Having given him some practice in socializing with a woman (as part of the couple), MHE suggested that Harold take swimming lessons at the YMCA and take dancing lessons. Harold resisted because he feared contact with women, but eventually he complied. MHE suggested that he thoroughly wash himself after contact with women.

Then MHE gave Harold a lecture about sexuality in animals as well as humans. This led to a great deal of reading about sex in the library. MHE gave Harold a cryptic assignment about discovering unhappy young people in the world who want someone to come along and help them. MHE told him to go to a public dance hall to execute this assignment. Harold saw many people there who were afraid to dance. He asked several wallflowers to dance.

After this experience MHE put therapy on hold so that Harold could think about all he had learned. While Harold was in college he lived in an apartment complex. One of his neighbors was a middle-aged divorcée. She began showing up at his door with groceries and insisting on cooking dinner for him. He was puzzled and annoyed by her. One evening, as she was leaving, she kissed him on the cheek. He got in the shower and scrubbed his face for quite a while.

When he told MHE this story MHE talked about the various meanings of a kiss. A week later MHE told Harold, "You sure as hell gotta find out what kinda critter a woman is. You ain't gonna let her sink no hooks into you, and you ain't gonna mess her up or get messed up yourself. All you gonna do is lay the answers right out on the line." Several weeks later Harold returned to report that he had made love to the woman. He knew it was the "answer" that MHE had spoken of.

After that experience the pleasure he took in life increased tremendously. After some time Harold and the woman decided to see people their own age. Harold had very specific goals for after he finished college; he had chosen a career and hoped to have a wife, a home and children.

Presenting Problem: Unhappiness; suicidal thoughts; poor self-image; fear of women

Age Group: Adult

Modality: Individual; outpatient

Problem Duration: Many years

Treatment Length: NA

Result: Success. Harold became happier and was enthusiastic about his future.

Follow-up: NA

Techniques: Task assignment (behavioral, perceptual and cognitive); hypnosis; utilization (of Harold's beliefs about himself); matching (Harold's language); direct suggestion

Source: *Uncommon Therapy*, pp. 120–148

Case #300

HYPNOTIC BLOCKS/RESISTANCE

Case Summary: A man who had previously participated in experimental studies on hypnosis and been an excellent subject was unable to develop the oral anesthesia required to have dental work done without chemical anesthesia. He was easily able to develop a glove anesthesia (numbness of the hand), but anytime the attempt was made to transfer the anesthesia to his mouth, it failed. MHE was consulted after several dentist/hypnotists failed to produce the oral anesthesia. MHE induced a trance and reminded the man of his desire to be comfortable in the dental chair. He then suggested to the man that his hand would become hyperesthetic (extremely sensitive) and that the dentist would take great care during the dental work to avoid contact with the sensitive hand. The man experienced the hand hyperesthesia and then spontaneously developed oral anesthesia. MHE commented that the man had a fixed belief that dental work must be associated with hypersensitivity; once that belief was taken into account, the work could proceed.

Presenting Problem: Inability to develop hypnotic anesthesia for dental work

Age Group: Adult

Modality: Individual; outpatient

Problem Duration: NA

Treatment Length: One session

Result: Success. The man was able to use oral anesthesia during his dental work.

Follow-up: The same procedure had to be used in the future to develop oral anesthesia for dental work with the man.

Techniques: Hypnosis; utilization (of hypersensitivity and of belief that pain sensitivity must be associated with dental work); linking (hypersensitivity with hand)

Sources: *Collected Papers I*, pp. 168–169; *Collected Papers IV*, pp. 215–218; *Hypnotherapy*, pp. 77–78 and pp. 225–226; *Life Reframing*, pp. 33–35

Case #301

Case Summary: A dentist's wife responded to all attempts to induce a trance with her by getting "scared stiff," unable to move or relax and unable to comply with suggestions. She would end up crying. She sought MHE's help and told him that she would like to be able to use trance to have dental work done. She gave him permission to use psychiatric treatment if it was necessary. MHE started to induce a trance by telling her that she would get stiff, even more stiff than she had gotten before. Then she should close her eyes and have them get so stiff that she wouldn't be able to open them. When she responded well to those suggestions, MHE told her that she could get scared silly and start to cry, but she could take a deep breath and go deeply into trance first. She took a deep breath and went into trance and relaxed. MHE reminded her that at any moment she could get scared and cry, but now that she knew how to relax and go deeply into trance, she might as well do that instead. He gave her a posthypnotic suggestion to insure that she could go into trance comfortably in the future. He then had her experience various deep trance phenomena.

Presenting Problem: Fear; muscular tension and crying during trance induction attempts

Age Group: Adult

Modality: Individual; outpatient

Problem Duration: NA

Treatment Length: One session

Result: Success. The woman was able to go into trance comfortably.

Follow-up: One year later, she was still able to go comfortably into trance.

Techniques: Hypnosis; linking (stiffness to eyelids); splitting (crying from stiffness); utilization (of stiffness)

Sources: *Collected Papers I*, pp. 169–170; *Hypnotherapy*, pp. 78–79

Case #302

Case Summary: A 25-year-old doctoral student in psychology was very interested in hypnotic alteration of sensory-perceptual processes such as anesthesia, hypnotic deafness and blindness, and color-blindness. At first skeptical that anyone could experience these phenomena, she had become convinced by observation and testing that others could experience them. She remained convinced, however, that she could not experience them herself. She asked MHE to attempt to help her experience them. She was generally a good trance subject. She was successfully able to develop glove anesthesia, and was surprised when it did not disappear when she focused on her hand. After experiencing several unsuccessful but creative and persistent efforts to induce hypnotic blindness, she expressed disappointment, but continued to urgently request that MHE continue his efforts.

He thought it over and decided that she really had an unrecognized fear of blindness and was using the experiments compulsively to deal with that fear. MHE therefore decided to use the experimental situation to produce within her an "acute hysterical obsessional compulsive mental state" which would give rise to blindness akin to pathological hysterical blindness that occurs spontaneously with some patients.

MHE found out that the woman had two traumatic incidents in her past relating to blindness, one in which her kitten had developed blindness and been killed in an accident (she had subsequently developed a cat phobia) and one in which a friend had gone blind as the result of an accident. He used those incidents, which she was very distressed about, and other incidents of the development of blindness, to induce in her an obsession about blindness connected with distress. This method proved so successful that she was terrified to find herself made blind. After some time in trance, MHE helped her redevelop her sight, although it took some time and effort. She was rehypnotized several weeks later to help develop blindness comfortably, which she was able to do. Several years later, when questioned, she remembered the blindness without distress and MHE also ascertained that she no longer had a cat phobia or distress over the incidence which resulted in her friend's blindness.

Presenting Problem: (Cat phobia; fear of blindness)

Age Group: Adult

Modality: Individual; outpatient

Problem Duration: (Since childhood for the cat phobia, probably at least 15 years)

Treatment Length: (Two or three sessions over the course of several months)

Result: Success. The fear of hypnotic blindness dissipated and the cat phobia and distress about her friend's accident were removed.

Follow-up: "Several years later" the cat phobia had disappeared.

Techniques: Hypnosis; anesthesia; hypnotic blindness

Source: *Collected Papers II*, pp. 51–65

Case #303

Case Summary: A woman was married to a physician. She needed a painful medical procedure which her husband was going to do for her. Rather than using general anesthesia, they were going to use a hypnotic anesthesia. The woman was an excellent hypnotic subject. She could develop a perfect anesthesia but just before the procedure began she would lose it. MHE asked her some questions about her sexual history: Was she a virgin when she married? What did she wear to bed? The woman turned out to be quite modest. MHE asked her how she would feel if he put his hand on her knee. She said she wouldn't mind if he had some legitimate reason. MHE put his hand on her knee. He then told her he was going to do it again, only this time it was going to be underneath her dress. "Do you feel it?" he asked.

"Yes, and I don't like it." "You're a good hypnotic subject, why do you feel it?" "I don't." The woman found she had anesthesia all the way up to her waist. She couldn't move her legs. MHE told her to let the anesthesia disappear. MHE gave her two choices. The first was to permit the medical procedure. The alternative was to braid her pubic hair into pigtails, have her husband take color snapshots of it, and then to destroy the film. She allowed the procedure to take place.

Presenting Problem: Inability to maintain a hypnotic anesthesia

Age Group: Adult

Modality: Individual; outpatient

Problem Duration: (A few days to a few weeks)

Treatment Length: (One session)

Result: Success. The woman was able to maintain an anesthesia.

Follow-up: "Braids" became a family word for something funny and absurd.

Techniques: Task assignment (behavioral); implication (that the woman would not be able to feel the touch and would develop anesthesia); shock

Source: *Conversations II*, pp. 99–103

Case #304

ATHLETIC PERFORMANCE PROBLEMS

Case Summary: Donald Lawrence [or Dallas Long, in another version] was a 6'6", 260 lb., high school student. The coach at the high school had been working with him all year on shotputting. The coach hoped the boy would break the national high school record. The boy's progress had reached a plateau that he was having trouble overcoming. Donald's father brought him to MHE. MHE told Donald how Roger Banister had broken the world record for the mile. Bannister had realized that the difference between a 240-second mile and 239.5-second mile was really very slight. Donald had already thrown the shot 58 ft. MHE asked him if he could tell a difference between 58 ft. and 58 1/6 ft. Donald said no. Gradually MHE kept increasing the difference. He continued to "slowly enlarge the possibility" for the next few sessions. Two weeks later Donald broke the national high school record. That summer he told MHE he was going to the Olympics. MHE told him that he should just take the bronze medal since he was only 18 years old. For each subsequent competition he went to, MHE told him what goal he could reasonably achieve. Donald eventually broke the world record by 6 ft. 10 in., as per MHE's instructions.

Presenting Problem: Athletic plateau

Age Group: Adolescent

Modality: Individual; outpatient

Problem Duration: NA

Treatment Length: NA

Result: Success. Donald's athletic performance improved.

Follow-up: NA

Techniques: Reframing; direct suggestion

Sources: *Healing in Hypnosis*, p. 235; *My Voice Will Go With You*, pp. 103–105

Case #305

Case Summary: A golfer wanted to win the Arizona Amateur golfing championship before becoming a professional golfer. He found that in every tournament he shot in the 90s but when he was alone his score would be in the low 70s. MHE put him in trance and told him that he would only remember playing the first hole and then he would be alone when he played tournaments. He played in the next state tournament. After the 18th hole he thought he'd just finished the first and he wondered where all the people had come from.

Presenting Problem: Unsatisfactory golf performance; athletic performance difficulties

Age Group: Adult

Modality: Individual

Problem Duration: NA

Treatment Length: NA

Result: (Success. It is implied that the man's performance improved.)

Follow-up: NA

Techniques: Hypnosis; negative hallucination

Source: *My Voice Will Go With You*, p. 105

Case #306

MISCELLANEOUS CASES

Case Summary: MHE was treating an artist in his thirties for marital and personality problems and was making good progress, but the man complained that he had been trying for some years to paint a circus picture and had not even succeeded in sketching one out. MHE gave him posthypnotic suggestions regarding painting such a picture. The man called MHE after completing the picture in an amazingly short time without even having a conscious memory of having painted it. Various aspects of the picture represented significant people in his life. In trance, he remembered painting it. In trance and out of trance, he and art judges who viewed it were satisfied and impressed with the quality of the work. Therapy was terminated several sessions after the picture was painted.

Presenting Problem: Marital problem; personality problem; artistic block

Age Group: Adult

Modality: Individual; outpatient

Problem Duration: 10 years

Treatment Length: NA

Result: Success. The man painted the picture he had been blocked on and finished therapy.

Follow-up: NA

Techniques: Hypnosis; posthypnotic suggestion; direct suggestion

Source: *Collected Papers II*, pp. 269–272

Case #307

Case Summary: A social service worker who had acted as a hypnotic demonstration subject for MHE sought his help for breaking through her block in psychoanalysis. She was told that, since she was under the care of another psychiatrist, this would be unethical. She was disappointed and had hoped that MHE would return the favor she had done him by acting as a demonstration subject. MHE then asked her if she would again serve as a demonstration subject that week. She assented. MHE had a guess as to what her hidden problem was, so at the demonstration he had her forget her identity and take on that of one of her office mates, a most attractive and very "feminine" woman. The week after the demonstration, the woman had a breakthrough in her analysis and discovered that she had latent homosexual impulses that she was constantly struggling to repress. This insight was initiated by thinking about the office mate whose identity she had assumed during the hypnotic demonstration. After she had successfully completed her analysis, she told MHE that her progress had something to do with him and with the office mate, but she didn't know exactly what. MHE hypnotized her and had her remember the demonstration. She realized that he had known her conflict all along.

Presenting Problem: Block/resistance in psychoanalysis

Age Group: Adult

Modality: Individual; outpatient (demonstration)

Problem Duration: One year

Treatment Length: One session

Result: Success. The woman was able to overcome the block, resolve her issues, and complete her analysis.

Follow-up: The woman subsequently married and raised a family in addition to having a career. She abandoned social service work once she realized she had pursued it because of her problems.

Techniques: Hypnosis; depersonalization; trance identification

Source: *Collected Papers IV*, pp. 383–385

Case #308

Case Summary: An orthodox Jewish woman whose family had fled from Nazi persecution in Europe came to America. The parents wanted their daughter to assimilate in America, but when a Jewish doctor proposed to her, she had difficulty accepting because he did not keep a kosher home. MHE had her leave his office and buy a ham sandwich across the street. He had her unwrap it in his office and take a bite. He told her he had never seen a person die, which she was afraid might happen to her if she ate ham. Under his gaze, she ate the ham and didn't die. MHE suggested that it would be just terrible if she happened to like the sandwich. She married the non-kosher doctor and did fine.

Presenting Problem: Inhibition about breaking tradition

Age Group: Adult

Modality: Individual; outpatient

Problem Duration: NA

Treatment Length: (One session)

Result: Success. The woman lost her inhibition and was able to marry a man who did not share her traditions.

Follow-up: MHE mentions that the woman was happily married at the time of the case report.

Technique: Task assignment (behavioral); indirect suggestion

Source: *Collected Papers IV*, pp. 456–457

Case #309

Case Summary: A man named Tom came to MHE because he sat alone in a room all day and did nothing. MHE asked him, "Can't you waste time

elsewhere?" He suggested that the man waste his time at the library. Once at the library Tom idled away his time by picking up magazines. Someone saw him reading an article on speleology and struck up a conversation about it with him. Soon Tom went on a spelunking trip and met someone who liked skiing. That person took Tom to Flagstaff to ski. Tom's social life continued in a similar fashion.

Presenting Problem: Loneliness and boredom

Age Group: Adult

Modality: Individual; outpatient

Problem Duration: NA

Treatment Length: NA

Result: Success. Tom's social life improved.

Follow-up: NA

Techniques: Task assignment (behavioral); pattern intervention (changing the location of the symptom)

Source: *Conversations I*, pp. 286–287

Case #310

Case Summary: A woman whose husband had been successfully treated by MHE with hypnosis for repeated examination failures (see Case #205) sought hypnosis from MHE as she was on her way to the hospital to deliver her first child. [In another version, she came in a month before.] MHE gently hinted that she should allow more preparation for this, but he hypnotized her. When she was in trance, he taught her the use of hypnotic anesthesia and analgesia by using common everyday analogies for those experiences. He also helped her to develop a body dissociation. While she was in trance, he told her that she should go to the hospital and cooperate in every way, explaining to the medical personnel that she wanted no medications or chemical anesthesia. While she was on the delivery table, she should think about the baby. She could wonder about the gender, the weight, the length, the hair color, the eye color, the name, etc. of the baby. She should enjoy all the happy thoughts she had about having a baby. She did as he suggested and was startled to hear the obstetrician say, "Here is your baby boy." She returned to MHE two years later, several days before her next child was to be born, for more hypnotic preparation. MHE instructed her to go deeply into trance and repeat what she had done the first time.

Presenting Problem: Childbirth preparation

Age Group: Adult

Modality: Individual; outpatient

Problem Duration: NA

Treatment Length: Two or three sessions

Result: Success. The woman had an easy delivery.

Follow-up: NA

Techniques: Hypnosis; anesthesia; analgesia; dissociation; redirecting attention; analogy

Sources: *Experiencing Erickson*, p. 152; *Healing in Hypnosis*, p. 267; *Mind-Body Communication*, pp. 26–28; *Teaching Seminar*, p. 60

Case #311

Case Summary: A man came to MHE because he could not learn to dance; he said he had "three left feet." MHE got him to be intensely interested in and to describe the sensations in one foot at a time as he moved it slightly. In this way the man learned to dance.

Presenting Problem: Inability to dance

Age Group: Adult

Modality: Individual; outpatient

Problem Duration: NA

Treatment Length: NA

Result: Success. The man learned to dance.

Follow-up: NA

Techniques: Redirecting attention; task assignment (behavioral and perceptual)

Source: *Healing in Hypnosis*, p. 123

Case #312

꙯

Case Summary: A woman came to see MHE because she hated living in Phoenix but refused to go on vacation to Flagstaff. MHE suggested that she might develop a curiosity about why she liked to punish herself. He also suggested an even more profound curiosity about the "flash of color" she would see if she spent a week in Flagstaff. The woman went to Flagstaff intending to stay for a week and stayed for a month. The flash of color she saw was a red-headed woodpecker flying past an evergreen. After that trip the woman began traveling frequently.

Presenting Problem: Dissatisfaction with living in Phoenix

Age Group: Adult

Modality: Individual; outpatient

Problem Duration: NA

Treatment Length: NA

Result: Success. The woman got away from Phoenix frequently.

Follow-up: NA

Techniques: Hypnosis; implication (that she would see something interesting in Flagstaff); redirecting attention

Source: *My Voice Will Go With You*, pp. 108–109

Case #313

꙯

Case Summary: A six-year-old [seven-year-old in another version] girl had a problem with stealing. She stole things from her parents and other children. Her parents asked MHE to help them with her. MHE wrote her a letter that he sent to the father's office and had the father drop on the child's floor at midnight. It began, "Dear Heidi-Ho, I am your six-year-old-growing-up fairy." In the letter, MHE described himself as having many eyes and ears to watch and hear the little girl with. He told her that each year she had another growing up fairy and that her previous fairies had told him many good things about her. He had heard that she was making some mistakes and that was to be expected. It was also expected that she would correct her mistakes. The girl wrote back and invited him to her seventh birthday party, but he declined because he was the "six-year-old-growing-up fairy." The girl stopped stealing.

Presenting Problem: Stealing

Age Group: Child

Modality: Individual; outpatient (by mail)

Problem Duration: NA

Treatment Length: NA

Result: Success. The girl stopped stealing.

Follow-up: NA

Techniques: Indirect suggestion; interpersonal evocation

Sources: *My Voice Will Go With You*, pp. 241–242; *Phoenix*, 52–53

Case #314

Case Summary: A man who was committed to the mental hospital pestered everyone by telling them he didn't belong there. MHE instructed the staff to reply, "But you are here!" After getting this response for six months, the man finally exclaimed in frustration, "I know I'm here!" When MHE heard about this, he went to see the man. When the man told him that he didn't belong there, MHE replied, "But you are here," and the man answered that he knew he was. MHE then asked him what he was going to do about getting out of there. Within nine months the man was out of the hospital, working and helping to put his sister through college.

Presenting Problem: Obnoxious behavior; not wanting to be in the hospital

Age Group: Adult

Modality: Individual; inpatient

Problem Duration: NA

Treatment Length: 15 months

Result: Success. The man got out of the hospital and was working.

Follow-up: NA

Techniques: Interpersonal evocation (of frustration); utilization (of repetitive claims)

Source: *Phoenix*, p. 31

Case #315

Case Summary: Juan was a young Mexican man who felt that nobody would hire him because of his ethnic background. MHE told him that if he followed his instructions he would get a job. MHE told Juan to go to a restaurant and volunteer to mop up the kitchen for free. Juan followed his instructions daily and in time the restaurant began using him for a variety of jobs, but still without pay. Finally, MHE had Juan tell the manager that he thought he could get a paying job in Tucson. The manager offered him a good wage to stay. Later Juan got a substantial raise through similar means.

Presenting Problem: Lack of employment

Age Group: Adolescent

Modality: Individual; outpatient

Problem Duration: NA

Treatment Length: NA

Result: Success. Juan was able to obtain a good job in a restaurant.

Follow-up: NA

Techniques: Task assignment (behavioral)

Source: *Teaching Seminar*, pp. 249–250

Case #316

Glossary of Techniques

Age progression: Hypnotically reorienting a person to his/her future. Also called "future projection."

Age regression: Hypnotically reorienting a person to his/her past.

Alteration of sensation: Hypnotically changing a person's perception or experience of some sensation, e.g., pain into tingling.

Ambiguity: Not giving enough information or cues for the person to be able to interpret clearly the meaning of some action or statement.

Analgesia: Hypnotic elimination of pain.

Analogy: When something is likened to something else, either explicitly, as in simile ("Your eyes are *like* the moon") or implicitly ("You can make a *bridge* between your unconscious and conscious").

Anchoring the resistance: Linking the person's objections or difficulties co-operating with some location, aspect of his/her experience, or area of his/her body.

Anchoring the symptom: Linking the person's symptom with some location, aspect of his/her experience or area of his/her body.

Anesthesia: Hypnotic elimination of sensation.

Apposition of opposites: Putting two opposite concepts together in the same phrase, suggestion or sentence. For example, "You can be *comfortable* about being *uncomfortable* at times."

Arm levitation: Automatic lifting of the hand and arm during hypnosis, usually suggested or induced by the hypnotist. Also called "hand levitation."

Automatic handwriting: Writing done while in trance that is not under the person's deliberate control.

Body dissociation: A sense of detachment from the body that can be suggested or can happen spontaneously in trance.

Catalepsy: The immobility of certain parts or all of the body.

Confusion technique: A technique, originated by MHE, that involves inducing trance by overwhelming the person's conscious ability to make sense of what the hypnotist is saying or doing.

Depersonalization: A sense that one is not oneself. In this book, the term is used to describe the deliberate induction of such a sense.

Direct suggestion: Telling someone, in trance or out of trance, what to do very directly.

Dissociation: A splitting of one part of a person's experience or behavior from any other part.

Evoking abilities/resources: Helping people gain access to their strengths and capabilities.

Future projection: *See* age progression.

Hand levitation: *See* arm levitation.

Hypnosis: An altered state of awareness or the induction of an altered state of awareness. This state is usually characterized by a sense of dissociation and a narrowing of the focus of attention.

Implication: Suggestion that something may be the case without explicitly stating it.

Indirect suggestion: Telling someone to do something in a roundabout way, without stating it directly. Includes the use of metaphor, implication, and nonverbal suggestions.

Interpersonal evocation: Using the therapeutic relationship to evoke certain responses from people, usually either emotions or behavior.

Interspersal: Nonverbally emphasizing certain words, phrases or sentences to make an indirect suggestion.

Linking (of . . .): Joining two concepts, actions or experiences together.

Matching (of . . .): The therapist using the same language, syntax, gestures, breathing rates, beliefs or other aspects of the person.

Metaphor: Any action or figure of speech that uses one thing to speak about another. This category includes anecdotes, analogies, stories, puns, riddles, jokes, and idiomatic phrases.

Negative hallucination: When the person drops something out of his/her sensory field, such as not hearing a loud noise or seeing someone nearby. This can be deliberately induced during hypnosis or may occur spontaneously.

Normalizing: Giving a person the message that his/her behavior or experience is normal, not pathological or highly unusual.

Ordeal: Having someone perform some burdensome action when a symptom occurs or to stave off the symptom.

Oxymoron: Phrases in which two opposite concepts are placed together, such as "burning cold" or "vicious pleasure."

Paradoxical intervention: Telling the person to do the opposite of what he/she has been doing to try to get rid of the symptom or problem.

Parallel treatment: When one person is treated to indirectly treat another.

Pattern intervention: Breaking the usual symptom pattern into pieces or changing some minor or major aspect of the symptom performance.

Positive hallucination: When the person adds something to his/her sensory field that observers cannot perceive, such as seeing puppies playing on the floor. This can be deliberately induced or may occur spontaneously in hypnosis.

Posthypnotic suggestion: While the person is in trance, directing him/her to do some action, to think something, or to perceive something after he/she comes out of trance.

Prescribing resistance: Directing the person to resist hypnosis or treatment.

Redirecting attention: Refocusing attention or perception on other aspects of the person's behavior, experience, or situation.

Reframing: Suggesting an alternative frame of reference for or way of thinking about some situation.

Shock: Jarring someone with an unexpected action or talk; usually used to focus attention and/or to rapidly induce trance.

Skill building: Giving people tasks to increase or attain life skills.

Surprise: *See* shock.

Splitting (of . . .): Dividing a concept, experience, or action into two or more components.

Symptom displacement: Changing the location of the symptom, within the body or the world.

Symptom prescription: Directing the person to perform a symptom deliberately.

Symptom scheduling: Directing the person to perform a symptom at specific times only.

Symptom transformation: Taking the underlying energy of the symptom and changing its direction or application.

Structured amnesia: Deliberately creating forgetfulness by reorienting the person to the moment he/she went into trance.

Task assignment (behavioral): Directing the person to do something between sessions or after a session.

Task assignment (cognitive): Directing the person to think something between sessions or after a session.

Task assignment (perceptual): Directing the person to perceive something between sessions or after a session.

Task assignment (symbolic): Directing the person to do something that symbolizes his/her problem or a solution between sessions or after a session.

Time distortion: Changing the person's subjective experience of time while he/she is in trance. This can entail time contraction or condensation (making time seem shorter than clock or calendar time) or time expansion (making time seem longer than clock or calendar time).

Time framing: Suggesting a time period in which something, usually symptom resolution, will occur.

Trance identification: Having the person in trance take on the identity of someone else while in trance.

Utilization (of . . .): The therapist/hypnotist uses the person's usual mental habits, resistance, symptoms, behavior, delusions, or any other aspect of the person's internal or external behavior in service of treatment or trance induction.

Source Materials

"Advanced Techniques I," (Undated audiotape). Phoenix, Arizona: Milton Erickson Foundation. ["Advanced Techniques"]

Alexander, Leo. (1965) "Clinical Experiences with Hypnosis in Psychiatric Therapy," *The American Journal of Clinical Hypnosis*, 7, 190–206. ["Clinical Experiences"]

"Caring and Clarity," (1975) *The Co-Evolution Quarterly*, Fall, 32–33. ["Caring and Clarity"]

"Double Binds (Advanced Techniques II)," (Undated audiotape). Phoenix, Arizona: Milton Erickson Foundation. ["Double Binds"]

Erickson, Milton H. and Rossi, Ernest L. (1981) *Experiencing hypnosis: therapeutic approaches to altered states*. New York: Irvington. [*Experiencing Hypnosis*]

Erickson, Milton H. and Rossi, Ernest L. (1979) *Hypnotherapy: An exploratory casebook*. New York: Irvington. [*Hypnotherapy*]

Erickson, Milton H. and Rossi, Ernest L. (1989) *The february man: Evolving consciousness and identity in hypnotherapy*. New York: Brunner/Mazel. [*The February Man*]

Gordon, David and Myers-Anderson, Maribeth. (1981) *Phoenix: Therapeutic patterns of Milton H. Erickson*. Cupertino, California: Meta. [*Phoenix*]

Haley, Jay. (1963) *Strategies of psychotherapy*. New York: Grune and Stratton. [*Strategies of Psychotherapy*]

Haley, Jay. (1973) *Uncommon therapy: The psychiatric techniques of Milton H. Erickson, M.D.* New York: Norton. [*Uncommon Therapy*]

Haley, Jay. (1984) *Ordeal therapy: Unusual ways to change behavior*. San Francisco: Jossey-Bass. [*Ordeal Therapy*]

Haley, Jay. (1985) *Conversations with Milton H. Erickson, M.D. Volume I: Changing individuals; Volume II: Changing couples; Volume III: Changing children and families*. New York: Triangle (Norton). [*Conversations I, II, III*]

Rosen, Sidney. (1982) *My voice will go with you: The teaching tales of Milton H. Erickson*. New York: Norton. [*My Voice Will Go With You*]

Rossi, Ernest L. (1980) *The collected papers of Milton Erickson on hypnosis, Volumes I-IV*. New York: Irvington. [*Collected Papers I, II, III, IV*]

Rossi, Ernest L., Ryan, Margaret O., and Sharp, Florence A. (1983) *Healing in hypnosis : The seminars, workshops and lectures of Milton H. Erickson, Volume I.* New York: Irvington. [*Healing in Hypnosis*]

Rossi, Ernest L., and Ryan, Margaret O. (1985) *Life reframing in hypnosis: The seminars, workshops and lectures of Milton H. Erickson, Volume II.* New York: Irvington. [*Life Reframing*]

Rossi, Ernest L., and Ryan, Margaret O. (1986) *Mind-body communication in hypnosis: The seminars, workshops and lectures of Milton H. Erickson, Volume III.* New York: Irvington. [*Mind-Body Communication*]

Zeig, Jeffrey K. (Editor). (1982) *Ericksonian approaches to hypnosis and psychotherapy.* New York: Brunner/Mazel. [*Ericksonian Approaches*]

Zeig, Jeffrey K. (1985) *Experiencing Erickson: An introduction to the man and his work.* New York: Brunner/Mazel. [*Experiencing Erickson*]

Zeig, Jeffrey K. (1980) *A teaching seminar with Milton Erickson.* New York: Brunner/Mazel. [*Teaching Seminar*]

Index

GENERAL INDEX

mother-in-law, 255
motor impairment, 204
movies, 247
mow the lawn, 114, 155
muscle control, 108
muscular tension and crying, 318
music, 1, 3, 67, 157, 159, 204
mustache, 217, 301
mutism, 54, 55, 209

nailbiting, 3–4
narcotic stupor, 64–65, 71
narcotics, 64, 69, 71, 76
nasty letters, 57
nausea, 136, 187, 261
Naval Academy, 113, 231
Navy, 162
Nazi(s), 207, 325
neurodermatitis, 95–96
neurologist, 67
New England, 83, 244, 277
New Mexico, 30, 91
New Year's Day, 115
New York, 10
New York Symphony, 236
newspaper, 11, 93
no memory of father, 220
nonsense, 203, 209
Norskys (*see* Norwegian)
North Dakota, 256
Norwegian, 7
nude, 11
    dancing girls, 281–282
    young men, 282
nursery rhymes, 204, 206
nursing a pickle, 255

oatmeal, 273
obesity, 14, 20, 21–30, 92, 154
obnoxious behavior, 329
obscenity, 13
obsession(s), 234–235, 281
    for killing self and son, 43
obsessive-compulsive, 123, 233
one simple question, 108
operation(s), 73, 81
oral anesthesia, 317
orange juice, 183
orgasm, 142, 160, 263
orthodox Jew, 325
outpatient, 2–4, 6, 8–20, 22–29, 33, 36, 39,
    41–44, 47–55, 57–62, 64, 66–67, 69–
    74, 76–79, 81, 83–84, 86, 88–90, 92–
    99, 101–108, 110–113, 115–125, 127–

128, 130–134, 136, 138–140, 142,
144–146, 148–150, 152–153, 155–158,
160, 162, 164–166, 168–169, 171–
174, 176–180, 183–187, 189, 191–
193, 195–198, 200, 202, 204, 206,
208, 210–212, 214–216, 218–219,
221, 223–226, 228, 230–233, 235–
262, 264–268, 272, 274, 276, 278–
284, 286, 289–290, 292, 295–297,
299–300, 302, 304–306, 308, 310–
314, 317–330
overinvolvement with food, 30
overuse of tranquilizers, 13
overweight (*see* obesity)

pain, 50, 64–84, 203–204
    phantom limb, 68
    underneath her dress, 80
painted cigarette box, 219
panic, 132–133, 154, 156
    attacks, 5–6
panties, 103
paralysis, 51, 54–55, 203–204
paranoia, 285
paranoid schizophrenia, 278
parasite, 309
Parkinson's disease, 206
partial success, 9, 26–27, 43, 58, 69, 82,
    90, 95, 116, 129, 173, 179, 205, 218,
    232, 250–251, 255–256, 282, 285,
    289, 291
peeing semen, 149
penis, 111, 113
Pennsylvania, 256
peptic ulcer, 50
Percodan, 92
personality problem, 323
perversion, 139
Petrified Forest, 30
Ph.D. student, 158
phantom limb pain, 68
Philadelphia, 113
phobias (*see* fears)
Phoenix, 33, 56, 91, 165, 169, 173, 176,
    190, 292, 310, 312, 328
Phoenix police, 217
piano lessons, 316
piece of ass, 268
pilot, 7
playing in the leaves, 177
pneumonia, 135
policeman, 19
polka dots, 21
Pond, Janice, 160–162

SOURCE INDEX

TECHNIQUE INDEX